THE FINGER LAKES

DRINKING GUIDE

THE ULTIMATE COMPANION TO
UPSTATE NEW YORK'S
WINERIES, BREWERIES,
CIDERIES, AND DISTILLERIES

T0283884

MICHAEL TURBACK

BOOKS

North Country Books
An imprint of The Globe Pequot Publishing Group, Inc.
64 South Main Street
Essex, CT 06426
www.globepequot.com

Distributed by NATIONAL BOOK NETWORK

British Library Cataloguing in Publication Information Available

Library of Congress Cataloging-in-Publication Data

Names: Turback, Michael, author.
Title: The Finger Lakes drinking guide : the ultimate companion to upstate New York's
  wineries, breweries, cideries, and distilleries / Michael Turback.
Description: Lanham, MD : North Country Books, an imprint of Globe Pequot,
  the trade division of The Rowman & Littlefield Publishing Group, Inc., [2024] |
  Includes index. | Summary: "The Finger Lakes Drinking Guide is a comprehensive
  guidebook to every major winery, brewery, cidery, and distillery in New York State's
  Finger Lakes region—a world-class wine destination and rising star in beers, ciders,
  and spirits alike"—Provided by publisher.
Identifiers: LCCN 2024010636 (print) | LCCN 2024010637 (ebook) |
  ISBN 9781493078394 (paperback) | ISBN 9781493078400 (epub)
Subjects: LCSH: Wine and wine making—New York (State)—Finger Lakes—
  Guidebooks. | Wineries—New York (State)—Finger Lakes—Guidebooks. |
  Breweries—New York (State)—Finger Lakes—Guidebooks. | Distilleries—
  New York (State)—Finger Lakes—Guidebooks.
Classification: LCC TX907.3.N72 F5575 2024 (print) | LCC TX907.3.N72 (ebook) |
  DDC 641.2/2097478—dc23/eng/20240524
LC record available at https://lccn.loc.gov/2024010636
LC ebook record available at https://lccn.loc.gov/2024010637

♾️™ The paper used in this publication meets the minimum requirements of American
National Standard for Information Sciences—Permanence of Paper for Printed Library
Materials, ANSI/NISO Z39.48-1992

To LD and shared pleasures

CONTENTS

BEST OF THE REST

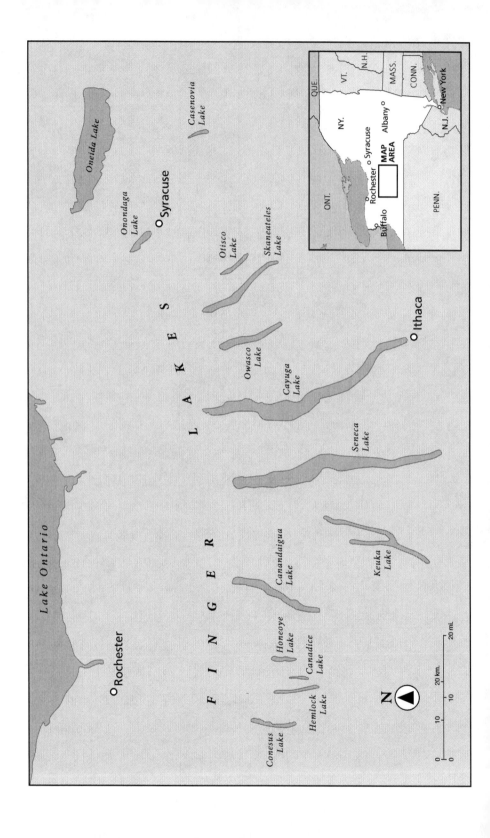

INTRODUCTION

Connecting Past to the Present

There's no place on earth quite like the Finger Lakes of New York State. Encompassing more than nine thousand square miles and fourteen counties, the region is bordered on the north from Rochester to Syracuse and nearly as far south as the Pennsylvania state line, dotted with historic cities, dramatic gorges and waterways, and vast farmland and vineyards.

The major lakes from west to east are Canandaigua, Keuka, Seneca, Cayuga, and Skaneateles. Cities and villages, including Skaneateles, Ithaca, Geneva, Watkins Glen, Penn Yan, Hammondsport, and Canandaigua, are located at the head or foot of lakes, reminding early map makers of the fingers of a hand.

For all the decidedly contemporary people and places you'll find here, visiting the Finger Lakes inevitably involves interacting with history. During the ancient Ice Age, up to a mile-high mass of ice plowed into this terrain from the north like a giant bulldozer, carving deep canyons into the bedrock and depositing a shallow layer of topsoil on sloping shale beds. As the glaciers retreated, melting ice sheets filled deep claw marks to form a series of parallel lakes surrounded by copious deposits of mineral-rich soils and a terroir characterized by a wide-ranging variety of microclimates. The earliest immigrants understood that the agricultural abundance of this land was a precious gift. Enabled by the moderating effects of the deep, narrow bodies of water, they were able to harvest bumper crops of produce not otherwise expected to prosper this far north.

Hammondsport, at the southern end of Keuka Lake, is the site of both the birth and rebirth of the wine industry in the region. In 1855, the cultivation of grapes attracted an enterprising Frenchman by the name of Charles D. Champlin, and by 1860, he had become the principal organizer of the Pleasant Valley Wine Company, producing bottle-fermented sparkling wines from hillside-grown Catawba grapes.

Then, almost exactly one hundred years after Champlin first persisted with the grapey native wines, an eccentric Ukrainian-born professor of plant science challenged prevailing wisdom by cultivating classic European grapes in his

Hammondsport vineyard. With the experience he gained coping with the extreme winters of his homeland, Konstantin Frank produced remarkable wines from vinifera grapes planted on a thermally stable slope of Keuka Lake. He developed his own rootstock mother blocks and tinkered with various clones, successfully igniting a movement that dramatically changed the course of the Finger Lakes wine industry.

In 1976, the New York State legislature passed the Farm Winery Act, and aided by the viticultural research of nearby Cornell University, farm wineries began dotting lakesides. Thanks to the confluence of circumstances—habitable climate, the earth in which the grapes are grown, and a new generation of winemaking talent—the Finger Lakes region has become home to some of the most exciting wines made today.

Since the early days of European settlement through much of the nineteenth century, brewing was a vital industry in the Finger Lakes. During the mid-1800s, the region boasted dozens of breweries, and hop fields covered acres of farmland, producing hop flowers—the source of bitterness, aroma, and flavor in beer. The arrival of Prohibition in 1920 resulted in the demise of hometown breweries and commercial hopyards throughout the state, and by the time beer drinking was legal again in 1933, it was only the large national breweries who survived being closed for more than a decade.

Early in the aughts, as craft brewers began to enter the market, regional upstarts began filling a product niche in a market of mass-produced uniformity. The Finger Lakes microbrew industry has seen a steady increase in recent years, now boasting nearly one-half as many breweries as there are wineries. More than one-third of New York's total breweries are located in the region. And the popularity of craft beer has produced a resurgence of hop growing, abetted by state legislation that provides incentives to breweries for using local ingredients.

Apple trees for cider production were among the first fruits planted by colonists who resettled the Finger Lakes region, and practically every home in early America set aside a barrel of cider for wintertime. Hard cider continued as the country's most popular alcoholic drink until Prohibition, but with the return of legal drinking, America had acquired a robust appetite for beer. Cider making became a virtually lost art.

As the second-largest apple-producing state in America, New York has taken a leading role in the past decade's cider renaissance. Hard cider is the fastest-growing beverage sector in the country, and the Finger Lakes not only has ideal climate, soils, and weather patterns, but also a Cornell University program is dedicated to research, science, and cider production. Making artisanal cider from heirloom varieties and European cider apples, pioneering enterprises have established the region's sense of place. *Travel and Leisure* magazine recently called the Finger Lakes the "Napa Valley of Cider."

It was Dutch settlers who introduced distilling to America with the first commercial distillery on New York's Staten Island in 1640, producing a grain-based gin infused with locally sourced botanicals. Repeal of the whiskey tax in 1802 brought about the golden age of New York distillation, as farm distilleries flourished across the state. But, of course, legal distilling was crippled by Prohibition, with traditions and methodologies seemingly lost forever.

Then in 2007, less than a century after repeal of the "noble experiment," New York lawmakers passed the Farm Distillery Act, reviving the art of distilling whiskey, rye, gin, vodka, and rum. It was the fuse that ignited an explosion of craft enterprises, allowing a number of upstate farms to become full-on distilleries, a natural outgrowth of New York's agricultural bounty and the locavore movement.

While New York's Finger Lakes may seem like halfway to nowhere, locals will remind you that our region sits within three hundred miles of 30 percent of the entire US population. If you think of the territory as a giant rectangle, almost any traveler will enter through a city, town, or village—a portal at each of the four corners. Travelers from New York City, the New York–New Jersey–Connecticut metropolitan area, Philadelphia, and all points southeast enter through Ithaca. From Syracuse, Albany, Montreal, Boston, New England, and all points northeast, travelers enter through Skaneateles. From Rochester, Buffalo, Niagara Falls, Toronto, and all points northwest, travelers enter through Canandaigua. If arriving from Pittsburgh, Cleveland, Indianapolis, Chicago, and other points southwest, travelers enter through Hammondsport.

The region offers plenty of liquid pleasures, and this book will help you get right to them. Listings in each section generally run north to south for itinerary-based travelers, but always allow for spontaneity on your visit. Carole King crooned that life is a tapestry, and that's certainly true for the Finger Lakes of New York. Consider the book you hold in your hands as my personal invitation to the awesome tapestry of the region.

Read on, my friends, as you begin your journey to this remarkable place.

CONESUS LAKE

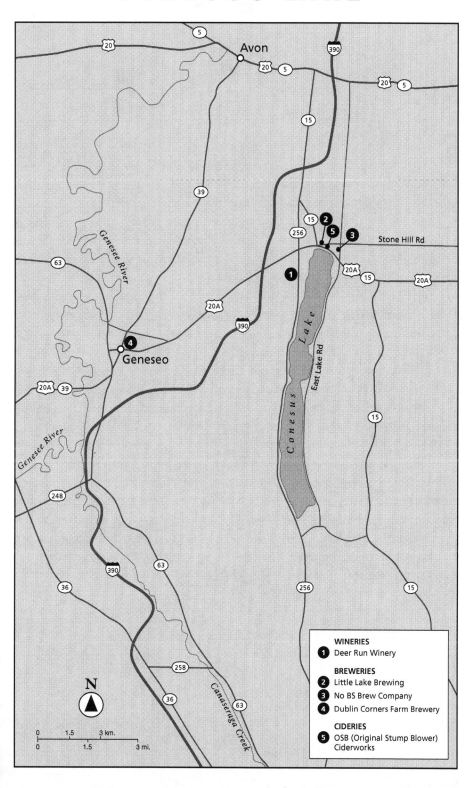

WINERIES
1. Deer Run Winery

BREWERIES
2. Little Lake Brewing
3. No BS Brew Company
4. Dublin Corners Farm Brewery

CIDERIES
5. OSB (Original Stump Blower) Ciderworks

WINERIES

DEER RUN WINERY
3772 West Lake Road
Geneseo, NY 14454
www.deerrunwinery.com

Westernmost of New York's eleven Finger Lakes, Conesus derives its name from the Native American word *Gah-Ne-A-Sos*, meaning "beautiful valley," where the people of the Seneca Nation cultivated orchards, vineyards, and fields of maize and vegetables. In 2003, after retiring as a quality control manager at Kodak, George Kuyon, along with his son Scott, a marine technician, began planting grapes on a five-acre parcel of rich farmland. It was the beginning of Deer Run, flourishing in splendid isolation as the only winery on Conesus Lake, a family-owned and -operated enterprise where Scott now tends the vines and manages winemaking chores. Twenty percent of estate-grown grapes are used for Deer Run wines, with the remainder purchased from vineyards on other lakes.

Because Conesus is only eight miles long with a maximum depth of sixty-six feet, the shallow depths can't provide the moderate temperatures of the larger, deeper lakes. Yet the Kuyons have had success with several cold-hardy wine varieties developed at Cornell AgriTech, each lending special, complementary qualities to proprietary blends.

Runway Red, the name inspired by a private airport across from the winery grounds, combines deeply colored, Syrah-like Noiret (pronounced *nwahr-AY*) with the berry and cherry aromas of Corot Noir. Max Black, named for the winery's Scottish terrier, unites native, grapey Niagara with the Chianti-like, French-American hybrid Vincent.

Perhaps the best way to enjoy the full experience here is by having lunch in the Tankroom Café. Enjoy salads, burgers, flatbreads, and cheese and charcuterie plates with curated flights for sampling wines from current releases.

BREWERIES

LITTLE LAKE BREWING
5857 Big Tree Road
Lakeville, NY 14480
www.littlelakebrewing.com

From 1989 to 1993, culinary professional Don Carll traveled in a sixty-five-foot mobile kitchen, cooking and baking on the road for the Grateful Dead and their entourage, the top-selling concert tour group in the United States during those years. He later worked as head chef at the Conesus Inn until it closed in 2012, then rented a small building on nearby Big Tree Road across from the lake. In 2018, Don squeezed Little Lake Brewing into that space, and the operative word here is *small*. Everything at this village gathering place is done on a small scale.

Early in the day, Don roasts single-origin coffee beans in a small commercial roaster, bakes pastries, and prepares breakfast dishes to order. In the evening, the place transforms from a coffee shop to a nanobrewery, offering small-batch, house-brewed IPAs, rye PAs, and light-bodied lagers, crafted on a one-and-a-half-barrel brewhouse, along with a limited dinner menu. Small-size production affords Don an unusual degree of freedom to experiment with more eccentric brews, including a black IPA made with roasted grain and chocolate malt.

Local folks like to talk about the hamlet of Lakeville in the 1800s when visitors arrived here by train and boarded lake steamers for various destinations on the lake.

If you're wondering about the fishhook in the Little Lake Brewing logo, it's a reminder that Conesus Lake provides excellent fishing for both bass species, northern pike, bluegills, and sunfish.

NO BS BREW COMPANY

3474 Bronson Hill Road
Livonia, NY 14487
www.bsbrewcompany.com

The origin of the name is not exactly what you think. The *B* is for *Ben Noragong*, and the *S* is for *Steve Gray*, partners who cofounded this buzzing beerhouse, locally renowned for the warmth of its welcome, with knowledgeable bar staff happy to help visitors negotiate a range of microbrews that capture the spirit of where they were born.

No BS is arguably best known for their retro-style cream ales, a category long popular in western New York. First brewed in the 1960s by Rochester's Genesee Brewing Company, Genny Cream, a refreshing, easy-drinking brew with a creamy mouthfeel, maintains a devoted cult following.

His background in biochemistry prepared Ben for the science and discipline of craft beer brewing. He works his magic in the seven-barrel brewhouse with creative interpretations of the hybrid classic "lawnmower beer," adding corn to the grain bill to lighten the color and body of North End Cream Ale, low-ABV Lawnmower Ale, and Jamaican Me Happy Cream Ale, brewed with a signature roast from Evening Star Coffee in nearby Avon.

Because nothing goes better with beer than pizza, BS houses a serious kitchen, stretching its offerings with Buffalo wings and a Friday-night beer-battered fish fry.

Outside, there is a patio drinking area and an open stage where it hosts bluegrass and roots bands during the summer.

No BS Brew Company operates a sister taproom at 49 West Main Street in Victor.

DUBLIN CORNERS FARM BREWERY

116 Main Street
Geneseo, NY 14454
www.dublincornersfarm.com

Small-town America is alive and well along Geneseo's charming Main Street, including a row of shops, restaurants, and the locally popular taproom of Dublin Corners Farm Brewery. In a storefront that once housed a flower shop, servers pour beers from the home brewery in nearby Linwood. Among the offerings, an IPA called Devil's ½ Acre is a nod to the area's early Irish immigrants, and Tree

Tapper is a porter brewed with local maple syrup. Pay special attention to Better Red than Dead, an amber ale that ran away with a gold medal at the New York State Craft Brewers Association Beer Competition.

The mothership brewery and tasting room (see page 200) is at 1906 Main Street (Route 36) in Linwood.

CIDERIES

OSB (ORIGINAL STUMP BLOWER) CIDERWORKS
5901 Big Tree Road
Lakeville, NY 14480
www.osbciderworks.com

Inspired by family folklore, in 2016, siblings Eric Smith and Elise Barnard established OSB at the north end of Conesus Lake. As the story is told, great-uncle Charlie hid his homemade cider in tree stumps, and the notion "Let's go blow up some stumps" became code for an excuse to indulge in the powerful backyard stash.

Eric studied at the Institute of Culinary Education (ICE) in New York City, tutored at the Michelin-starred Taillevent in Paris, and cooked at Eleven Madison Park in Manhattan. His culinary background provides a unique edge into crafting a range of balanced and complex ciders and experimenting with techniques and styles.

Sourcing a mix of sweet, acidic, and tannic apples from nearby orchards, Eric applies a trained chef's sense of flavor and kitchen skills to his recipes for forty different blends. There are as many as a dozen different ciders on tap in the tasting room, rotating according to the season. Depending on his preferences and creativity, Eric's blending ingredients might include pears, cherries, raspberries, cranberries, hibiscus, chamomile, Concord and Niagara grapes, honey, maple syrup, matcha tea, or even espresso from Underground Coffee in Buffalo.

Among popular ciders with witty names, Cherry Cherry Why Ya Buggin? is a mix of culinary apples and local tart cherries. The Original is a high-ABV cider, a fusion of apples and Concord grapes aged in used whiskey barrels from Black Button Distilling in Rochester.

The production space and unpretentious tasting quarters are a stone's throw from the lake, just off Big Tree Road. While ciders steal the show here, there's plenty of local beer on tap, a selection of canned cocktails, and something called the Poor Man's Charcuterie, a meat stick, a cheese stick, and a plate of Ritz crackers.

OSB operates a satellite tasting room location at 517 Main Street in downtown Buffalo.

HEMLOCK LAKE

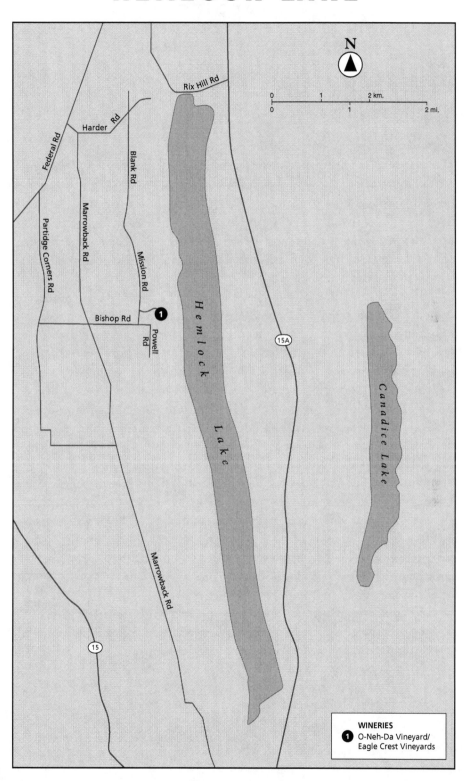

Rix Hill Rd

Federal Rd

Harder Rd

Blank Rd

Marrowback Rd

Mission Rd

Partidge Corners Rd

Bishop Rd

Powell Rd

1

Hemlock Lake

Canadice Lake

15A

Marrowback Rd

15

N

0   1   2 km.
0   1   2 mi.

WINERIES

1 O-Neh-Da Vineyard/
Eagle Crest Vineyards

WINERIES

O-NEH-DA VINEYARD/EAGLE CREST VINEYARDS
7107 Vineyard Road
Conesus, NY 14435
www.eaglecrestvineyards.com

The third-oldest winery in America and the very oldest winery dedicated to making sacramental wines, O-Neh-Da was established in 1872 by Rochester's founding Catholic bishop, Bernard J. McQuaid, to supply wine for churches in his diocese. While all the other Finger Lakes have Native American names, Hemlock Lake was named by European settlers after the hemlock trees shading gorges around the lake. Bishop McQuaid called his vineyard O·Neh·Da to honor the culture of the Native people.

The majority of liturgical churches, such as the Catholic Church and Eastern Orthodox Church, require sacramental wine made from certified sustainable and organically grown grapes using wild fermentation, without such additives or preservatives as sulfites. In the past few years there has been a growing trend among mainstream vintners toward natural wines, adopting the same clean methods O-Neh-Da has been using for 150 years. Their winemaking process is a veneration of tradition, taught and handed down from one generation to the next throughout the winery's history, and they produce sacramental wine for Catholic parishes all over the eastern United States. O-Neh-Da Chalice Wine, a blend of Marquette, Chancellor, and Noiret (pronounced *nwahr-AY*), was used during the celebration of Mass at Madison Square Garden by Pope Francis on his visit to America in 2015.

The winery's second label, Eagle Crest, established in 2005, was named for Hemlock Lake's two pairs of bald eagles, the sole remaining breeding pairs in New York State. While the sacramental wine is sold directly to parishes, the Eagle Crest brand's portfolio of mostly French-American hybrid blends are intended for sale to the general public in the tasting room.

Among exceptional white wines, On-No-Lee is made from 100 percent Cayuga white, its name a reference to the local legend of the young bride of the chief of the Munsee band of the Mohican tribe.

HONEOYE LAKE

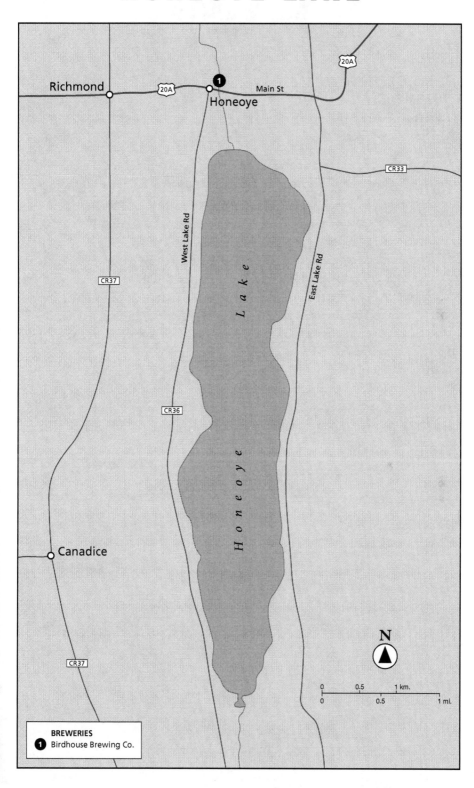

Richmond

20A

Main St

Honeoye

20A

CR33

West Lake Rd

East Lake Rd

CR37

L a k e

CR36

H o n e o y e

Canadice

CR37

N

BREWERIES
1 Birdhouse Brewing Co.

0   0.5   1 km.
0   0.5   1 mi.

BREWERIES

BIRDHOUSE BREWING CO.
8716 Main Street
Honeoye, NY 14471
www.birdhousebrewing.beer

You're probably wondering about the name. For many years, a home on the village Main Street was owned by a bird enthusiast who built birdhouses and bird feeders in his backyard and hung them across the front porch. Locals called it the "birdhouse place." So when Scott Gillen and Greg Searles purchased that house and repurposed it as a microbrewery, the name stuck.

Birdhouse Brewing was launched in 2020, operating from a one-barrel system, cranking out recipes, and developing beer styles. One of those experiments, Hazy Bird IPA, became the brewery's flagship beer, crafted with hops grown on nearby Drumlin Hop Farm. Approachable and easy-drinking, Honey Cream Ale is true to style, brewed with New York State corn and honey from Bristol Hills. Other house-made, rotating taps include seasonal and one-off beers, plus take-out options in four-packs.

The fledgling enterprise has become a community gathering place and has grown from a nanobrewery to a microbrewery. When hunger strikes, an eclectic menu includes mac and cheese, chicken and biscuits, and Hungarian paprikas.

CANANDAIGUA LAKE

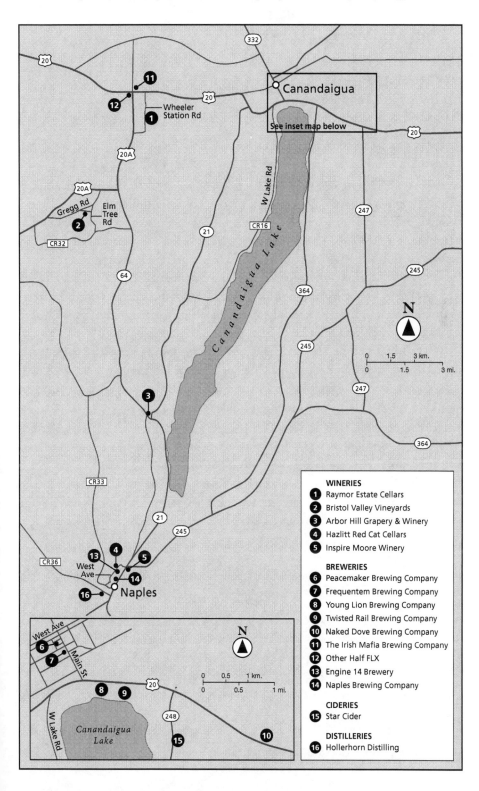

WINERIES
1. Raymor Estate Cellars
2. Bristol Valley Vineyards
3. Arbor Hill Grapery & Winery
4. Hazlitt Red Cat Cellars
5. Inspire Moore Winery

BREWERIES
6. Peacemaker Brewing Company
7. Frequentem Brewing Company
8. Young Lion Brewing Company
9. Twisted Rail Brewing Company
10. Naked Dove Brewing Company
11. The Irish Mafia Brewing Company
12. Other Half FLX
13. Engine 14 Brewery
14. Naples Brewing Company

CIDERIES
15. Star Cider

DISTILLERIES
16. Hollerhorn Distilling

WINERIES

RAYMOR ESTATE CELLARS
3263 Wheeler Station Road
Bloomfield, NY 14469
www.raymorcellars.com

He is a one-man band—winemaker, cidermaker, brewer. After working as a systems engineer for more than twenty years, in 2011 Herb Raymor returned to his roots as a farm boy. On a modest homestead in the rolling hills near Bristol, his small-scale venture produces wines from grapes grown at nearby Randall-Standish Vineyards and sources apples grown on the Noto Fruit Farm in Williamson for his handcrafted hard ciders.

It's said that Iona, a hybrid wine variety developed in 1885 in New York's Hudson Valley, tastes like Riesling with the volume turned up. Raymor Estate's semisweet Iona, sourced specifically from John Cicero's three-acre Iona vineyard, regularly captures medals in New York State wine competitions.

Sugar Maple Apple Hard Cider, blended with locally harvested dark amber maple syrup, has become the signature cider here, and a unique wine-cider hybrid called Fusion is a mix of separately fermented Noiret (pronounced *nwahr-AY*) red wine and the Northern Spy–dominant cider. Among the beers on display, pay special attention to Herb's Amber Ale.

The tasting room is a small, knotty pine–lined shack just behind the residence. Visitors obtain access by appointment for category-specific tastings. Inside, while popcorn is popping, you'll be greeted by Herb Raymor himself, a man whose infectious enthusiasm and joy is mirrored in his craft. When you get around to purchasing a favorite, ask Herb to personally sign the bottle.

BRISTOL VALLEY VINEYARDS
7235 Lane Road
Bloomfield, NY 14469
www.bristolvalleyvineyards.com

An image of the snowy owl, a bird that migrates from Canada to the Finger Lakes in winter, appears on labels of Bristol Valley Vineyards wines. On a visit to this scenic backwater, a member of the Anselm family will tell you how it became a symbol of the farm winery. After a marketing career at Xerox, Barbara Anselm began a new chapter in life, along with her son Nickolas. With determination and heart, in 2015 they planted their first grapes, Riesling and Vidal Blanc; produced their first wines in 2017; and added fruited meads a few years later.

High points include estate-grown Léon Millot (pronounced *MEE-yo*), a medium-bodied, bright cherry-red wine aged with French toast oak chips, mimicking a flavor profile that compares to a rustic Pinot Noir. And most notable among the meads produced from regional wildflower honey is a gold-medal-winning Orange Spice Mead.

ARBOR HILL GRAPERY & WINERY
6461 Route 64
Naples, NY 14512
www.thegrapery.com

Arbor Hill Grapery has mounted a challenge to skeptics who insist that temperatures near Canandaigua Lake are too cold to grow fine wine grapes. Cornell University–trained pomologist John Brahm became fascinated with the potential of a cross between Joannes Seyve and Gewürztraminer wine grapes during field trials conducted at the Geneva Experiment Station in 1985. As a senior vice president at Widmer's Wine Cellars for many years, John was the viticultural innovator who pioneered the commercial production of Cayuga, a successful hybrid variety developed at Geneva, and he was eager to blaze another trail with Traminette, created as part of the breeding program at the University of Illinois, originally intended as a table grape. Although the hybrid produces wine with pronounced varietal characters likened to its acclaimed parent, the vines are more prolific, at least partially resistant to disease, and designed to outwit the region's notorious winters.

In 1986, John opened Arbor Hill Grapery to showcase the experimental grape variety that would become the trademark of his enterprise. Now in the hands of Sherry and John French, the winery continues to demonstrate Traminette's versatility in both dry and semisweet versions.

Housed in the cluster of vintage buildings dating to the 1800s, shelves of the Arbor Hill gift shop are filled with an eclectic range of wines, as well as wine sauces, jams, jellies and preserves, flavored vinegars, barbecue sauces, and salad dressings—all made one batch at a time on the property.

HAZLITT RED CAT CELLARS
1 Lake Niagara Lane
Naples, NY 14512
www.hazlitt1852/naples

John Jacob Widmer played an important role in the formative years of the Finger Lakes wine industry. He traveled from his home in Switzerland to the village of Naples in 1882, and finding the fertile slopes above Canandaigua Lake suited to grape growing, he decided to make wine his life's work. He purchased his first plot of hillside woodland with borrowed money, cleared it, planted vines in the spring of 1883, and began production of wines five years later. During Prohibition, Widmer survived by producing unfermented grape juice, and upon repeal in 1933, the company was able to quickly revive its winemaking, and reestablish its brand among wine consumers. The winery changed hands several times in the late twentieth century and is now owned by the Hazlitt family, an important name in Finger Lakes wine country, specifically for their large-scale production of a pop wine called Red Cat.

With century-old native Catawba grapevines and eight acres of hybrid Baco Noir on the original Hazlitt property, one of the first wines produced was a proprietary blend of the two. Combining both of these early-ripening, high-acid varieties proved much better than either one on its own, especially with added sugar for balance. Red Cat (named for the *Cat* in *Catawba*) has become the best-selling wine produced in New York State. The popularity of Red Cat has been explained as a beginning drinker's bridge between Coca-Cola and wine. Promoted as the "original hot tub wine," its continued success in the growing low-price-point, sweet-wine category has spawned a line of products, including Red Cat Sangria, Red Cat Fizz, White Cat, and Pink Cat.

The Naples complex was acquired to keep up with the demand for these fan favorites; however, if you visit the tasting room, you'll also have the opportunity to sample Riesling, Cabernet Franc, and Pinot Gris, among Hazlitt's more serious varietals.

INSPIRE MOORE WINERY
197 North Main Street
Naples, NY 14512
www.inspiremoorewinery.com

Tim Moore grew up in California, studied viticulture and enology at UC Davis, and worked on the winemaking team at Constellation Brands for a dozen years. In 2007, Tim and his wife, Diane, purchased a seven-acre vineyard first planted by the Widmer family in the 1930s and set out on their own. Originally a tavern, a stagecoach stop, and then a carriage house, the Moores transformed that historic building on Main Street in Naples into a brightly painted boutique winery, quaint tasting room, and rustic café. From the outside, it looks like something out of a fairy tale. Inside, the vibe is a compelling mix of influences reminiscent of 1960s hippie culture.

This is intended to be a place for mindful wine lovers, inspired by shared values of peace, love, and respect for the earth. The *inspire* of *Inspire Moore Winery* includes a message of positivity on the label of each bottle from the handcrafted, small-lot production. Semi-dry Riesling is called Love; unoaked Chardonnay, Gratitude; and Blaufränkisch, Change.

Winemaking is now in the hands of Nate Moore, who follows in his father's footsteps and maintains the attributes and ethos of the family enterprise. Since taking charge, he has introduced Traminette, a promising varietal from the Gewürztraminer family sourced from fruit grown on the Simmons Vineyard on Keuka Lake and released under the Nathaniel J. Moore designation.

Roots Cafe, a community-driven restaurant located in the main house, serves lunch and dinner in a rustic setting. The eclectic menu includes seasonal salads, grass-fed beef burgers, and vegetarian dishes.

BREWERIES

PEACEMAKER BREWING COMPANY
39 Coach Street
Canandaigua, NY 14424
www.peacemakerbrewing.com

Roger Clyne and the Peacemakers emerged on the music scene in 1999, blending punk rock, country-western, and mariachi. Among their devoted legion of fans, Todd Reardon not only received the group's blessing to use their name for his brewery start-up, but also each of his beers is named after one of the group's songs or a snippet of lyrics. And of course, you can probably guess whose music is blaring on the sound system.

But first you have to find Peacemaker Brewing. It's just off the city's Main Street, once the home of a working ceramic studio equipped with eight potter's wheels, three electric kilns, and a glaze lab. Reimagined as a snug, rustic pub, it's now a meeting place where enthusiasts sip and savor weird and wonderful craft beers.

Ryan Rahm is a brewer who can take a light hand, as he does with Semi-Professional Tourist, a dry-hopped, light-bodied Italian pilsner, or use a deft touch with the heavy-metal flavors of Wake Up Call Coffee Stout.

In the warmer months, a highlight of Peacemaker is the hometown version of a biergarten in the backyard.

FREQUENTEM BREWING COMPANY
254 Main Street
Canandaigua, NY 14424
www.frequentembrewing.com

Much of the credit for Canandaigua's status as a pilgrimage-worthy craft-beer destination is due to its grassroots home-brewing scene. David and Meagan D'Allesandro jumped from making beer for enthusiastic friends to opening a brewery on the city's pedestrian-friendly Main Street.

The name, Frequentem, derived from Latin, translates roughly into "a busy or crowded space to gather." That gathering space, a former Byrne Dairy convenience store, has been transformed into a sleek, industrial-inspired taproom with

Euro-style tables, rolling garage-style doors that open up to a side patio with options for outdoor seating, umbrellas for warm summer days, and heating lamps for chilly nights.

You'll have the opportunity to chat with knowledgeable staff at the long bar, peer through glass windows to the brewing vats, and experience the friendly local ambiance. In its short history, the brewery has developed a reputation for an impressive arsenal of beers, among the best in the region.

Frequentem separates from the pack with a dedicated lager program. Unlike traditional tanks that stand vertically, the brewery's unique horizontal tank provides a larger ratio of surface area to beer depth, so the yeast doesn't have to travel as far to settle on the bottom. Pay special attention to Black Rice Dark Lager, brewed with cereal mash and heirloom forbidden rice.

The fruity beers, reminiscent of spiked smoothies, shouldn't be missed here. In blueberry, tangerine, plum, cranberry, apricot, and pineapple versions, fruit takes the lead, gently backed up with hops. People who don't usually like beer might find this category a stepping stone into craft beer's eclectic and flavorful world.

Visitors can soak up a favorite brew with simple bar food—ciabatta pizzas, pretzel sticks, and bags of flavored popcorn. For the occasional nonbeer drinker, wines and hard ciders made by regional producers supplement the offerings.

When in Buffalo, stop by the Frequentem satellite tasting room at 225 Louisiana Street in the Old First Ward District.

YOUNG LION BREWING COMPANY
24 Lakeshore Drive
Canandaigua, NY 14424
www.younglionbrewing.com

With the completion of the Erie Canal in 1825, Rochester prospered into a bustling agricultural and milling boomtown, garnering the city's first nickname, Young Lion of the West. Young Lion provided an appropriate name for this start-up by a focused, high-energy group of Rochesterians and a women-managed team led by serial entrepreneur Jennifer Newman. Anchored at the Pinnacle North complex on Canandaigua Lake, with a view of the lake across Lakeshore Drive, in 2017 the team set out to catch the craft-beer wave, poised to serve the local community and beyond the home market.

With a UC Davis degree, strong technical background, and more than a decade of production experience, head brewer Phillip Platz set the enterprise on an upward course, overseeing the thirty-five-barrel brewhouse and producing a diverse portfolio of beers. His successor, Dan McCumiskey, trained at the legendary Siebel Institute, earned his credentials at the Genesee Brewing Company, and has maintained Young Lion's high standards of quality and consistency.

Core beers include a crisp, pale-gold Czech pilsner, crafted with Czech Saaz hops, as well as eminently drinkable IPAs and double IPAs. Rotating seasonal and specialty offerings include a range of expressive fruited sours, beers that combine the tartness and acidity of sour beers with the sweetness and juiciness of fruit. These complex flavor profiles make them excellent for sipping and perfect for pairing with food.

If you visit the handsome tasting room, you'll be invited to curate a flight, four glasses of your choice from a dozen or so current offerings on draught. And besides the Canandaigua stronghold, Young Lion brews are available in supermarkets and bottle shops throughout central and western New York.

TWISTED RAIL BREWING COMPANY
169 Lakeshore Drive
Canandaigua, NY 14424
www.twistedrailbrewing.com

From little things, big things grow. The ambitious partnership of Ian Boni, John McMullen, and Rich Russ began in 2013 as a three-barrel microbrewery housed in part of the old railroad depot on Pleasant Street. Over recent years the enterprise has multiplied, both in their range of beers and in locations. The Twisted Rail mothership brewhouse is now headquartered in the former Regent Theatre space in Geneva, with outpost tasting rooms in Honeoye, Macedon, and here at the Lakeshore Drive location near Kershaw Park, all under the same beer-mad ownership.

You can belly up to the tasting bar for a convivial experience or at café tables in the next room if you're looking to set a more leisurely pace. Sip easy-drinking Lake to Lake Lager or Pancake Breakfast, a maple-infused oatmeal stout, among other options from the nearly twenty taps in a casual setting overlooking picturesque Canandaigua Lake.

There's at least one thing you should order from the food menu: the soft Bavarian pretzels with beer cheese.

NAKED DOVE BREWING COMPANY
4048 Routes 5 and 20
Canandaigua, NY 14424
www.nakeddovebrewing.com

In 2010, Dave Schlosser and two partners converted a building vacated by NAPA Auto Parts, installed a fifteen-barrel brewhouse, and launched the first craft brewery in Ontario County. Schlosser earned his credentials at Rochester's three local stalwarts: Genesee; Custom Brewcrafters; and most notably Rohrbach, where he was responsible for a rich, supermalty Scotch Ale, arguably the city's most famous craft beer.

The Canandaigua venture was named Naked Dove not accidently since the dove is symbolic of new beginnings, luck, and prosperity. While the atmosphere here is basic and unassuming, the beers aspire to greater things. Grab a seat at the stainless-steel counter and browse the offerings. Scott Guest or Mike Stahlbrodt, members of the brewing team, will talk you through a custom flight from among ten beers on tap.

Core offerings are Starkers India Pale Ale, Wind Blown Amber Ale, and Berry Naked Black Raspberry Ale, but the beer that changed everything here is 45 Fathoms Porter, brewed with a magical combination of five specialty malts. Named for the deepest point in Canandaigua Lake, the robust, aromatic dark beer was awarded a gold medal at the New York State Craft Beer Competition in 2022.

THE IRISH MAFIA BREWING COMPANY
2971 Whalen Road
Bloomfield, NY 14469
www.irishmafiabrewing.com

It's not what you're thinking. This isn't the headquarters of a crime syndicate composed of ethnic Irish members. Yet Mark Mansfield's establishment does indeed have the culture of an Irish pub–cum–sports bar centered around a casual and friendly atmosphere with hearty food and a mix of house-brewed and contract beers. The unlikely setting, seemingly in the middle of nowhere, is actually just off Routes 5 and 20, a few miles west of Canandaigua.

The kitchen serves generous plates of potato cakes, corned beef poutine, IPA-beer-battered onion rings, and a piled-high fish-fry sandwich called Swimming with the Fishes.

OTHER HALF FLX

6621 Routes 5 and 20
Bloomfield, NY 14469
www.otherhalfbrewing.com

The enterprise was hatched in Brooklyn by partners Sam Richardson, Matt Monahan, and Andrew Burman, its name inspired by the craft-culture half of the beer industry. As Other Half Brewing, they've been turning heads and disrupting the movement since 2014.

Since opening the first taproom in an industrial garage beneath the Gowanus Expressway, the trio has added satellite locations in New York City; Washington, DC; Philadelphia; Buffalo; and, lucky for us, here in the Finger Lakes village of Bloomfield, just west of Canandaigua in 2018, shaking up the region's craft-beer scene.

Fans of IPAs might race you to the door. After earning a degree at Oregon State's Fermentation Science Program, Richardson moved to Brooklyn and began making beer at Greenpoint Beerworks. He developed a passion for bold IPAs, and at Other Half, he has earned an international reputation in the juicy IPA game. In fact, 85 percent of his rotating portfolio are IPAs, and he is responsible for making double-dry hopping a standard technique for many IPA brewers.

Bloomfield's vibrant taproom rests on ten sprawling acres the boys from Brooklyn must think of as idyllic wilderness. Come to taste flagship beers that have a cult following: Green City, a double-dry-hopped IPA, and Forever Ever, a lower-alcohol yet hop-dominant-profile session IPA. Can labels differ based on the brew, but all have whimsical, attention-grabbing designs.

Parked next door, the Other Half food truck feeds hungry hipsters and local families on burgers, chicken tenders, BLTs, and other creative sammies for indoor or outdoor sipping and snacking.

ENGINE 14 BREWERY

52 West Avenue
Naples, NY 14512
www.engine14brewery.com

Upon retiring from twenty-two years as a firefighter with the Rochester Fire Department, Greg Borden set his sights on the beer business after homebrewing every Sunday for as long as he can remember. And the brewery he created in 2021 was not only inspired by his old firehouse, but also parked inside is the venture's mascot, a decommissioned Rochester fire truck—you guessed it, old Engine 14. Located in part of the former Widmer's Wine Cellars complex across from Hazlitt Red Cat Cellars (see page 14), Borden's bold, four-thousand-square-foot space includes a seven-barrel brewhouse producing a range of beer styles, each available for sipping in five-, ten-, or sixteen-ounce glasses.

The start-up's first batch of beer, a pilsner dubbed Golden Arm, has become the brewery's flagship. You'd be hard-pressed to find a more refreshing beer-drinking experience. Most of the beers are named after firefighter terms, and each speaks to the brewer's style. Greg's artistic choice leans to the traditional. Besides requisite IPAs, offerings include cream ale; English porter; and Schwarzbier, a style of black beer that dates to the Middle Ages.

The Engine 14 kitchen, helmed by Adam Borden, former chef at Oak Hill Country Club in Pittsford, sticks to tried and true pub grub, which means satisfying, if somewhat ordinary, options for the beer tourist with an appetite.

NAPLES BREWING COMPANY
104 North Main Street
Naples, NY 14512
www.naplesbrewco.com

Two local pals, Dan diGiovanna and Trevor Andrews, both RIT grads, decided to give craft brewing the old college try. And lucky for the village of Naples, they succeeded in creating a neighborhood gathering place for fellow beer enthusiasts. This small-scale microbrewery is set in a village storefront that once housed a jewelry shop, but the gems here are now distinctive craft beers made with ingredients sourced as locally as possible, including malts from Murmuration Malts in Bloomfield and hops and fruit from dependable growers in the region.

The house beer is called NYIPA, a double-dry-hopped New England–style IPA brewed with New York–grown Chinook hops and local grains. In a sister brew, crafted with locally picked peaches and apricots, the NYIPA becomes Stonefruit Sour IPA, propelling this little but pioneering micro into the spotlight.

Experimental beers are made available to customers either weekly or twice a month or until the single keg is kicked. While the tasting room is stylish and friendly, the beer garden out back is the place to savor these ambitious brews.

In addition to the beers, Dan and Trevor handcraft a distinctive hard cider from hand-foraged wild apples, abandoned orchards, and heirloom varieties.

Once you're done swilling, wander Naples's Main Street past restaurants, shops, and galleries.

CIDERIES

STAR CIDER
3365 East Lake Road (Route 364)
Canandaigua, NY 14424
www.starcidery.com

Cornell grad Cortni Stahl is a credentialed technician at the university's Enology Extension Laboratory, providing support to large and small craft wineries, cideries, and breweries in the Finger Lakes and across the United States. In 2014, she and husband, Adam, launched Star Cider, developing blends, producing small-batch ciders, wholesaling to bars and restaurants, and eventually outgrowing two different production spaces. By 2019 the flourishing enterprise moved into a destination facility just south of the city, set to make hard ciders a significant part of the regional craft scene.

Star Cider has become a popular gathering spot where you can sip your way through flights of four or eight thirst-quenching ciders, discover the world of cider cocktails, listen to live music on the lawn, and create cider and food pairings from a menu of Mexican dishes.

Five Point is the star here, a blend of five varieties—McIntosh, Empire, Crispin, Northern Spy, and Jonagold—sourced from Finger Lakes growers. Enchanted is an aromatic, bone-dry cider made from 100 percent Newtown Pippins, the oldest commercially grown variety to have been bred in America.

Don't miss Frisky Whisky. It's made from a blend of wild apples and vanilla, then gets a swim in used whiskey barrels from local distilleries, challenging the palate with notes reminiscent of whiskey's most familiar flavors.

DISTILLERIES

HOLLERHORN DISTILLING
8443 Spirit Run
Naples, NY 14512
www.hollerhorn.com

Although Naples is better known for wine than anything else, it was refreshing in 2018 when Karl and Melissa Neubauer opened Hollerhorn Distilling among the grapevines. Following along a path of artistic endeavors, the husband-and-wife team set out on a long-plotted dream of combining a dash of wine-country elegance with a cutting-edge craft-spirit experience. Karl, whose educational background includes Alfred University School of Art and Design and Yestermorrow Design/Build School, became an avid home brewer and home distiller, researching traditional methods of distillation and blending. As his creative itch grew, he enrolled in Springbank Whiskey School at the renowned distillery in Campbeltown, on the Kintyre Peninsula in western Scotland. A self-described maker of things, Karl combined his cultivated passions to create this visionary enterprise. Hollerhorn Distilling is a category unto itself, truly an art piece that provides fertile ground for experimentation.

In a series called Tree Spirits, Karl does what all great artists do: reinvigorating and reinventing forms and making them his own. While rum is made by fermenting sugarcane juice, his originally conceived notion starts with locally sourced maple syrup as the sugar source to produce these terroir-driven spirits.

Single-malt whiskeys include Malt in Motion, made from Naples Valley–grown barley, malted by Murmuration Malts in Bloomfield, and finished in multiple casks. Heavily peated Devil's Bedroom is made with hot pepper–infused honey from Frog's Point near Canadice Lake.

A handful of tasty liqueurs include Kirsch, an unaged cherry brandy, and Grappa, a collaboration using Riesling grapes from McGregor Vineyard (see page 49).

Come hungry and thirsty. The Spirit Room menu, created by Melissa, will inspire you to linger over a long lunch. Small plates include baked camembert and a ploughman's board and, among the main dishes, smoked pork and chicken schnitzel. Save room for house-made ice creams.

KEUKA LAKE (WEST)

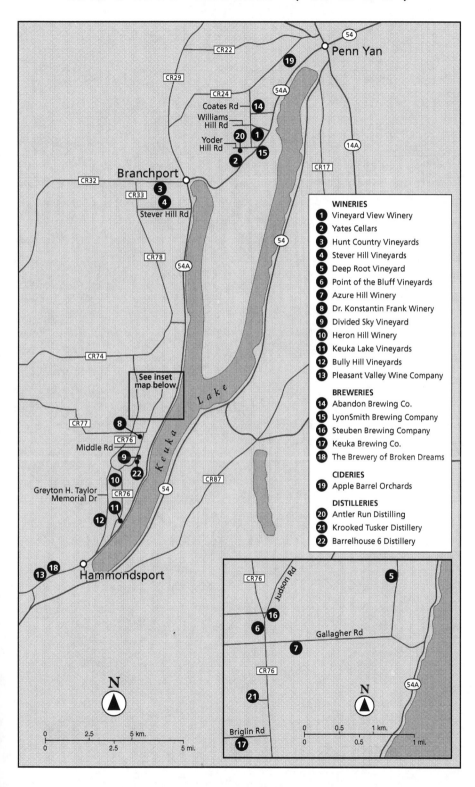

WINERIES
1. Vineyard View Winery
2. Yates Cellars
3. Hunt Country Vineyards
4. Stever Hill Vineyards
5. Deep Root Vineyard
6. Point of the Bluff Vineyards
7. Azure Hill Winery
8. Dr. Konstantin Frank Winery
9. Divided Sky Vineyard
10. Heron Hill Winery
11. Keuka Lake Vineyards
12. Bully Hill Vineyards
13. Pleasant Valley Wine Company

BREWERIES
14. Abandon Brewing Co.
15. LyonSmith Brewing Company
16. Steuben Brewing Company
17. Keuka Brewing Co.
18. The Brewery of Broken Dreams

CIDERIES
19. Apple Barrel Orchards

DISTILLERIES
20. Antler Run Distilling
21. Krooked Tusker Distillery
22. Barrelhouse 6 Distillery

WINERIES

VINEYARD VIEW WINERY
2971 Williams Hill Road
Keuka Park, NY 14478
www.vineyardviewwinery.com

Calling all shutterbugs. Nestled in a magical spot on a hillside draped in vineyards, the winery provides an abundance of fab backgrounds, all of which practically beg to be photographed. Visit for the views but not just for them.

Although its first vintage was 2012, the estate has a connection to five generations of grape growers. Adam Folts tends more than one hundred acres of grapes on the very same property his great-great-grandfather Sherman first cultivated more than a century ago. Early harvests of Concords were sold as table grapes, and over the years, as the farm expanded, the grapes were sold for wine production. More recent plantings have evolved beyond native Concords to include Traminette, Aromella, and Marquette, as well as vinifera varieties, including Riesling, Chardonnay, and Cabernet Franc.

In the early years, Adam's mentor in the cellar was Tim Moore of Inspire Moore Winery (see page 15). Winemaking is now in the capable hands of Paige Vinson, who comes from Three Brothers Wineries & Estates (see page 99) and whose previous experience includes stints at Rooster Hill Vineyards (see page 47) and Red Newt Cellars (see page 112).

The estate is best known for two wines that connect to the Folts grape-growing ancestry: Family White, made from fragrant Delaware grapes, and Family Red, made from robust Concords, staple varieties of the farmstead.

From May to October, Vineyard View Winery offers a "boxed lunch" from the nearby Flour Shop Cafe and Bakery for visitors to enjoy on the scenic, flat-out stunning estate grounds.

YATES CELLARS

3170 Route 54A
Keuka Park, NY 14478
www.yatescellars.com

There are acres of history here. The setting is a stately manor called the Hempstead Mansion, listed on the National Register of Historic Places. It was built in 1838 by Henry Rose, a physician who became interested in wool growing from Merino sheep and fruit growing on the five-hundred-acre estate. The Greek Revival edifice, surrounded by vineyards that date back to 1860, is now the setting of a winery and tasting parlor. Yates Cellars, established in 2003, is a personal, limited-production enterprise.

You'll find the owner of the estate, a gentleman winemaker by the name of Alan Hunt, in the parlor, pouring his wines and telling stories. He has more than fifty years of experience as a vineyardist, and at Yates Cellars he has become a small-scale vintner. He grows modest lots of native, French hybrid, and vinifera grapes, and although he sells most of his harvest to other wineries, he reserves the pick of the crop to make wines that suit his own palate.

For the Riesling seeker, he handcrafts Home Farm Dry Riesling, fermented in stainless steel, and Bluff Dry Riesling, barrel fermented in neutral oak.

Mr. Hunt's current obsession is Regent, a dark-skinned hybrid variety developed in Germany, counting Chambourcin, Silvaner, and Müller-Thurgau in its lineage. His plantings of a mere one hundred Regent vines are snatched away from the estate's hillside to produce rare and precious bottles of wine.

HUNT COUNTRY VINEYARDS

4021 Italy Hill Road
Branchport, NY 14418
www.huntwines.com

Branchport was already established as a farming community when Adam Hunt moved from the Hudson Valley and settled here in 1815. He built a simple but solid log cabin, took up residence, then planted fruit trees and grapevines on the rolling hillside. The farm has remained in the Hunt family for six generations and is now home to eighty acres of native, French-American hybrid, and vinifera wine grapes.

The winery was established by Art and Joyce Hunt in 1981, first as Finger Lakes Wine Cellars, then renamed Hunt Country Vineyards. In true farm-family fashion, young Jonathan Hunt was groomed to be the next-generation wine-grower. He studied viticulture and enology at Cornell; interned at St. Francis Winery and Vineyards in Sonoma Valley, California, and Delegat's Wine Estate in Auckland, New Zealand; before returning to the historic homestead and to family tradition.

Over the years, the vineyard has expanded; the wines have evolved; and most recently, a second label, Uncharted Terroir, provides the winemaking team an opportunity to experiment with the vineyard's "survivors," regionally adapted, climate-resilient varieties, including Vidal Blanc and Vignoles, grapes that work hard to survive, developing character in the process. As the oldest continuous producer of ice wine in the United States, Hunt Country has consistently excelled in the art of sculpting frozen fruit into these rare delicacies, so good they have accompanied dessert at White House dinners.

The Finger Lakes provides one of the few locales in the world ideal for producing these German-style *eisweins*. The production of this luxurious beverage is a daunting task, requiring specific weather conditions and climates. At Hunt Country, hardy Vidal grapes are left on the vines past traditional harvest time and picked when they are frozen. Vidal Ice Wine is an exceptional dessert wine with mouth-filling texture and explosive fruit flavors, on the high-sweetness end of the spectrum. Expect to pay dearly for this true ice wine, but it's well worth the splurge.

STEVER HILL VINEYARDS
3962 Stever Hill Road
Branchport, NY 14418
www.steverhillvineyards.com

The Tones have been developing vineyard expertise in the Finger Lakes since 1951, supplying regional wineries with thousands of tons of fruit each year from five hundred acres of family vineyards. When the owner of Stever Hill Vineyards, a small nearby winery, decided to retire in 2012, third-generation brothers Harold, Don, and Jim Tones got into the wine business. Stever Hill is both concept and wine born out of the collective energy and shared vision of the family. Sons Jon and Mike manage the vineyard, while daughter Liz and husband Jay, both graduates of Cal Poly's Wine and Viticulture Program, manage winemaking, contracting with Hunt Country Vineyards (see page 27) and Lakewood Vineyards (see page 84) for production.

Estate fruit includes a range of native and lesser-known hybrid varieties, among them Itasca, Marquette, and Petite Pearl, yielding wines that are uniquely flavorful and region-specific. Perhaps most interesting is the production of St. Croix, a dark-skinned, winter-hardy grape grown on a ten-acre block and used both for Old Barn Red and in a reserve program, aged in fifty-three-gallon Minnesota oak barrels, thought to provide a smoother finish than French oak. Besides their own holdings, the family uses a small quantity of purchased fruit to balance the Stever Hill portfolio with a few vinifera varieties.

The hillside tasting room, which has a spectacular view of vines that decorate the landscape, is housed in what's called the Crooked Barn, a renovated 1850s-era structure complete with rustic woodwork and original hand-hewn beams. A visit here represents the very picture of the Finger Lakes wine country many visitors imagine.

DEEP ROOT VINEYARD
10391 Cross Street
Hammondsport, NY 14840
www.deeprootvineyard.com

The color purple is the theme here—not the novel or the movie but the Concord grape and its distinctive purple color. The classic native grape variety is used to produce juices; jams; jellies; and, of course, sweet red table wines. For more than a century, this property has been planted with those native vines, so when Ben and Michelle Hartman purchased the vineyard in 2007, they inherited old-vine Concords. Culminating the couple's shared dream, Deep Root Vineyard was established as a microproduction farm winery in 2011, crafting estate-grown and purchased grapes into wines in small batches, perhaps no more than three hundred cases each year.

At this under-the-radar, small-scale winery, Ben makes his mark with Country Red, a Concord varietal; Flight, a Concord-Catawba blend; and a seasonal Concord infused with mulling spices. Sourced Chambourcin grapes are crafted into his oak-aged masterwork. This is real grassroots winemaking, and nearly every pour comes with a backstory.

Wines are sold onsite at the purple-painted barn, and for those who aren't able to make the journey, Deep Root wines are sold at a number of farmers markets throughout the region.

POINT OF THE BLUFF VINEYARDS

10489 County Road 76
Hammondsport, NY 14840
www.pointofthebluffvineyards.com

The bluff is an expansive, seven-mile promontory that divides the two branches of Keuka Lake's wishbone. Point of the Bluff, with stunning views overlooking the lake and lush hillside, is both a working winery and a hospitality-focused venue for weddings, concerts, and other special events. POBV concentrates on producing high-caliber wines, available for tasting in the property's repurposed 1800s-era schoolhouse.

Mike Countryman learned his trade at Casa Larga Vineyards and Winery (see page 189) under the wing of Andrew Colaruotolo. His vineyard and winemaking knowledge and experience deeply influenced the course of POBV and its ascendance among the region's important producers.

Estate wines are crafted from Riesling, Pinot Noir, and Frontenac grapes grown on sixteen acres of the Pulteney Vineyard and three acres in Keuka Park. The balance of fruit for the winery's portfolio are sourced from the Simmons Vineyard, Doyle Vineyards, and Anyela's Vineyards (see page 184). The winery has embraced the growing popularity of canned wines with its Hangar 17 brand, inspired by the owner's seaplane, once stored in Hangar 17 at the Penn Yan airport. Sales of the wine benefit the local Glenn H. Curtiss Aviation Museum.

In 2016, after studies at Finger Lakes Community College's Viticulture and Wine Technology Program, Devin Shomaker created an urban vineyard on the massive 65,000-square-foot roof of the Brooklyn Navy Yard towering over the East River. In collaboration with Point of the Bluff, he developed a high-density planter system filled with Keuka Lake soil for growing traditional Bordeaux grape varieties. After harvest, the fruit is transported to POBV winemaking facilities. While the Brooklyn venture only yields twenty or so cases of wine each year, the majority of the Rooftop Reds series of wines are produced here with Finger Lakes fruit.

Each summer, as many as 20,000 concertgoers from all over the country arrive at the estate for live music events at the impressive open-air pavilion, built with five-hundred-year-old reclaimed Douglas fir timbers.

AZURE HILL WINERY
8716 Gallagher Road
Hammondsport, NY 14840
www.azurehillwinery.com

Noël Coward, English writer, composer, and actor, once explained, "Why do I drink Champagne for breakfast? Doesn't everyone?" Taking a page from Sir Noël, Joseph Sheehy occasionally enjoys sipping his own bubbly with the first meal of the day, an exuberant sparkler called Riesling Brut, inspired by traditional German Sekt, made with grapes grown on this dramatic hillside. The best reason to come here isn't the views, fabulous as they are. Come for the serious, small-lot wines made by Sheehy, who followed a circuitous path on his way to winegrower.

After training in classical cooking at École de Cuisine La Varenne and working as a chef in Paris, he began rooting around in wider French tradition. His interest in wine was a natural outgrowth of his passion for the history of the great French chateaux. Back in the United States, he joined Stew Leonard's supermarket chain as buyer and wine educator, earned an online certificate in winemaking from UC Davis, then apprenticed under acclaimed winemaker Eric Fry at Lenz Winery on Long Island's North Fork. In 2004, Sheehy and his wife, Leslie Knipe, purchased this well-situated parcel of land above Keuka Lake and began hand-planting vines. The first bottles of Azure Hill wines were released in 2010, with stylish labels designed by Leslie, a former art director.

If you're spending the day in wine country, you can bring a picnic lunch to the lovely grounds. Of course, you'll need a bottle of wine to go with that picnic, and there are delicious options here. Besides the signature sparkling Riesling, best choices are the dry and sweet still versions and a delightfully complex red blend of Cabernet Franc, Léon Millot (pronounced *MEE-yo*), Marquette, and Chambourcin called Synthesis.

Wine aficionados will recognize Saperavi as an ancient grape variety from the most ancient winemaking region of the world. Sheehy's production of Saperavi rosé from hand-harvested, estate-grown grapes is extremely limited, even by boutique-winery standards. The lucky few who are able to secure a bottle will be amply rewarded.

DR. KONSTANTIN FRANK WINERY
9749 Middle Road
Hammondsport, NY 14840
www.drfrankwines.com

A Ukrainian-born professor of plant science, Konstantin Frank immigrated to New York City in 1951 after having successfully nurtured wine-producing vines through some of Ukraine's nastiest winters. His belief that the same vinifera plantings could do no worse in Upstate New York went unnoticed, even among the experts at Cornell who, when he arrived at the Agricultural Experiment Station, handed him a hoe and sent him into the blueberry field.

He was correct, of course, but it was not until he met Charles Fournier, wine master of Gold Seal Vineyards, that he would be given the opportunity to prove it. The two men collaborated on an experimental Pinot Noir vineyard near Hammondsport, and heady with success, Dr. Frank established his own winery in 1962. He planted as many as fifty different varieties, including Riesling; Chardonnay; Pinot Noir; Gewürztraminer; Cabernet Sauvignon; and Rkatsiteli, a favorite grape from his native Ukraine, at what grandson Frederick describes as "Dr. Frank's own experiment station." It was the wellspring of the Finger Lakes' modern wine industry.

The Frank family is the closest we have to royalty in the Finger Lakes. Meaghan, the great-granddaughter of the winery's namesake, armed with an MBA in the wine business from the University of Adelaide in Australia and a master's in enology from Cornell University, has become guardian of a revered legacy, working to preserve the historical accomplishments of her great-grandfather.

An exceptional single-vineyard Riesling, Eugenia Dry Riesling, is named after Konstantin's wife, and Hilda Chardonnay, from a single vineyard planted in 1985, is named after his daughter. Venerated by collectors, Old Vines Pinot Noir is made from original plantings, the second-oldest Pinot Noir vines in America. An absurdly high level of expectation attends tastings of Dr. Frank wines, yet they rarely, if ever, disappoint. The winery was named one of the top one hundred wineries in the world by *Wine & Spirits* magazine, one of America's eleven best wineries by *Men's Journal*, and the greatest wine producer in the Northeast by *Wine Report*.

The past is prologue, so an understanding of Finger Lakes wine culture wouldn't be complete without a visit here. There is a sense up here among the vineyards that you have entered a special, more magical place. You may end up drinking some of the best wines on the planet here and in one of the prettiest settings.

DIVIDED SKY VINEYARD
9570 Middle Road
Hammondsport, NY 14840
www.dividedskyvineyard.com

If Divided Sky seems focused on hospitality, it's because Megan Granata and Alek Ajder think of their boutique-size winery as an extension of their home. After training as a sommelier, Alek studied viticulture and wine technology at Finger Lakes Community College and now manages the Salon tasting room at Forge Cellars (see page 115). In 2016, the couple purchased a fifteen-acre property in the shadow of some of the most important wineries in the region. They built a home overlooking the lake in 2017 and began planting Riesling, Cabernet Franc, and Saperavi vines. Until the full three-acre vineyard matures, estate wines are extremely limited, and most bottles are currently made with fruit sourced from various Doyle family–owned vineyards.

Divided Sky Vineyard is focused on small-production, artisanal wines meant to celebrate the distinctive character of each terroir. Keep an eye out for the Dry Rosé, crafted from Blaufränkisch grapes grown at Caywood Vineyards (see page 106).

Tastings are intimate and personal, conducted by the winemaker at his home.

HERON HILL WINERY
9301 County Route 76
Hammondsport, NY 14840
www.heronhill.com

In 1972, John and Josephine Ford Ingle (she is the great-granddaughter of Henry Ford) first planted grapevines on farmland overlooking Canandaigua Lake, eventually joining forces with aspiring winemaker Peter Johnstone on Keuka Lake to turn grapes into fine wine. The collaboration called Heron Hill Winery was an important part in the formative years of the Finger Lakes wine industry. You're surely going to be wowed as you drive up the hill to the winery, where no matter the weather, you're treated to remarkable views of Keuka Lake.

This is where wine meets architecture. In 2000, the Ingles brought architect Charles Warren of New York City to Hammondsport to transform the Heron Hill facility. The result blends elements of the region's history into bold shapes with interesting materials, nothing the Finger Lakes had ever seen. Dramatic stonework was inspired by the cobblestone homes built by masons who came to the region to build the Erie Canal, and the rounded, vaulted ceilings of the tasting room are suggestive of a giant wine barrel. The family-owned winery is as much an architectural landmark as a destination for wine enthusiasts, arguably the grand dame of Keuka Lake.

A native of Ontario, Canada, Jordan Harris earned a degree in winemaking and viticulture from Niagara College, and as winemaker at Tarara Winery in Leesburg, Virginia, he was named among the top one hundred most influential winemakers in the United States by *Wine Enthusiast*. At Heron Hill he works with assistant Laura Zuzek to produce a broad range of exceptional wines. Besides sixteen acres onsite, grapes are sourced from Macri Vineyard on Canandaigua Lake and from the original Ingle Vineyard. Most noteworthy are the vineyard-designated bottles from the home property of John and Josephine.

Rieslings produced here are regarded as regional benchmarks, with no fewer than a half-dozen styles, from dry to semidry to semisweet; an old-vine reserve; and a blend of Muscat and Chardonnay.

With a supply of exceptional fruit, a state-of-the-art facility, and a formidable winemaker in the cellar, Heron Hill has become one of the Finger Lakes' most prominent wineries. And blessed with some of the area's most impressive views of the vineyards and lake, the winery was chosen as one of the ten most spectacular tasting rooms in the world by *Travel + Leisure* magazine.

KEUKA LAKE VINEYARDS

8882 County Route 76
Hammondsport, NY 14840
www.klvineyards.com

He studied mathematics at MIT and economic development at Princeton. After a career in industrial and agricultural development in developing countries, Melvin Goldman purchased a thirty-five-acre property, a former Taylor Wine Company vineyard. Goldman's first plantings were Riesling and Pinot Noir vines. The first vintage in 2005 was made under the guidance of Morten Hallgren of Ravines Wine Cellars (see page 50).

Since 2022, winemaking has been under the direction of Margot Federkiel, graduate of the Enology and Viticulture Program at Cal State Fresno. Starting out as a cellar rat in Napa Valley, she became winemaker at Heller Estate Organic Vineyard in Carmel Valley, California, then cheesemaker at Old Brooklyn Cheese Company in Cleveland, Ohio. She returned to winemaking at Firelands Winery in Sandusky, Ohio, and Gideon Owen Wine Company in Port Clinton, Ohio, before taking the helm at Keuka Lake Vineyards.

There are seven mature estate Riesling vineyards at KLV—Goldman, Evergreen Lek, Falling Man, Ernesto Lucie, 20 Rows, and Upper and Lower Eastside—and Margot leads a team to determine which will be bottled as vineyard specific and which remaining lots will become final blends for dry and semidry Rieslings.

All KLV wines are worthy of serious consideration, especially the Léon Millot (pronounced *MEE-yo*) from a grape developed in Alsace, France, in the early twentieth century. Legendary winemaker Charles Fournier, a champion of French-American hybrids, planted an experimental acre of Léon Millot here in the 1950s. Then in 2009 and 2014, Goldman planted another acre with cuttings from the Fournier Vineyard. Each year, wines produced from the two sites are blended to produce bottles that have gained something of a cult status due to their stellar quality and limited quantity.

The property's two-hundred-year-old white barn has been lovingly restored into a rustic tasting room, so charming and comfortable you'll never want to leave.

BULLY HILL VINEYARDS
8843 Greyton H. Taylor Memorial Drive
Hammondsport, NY 14840
www.bullyhill.com

It's hard to overstate the eccentricity of Bully Hill. The winery, situated on a terraced hillside overlooking Keuka Lake, is the inspiration and creation of a charismatic showman who turned disdain for his family's business into one of the Finger Lakes' most popular destinations. Bully Hill's founder, Walter Taylor, was a larger-than-life character in a sweeping epic of Finger Lakes wine country. The grandson of the founder of the Taylor Wine Company and eager provocateur, Walter railed against the "wine factory" the company had become by the time it was swallowed up by Coca-Cola in 1977.

A Barnum-like ability to capture public attention came naturally to Walter. After all, he was a distant cousin of Phineas Taylor (P. T.) Barnum, the man who built a circus empire with outrageous promotion and guile. When Coke enjoined him from using the family name on his labels, Walter started calling himself "Walter S. Blank." A talented artist, he drew his own winkingly irreverent labels. His most famous label was an image of a billy goat with the slogan "They have my name and my heritage, but they didn't get my goat."

He was a marketing genius whose roguish appeal and publicity stunts provided an antidote to wine snobbery. While the rascally, holy-terror personality of Walter Taylor is gone from his beloved winery, his antiestablishment winemaking and off-the-wall labels have earned him legendary status in the region.

Among the dizzying array of wines, Love My Goat Red is a blend of Baco Noir and Marechal Foch, midway on the winery's dry-to-sweet scale. Bully Hill was first in the region to offer a half-dozen unpretentious boxed wines.

Visit here if only to soak up a bit of the lore of the jester, philosopher, and ringmaster of Bully Hill, champion of the less-sophisticated palate. With one of the most extensive lists of wines (and labels) in the region, there's an air of amusement-park excitement here, and few Finger Lakes wineries are busier on a summer day than Bully Hill.

On the grounds of Bully Hill Vineyards, the first wine museum in America is devoted to the early history of New York State winemaking and the Taylor family endeavor that began in 1878. The Cooper Shop includes local memorabilia and winemaking equipment from the early days of the Finger Lakes wine industry. The Art Gallery houses some of Walter's original artwork, plus artifacts from the days of Prohibition, presidential glassware, and a collection of Taylor family photos.

PLEASANT VALLEY WINE COMPANY
8260 Pleasant Valley Road
Hammondsport, NY 14840
www.pleasantvalleywine.com

Picturesque Hammondsport, on the south end of the lake, has a long history as a vintner's enclave. The first wine grapes in the Finger Lakes were cultivated here in 1829 by William Bostwick, minister of St. James Episcopal Church, and commercial wine production began here in 1860. Many of the fine homes along Lake Street were built by winery owners and winemakers during the second half of the nineteenth century. Take a morning stroll around the village square of the 2012 coolest small town in America, according to *Budget Travel* magazine, then visit Pleasant Valley Wine Company, now home to the Great Western, Gold Seal, and Widmer brands, once-mighty giants in the wine industry, as well as Brickstone Cellars wines made from grapes harvested at the Doyle Family–Fournier Vineyard.

Most noteworthy is Gold Seal Blanc de Blanc, a blend of French-American hybrid varietals championed by Charles Fournier, the former chief winemaker at the French Champagne house of Veuve Clicquot who became president of Gold Seal. Napa Valley pioneer Louis Martini called Fournier "one of the greatest wine-makers we've had in this country."

Established in 1860, the winery proudly displays the designation US bonded winery no. 1 and has eight remarkable stone buildings listed on the National Register of Historic Places. Take a self-guided tour through the visitor center, which includes historic exhibits, winemaking displays from the original 1860 Great Western facility, and a display of artifacts from early winemaking in the region.

Outpost tasting rooms are located at Caywood Vineyards in Lodi (see page 106) and at the Seneca Harbor Wine Center in Watkins Glen.

BREWERIES

ABANDON BREWING CO.
2994 Merritt Hill Road
Penn Yan, NY 14527
www.abandonbrewing.com

All the way to the top of Merritt Hill, sheltered in a restored nineteenth-century barn amid acres of vineyards, apple orchards, walnut groves, and a hopyard with six varieties to flavor their beers, this farmhouse brewery is one of the region's charming pastoral retreats. The helpful staff receives brew pilgrims with open arms. Garry Sperrick, an RIT-trained engineer, opened Abandon in 2013, along with Jeff Hildebrandt, who studied brewing at schools in Chicago and Munich, Germany, then worked for Belgian beer specialist Brewery Ommegang.

The mastery of Hildebrandt's profession is on display in a range of undeniably eclectic offerings. Abandon's flagship, Reckless Abandon Double IPA, is a frontrunner as the region's cleanest, best-balanced IPA. Lower ABVs include Session IPA and Mild Ale, an English-style brown ale.

Belgian Wit Bier is a style that dates back hundreds of years yet in relative obscurity until revived by Belgian brewer Pierre Celis in the 1960s. Hildebrandt's take on this easy-drinking "white beer" is classically spiced with coriander and orange peel.

After sampling at the tasting bar, order a wood-fired pizza or wings, and take a pint of your favorite out on the deck overlooking the lake. At that moment, you'll feel that all is right with the world.

LYONSMITH BREWING COMPANY
2597 Assembly Avenue (off Route 54A)
Keuka Park, NY 14478
www.lyonsmithbrewing.com

Sara Lyon and Dave Smith established the namesake brewery in 2013 and served their first beers on Memorial Day weekend in 2015. In 2020, the couple relocated the brewhouse and tasting room from the village of Penn Yan to a bucolic setting along the Keuka Lake wine trail. An unabashed Anglophile, Dave finds inspiration in the brewing traditions of the United Kingdom. These are brews that spark conversation, a family of offerings in the pure style of English ales, from standards, including classic ales and robust porters, to specialties that embody qualities of the seasons (i.e., Nut Brown Ale in spring; Scotch Ale in summer; Braggot, a beer-mead hybrid, in fall; and Barleywine Ale in winter). For authenticity, Dave uses English hops, East Kent Golding and Fuggle, for earthy, stone-fruit aromatics, distinctly different from the more citrus-like notes of New World varieties.

LyonSmith is a must-visit in wine country for a "proper pint" to cure a wine taster's palate fatigue and lubricate the banter.

STEUBEN BREWING COMPANY
10286 Judson Road
Hammondsport, NY 14840
www.steubenbrewingcompany.com

Beer tourists will enjoy this outpost overlooking Keuka Lake's bluff at the northern edge of a county named in honor of Baron von Steuben, a German general who fought on the American side during the Revolutionary War. It's said that good beer tastes even better in a picturesque setting. In fact, *Men's Journal* named Steuben Brewing among the most scenic breweries in America to enjoy beers with a view.

With beer so often being the beverage of choice among people who work in the wine industry, a brewery smack dab in the middle of wine country came naturally to the Zimar family, headed by Jim Zimar, former winemaker at Prejean Winery. Son Chad, a former chef, takes charge of a seven-barrel system, turning out ales and lagers in two-hundred-gallon batches. In addition, a single-barrel pilot system produces a thirty-gallon supply for seasonals and experimentals. Sample fresh brews by the flight, half-pint, or pint.

While the brand's bread and butter has always been its pilsners, lightly hopped Hometown Brown Ale takes the cake. Grab a pint, sit outside, and soak up the views.

KEUKA BREWING CO.

8572 Briglin Road
Hammondsport, NY 14840
www.keukabrewingcompany.com

This back-lane venture, founded in 2008 by the father-and-son team of Rich and Mark Musso, was the first microbrewery on Keuka Lake and one of the first in the western Finger Lakes region. Sequestered among hills just off the wine trail, Mark takes charge of the ten-barrel brewhouse to produce a fine variety of crowd-pleasing beers, ranging from cream ale interpretations, including Pumpkin Cream Ale, Cookies & Cream Ale, and Strawberries & Cream Ale, to German-style Kölsch ale brewed with local honey and El Crispy, a Mexican-style lager scented with lime peel. In 2014, Keuka Brewing won the F. X. Matt Memorial Cup at the TAP New York Craft Beer Festival as best craft brewery.

If you're among those who think beer is the real breakfast of champions, Mark brews Fat Stack, a robust porter brewed with biscuit malt, local maple syrup, and pecans. It tastes like a stack of pancakes. Or, in place of morning coffee, Local Mocha Stout is made with roasted espresso and Dutch cocoa.

Keuka Brewing attracts IPA aficionados with a "polymorphic" rotation of New England–style IPAs, each inventive batch made with a different mix of hops, each with a unique flavor profile.

The taproom is the kind of place where local Bills fans gather on Sundays to sip beer and watch the games on TV.

THE BREWERY OF BROKEN DREAMS

8319 Pleasant Valley Road
Hammondsport, NY 14840
www.thebreweryofbrokendreams.com

Edward Hopper's 1942 painting *Nighthawks* depicts a diner with a waiter in a white uniform and three customers: a couple and a single man. In 1984, Gottfried Helnwein reworked the painting, replacing the waiter with Elvis Presley, the couple with Marilyn Monroe and Humphrey Bogart, and James Dean sitting alone. The painting, entitled *Boulevard of Broken Dreams*, brings to mind the theme of this unlikely brewery.

Although Douglas and Shelly Shuckers experienced challenges and setbacks over the years on their way to the brewing business, the extra time they spent chasing their dream allowed the couple the opportunity to find the right place at the right time, adopting an image of the resilient loon as a symbol for achieved goals. Above the convivial tasting room, housed in the historic Monarch Wine Company circa-1880 stone cellar, Doug, an engineer at Corning Glass, works his magic with a range of bespoke ales, all brewed using traditional techniques, including Old Antics, Wise Old Ale, and Crying Loon, the sessionable flagship.

Scottish ales originated in Edinburgh, Scotland, during the 1800s, a region unsuited for highlighting hops, so the style focuses on malt. At The Brewery of Broken Dreams, Unfinished Business is not only true to the style, but it also comes with the story of a feud between two Scottish families, one that hits close to home. Ask for the story when you visit the brewery.

Beers to go are available in bottles or in sixteen-ounce cans filled from the tap.

CIDERIES

APPLE BARREL ORCHARDS
2673 Sand Hill Road
Penn Yan, NY 14527
www.applebarrelorchards.com

When Michael and Allison Wager Hiller purchased the farm market and surrounding orchards from Allison's parents in 2020, they became the fourth generation of the Wager family to own the eighty-five-acre fruit farm started in 1922 by great-grandparents Forrest and Olive Wager. Some of the oldest apple trees were planted in the 1940s, with each generation of the family adding to the farm. Over the years, visiting the you-pick orchard has become a much-loved local tradition.

Beginning in 2023, the Hillers became artisan cidermakers, converting their pole barn into a production facility and the main barn into a tasting room. The first ciders from apples grown, harvested, and fermented on the farm include an unnamed dry cider made from estate-grown Empire culinary apples and a tart blend of apple cider and fresh-pressed Concord grapes.

With the planting of European cider apple varieties in 2021, the range of styles and offerings will expand as they mature and the business takes hold.

DISTILLERIES

ANTLER RUN DISTILLING
3133 Antler Run Road
Keuka Park, NY 14478
www.antlerrundistilling.com

It's all in the family. Doug and James Quade, a father-and-son team, not only enjoy hunting, fishing, and golfing together, but they also enjoy cooking up some of the best bourbons in the region. In a case of history repeating itself, James's great-great-great-grandfather William "Dandy" Rakes was a Virginia moonshiner back in the day.

To find Antler Run Distilling, drive up to Kinneys Corners Road, make an even steeper climb up Yoder Hill Road, then wind your way down Antler Run Road to the production space and tasting room. You'll receive a friendly greeting by Barkley, Finley, and Tucker, the distillery dogs.

Doug and James like to drink bourbon, so it's no surprise where the focus is here. Antler Run Bourbon is a Kentucky-style made with soft red wheat as the flavoring grain. A specialty malt typically used in beer brewing adds sweet and caramel notes to the roasted grain in Howling Dog Bourbon. Both bourbon styles are aged for twenty-four to thirty-six months in new American oak barrels. The bourbon barrels are then repurposed for Apple Whiskey, made with boiled cider. Buckwheat grown on nearby farms adds robust, nutty flavors to Buckwheat Moonshine.

Three years after opening in 2019, Antler Run was voted FLX finest distillery in the Distillery University and Great American International Spirits competition.

When he's not running the still, James brews ten-gallon batches of beer, mostly cream ales but sometimes red ales or stouts. Ask about the beer du jour.

KROOKED TUSKER DISTILLERY
10303 County Road 76
Hammondsport, NY 14840
www.krookedtusker.com

In 2016, Carlton Reeves opened Krooked Tusker Distillery in the heart of the Keuka Lake wine country. Its digs in an old airplane hangar suggests that something interesting is happening here. His small-batch distillery creates corn whiskeys, vodkas, bourbons, and even an absinthe, but gin holds a special place in the distiller's heart.

While gins are traditionally infused with juniper berries, Reeves mixes multiple botanicals to craft herbal-focused, boutique variations. In 2022, Chicago-based Beverage Testing Institute ranked QKA Navy Gin, comprised of fifty-one botanicals, among the world's best. BTI described the gin as "bold yet charming navy strength that will amp up robust cocktails."

Other offerings, available in tasting flights or mixed in cocktails, include South Pulteney Gin and Frolic; barrel-rested versions are called Sleepless in South Pulteney and Midnight Frolic.

Multicolored Adirondack chairs beckon visitors to the outside porch. If the weather's right, it's a pretty good place to while away an hour or so.

BARRELHOUSE 6 DISTILLERY
9558 Middle Road
Hammondsport, NY 14840
www.barrelhouse6.com

Although Kara Mackey began her career as an environmental engineer and attorney, she developed a passion for craft spirits that put her on a different pathway. She headed out to Edinburgh, Scotland, to study at Heriot-Watt University's International Centre for Brewing and Distilling, and in 2021, she staked her claim in a traditionally male-dominated industry.

B6D provides an appealing introduction to the region's spirits. On a property once part of the historic Gold Seal Vineyards, Kara and partner Joe Sorrentino launched this progressive distillery, crafting spirits using a mammoth five-hundred-gallon copper-pot still, the largest still ever made by Hillbilly Stills in Murray, Kentucky. A window in the upscale tasting room provides a glimpse of the experiments lab and the extraordinary vessel.

Kara quickly found success in producing award-winning products, and her signature work follows a Scottish tradition that began hundreds of years ago. B6D's bourbon and rye are aged in wooden sherry casks imported from Spain, allowing residue of sherry in the wood to impart sweet, fruity notes and soften the flavors.

Other offerings include Middle Finger Moonshine, a grain-forward corn whiskey, and Sisters' 1924 London Dry Gin, a juniper-forward sipper.

KEUKA LAKE (EAST)

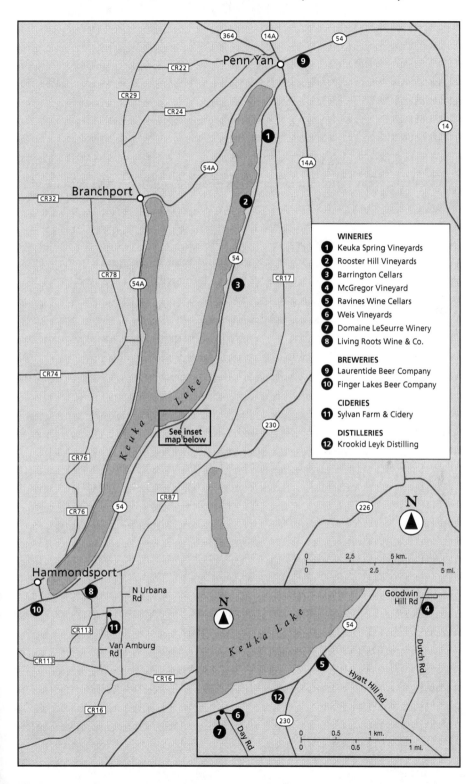

WINERIES
1. Keuka Spring Vineyards
2. Rooster Hill Vineyards
3. Barrington Cellars
4. McGregor Vineyard
5. Ravines Wine Cellars
6. Weis Vineyards
7. Domaine LeSeurre Winery
8. Living Roots Wine & Co.

BREWERIES
9. Laurentide Beer Company
10. Finger Lakes Beer Company

CIDERIES
11. Sylvan Farm & Cidery

DISTILLERIES
12. Krookid Leyk Distilling

Penn Yan

Branchport

Hammondsport

See inset
map below

Keuka Lake

N Urbana Rd
Van Amburg Rd

Goodwin Hill Rd
Dutch Rd
Hyatt Hill Rd
Day Rd

0   2.5   5 km.
0   2.5   5 mi.

0   0.5   1 km.
0   0.5   1 mi.

WINERIES

KEUKA SPRING VINEYARDS
243 Route 54 (East Lake Road)
Penn Yan, NY 14527
www.keukaspringwinery.com

In 1973, Rochesterians Len and Judy Wiltberger began transforming an over-grown property into an estate named for the meandering spring that provides natural irrigation to ten acres of vines. A dozen years later, Keuka Spring Vine-yards debuted its inaugural vintage. Seyval Blanc, Vignoles, Chardonnay, and Riesling—all white varieties—were the first wines, and early successes of these va-rieties in wine competitions attracted attention to the Wiltbergers. Then, over the next few years, they were able to slowly expand the production of red varieties.

If you're unfamiliar with the variety, Keuka Spring was one of the region's early believers in Blaufränkisch (also known as Lemberger), a cold-hearty Austri-an variety that dates to the days of Napoleon Bonaparte and Otto von Bismarck, both of whom enjoyed the wine. Also noteworthy is a Bordeaux-inspired, red-meat-friendly blend called Miller's Cove Red, named for an eighteenth-century farmer named Miller who grew fruit along a nearby inlet.

The agrarian, rustic tasting room fits comfortably into the rural setting, pro-viding a pergola and terrace with picnic tables for an unobstructed view of the vineyard and across the lake to Keuka College. Inside you'll find a knowledgeable staff happy to pour samples of wines that are fruity, balanced, and food friendly.

Former owner and cidermaker at Kashong Creek Craft Cider in Geneva Dan Bissell joined the Keuka Spring team for the 2020 harvest as assistant winemaker and became head winemaker in the summer of 2021. Dan works with estate-grown grapes from the Wiltberger Vineyard and the Dynamite Vineyard, named for the explosives used to break the rocky soil to make room for posts, and he supplements fruit from local growers.

For a dozen or so years, some of the highest-quality grapes used for Keuka Spring's high-scoring wines have been sourced from Simmons Vineyard. Started by Neil and Joyce Simmons in 1963 and now managed by Darren and Julie Simmons, these folks are among the leading grape growers of the region, culti-vating nearly five hundred acres of native, hybrid, and vinifera grapevines near the Keuka Lake bluff. In 2023, the Simmons family purchased the winery and vineyards from the Wiltberger family. Jeff and Annette Simmons will oversee the winery team, refreshed under new ownership, and plans for expansion are in the works.

ROOSTER HILL VINEYARDS
489 Route 54 (East Lake Road)
Penn Yan, NY 14527
www.roosterhill.com

Have you heard the story about the hardworking couple who gave up sensible careers and went all in to become grape growers and vintners? Business suits and briefcases were exchanged for overalls and work boots in 2002, when seven acres of overgrown grapevines on Keuka Lake came up for sale. David and Amy Hoffman restored a long-neglected vineyard on Keuka Lake and planted Cabernet Franc, Riesling, Pinot Noir, and Lemberger in the Savina Vineyard, named for Amy's Tuscan-born great-grandmother Savina Volpona Garbarino. Catherine Vineyard, honoring Savina's daughter, was planted at a slightly higher elevation in Cabernet Franc, Riesling, Gewürztraminer, and Lemberger.

Italian heritage inspired *Il Buon Gallo*, or the Good Rooster, as the winery's icon, a symbol of luck, abundance, and prosperity. The decidedly European tasting room is tastefully decorated with straw-colored walls surrounded by copper molding; the space is highlighted by an oval bar that cleverly provides a lake view to every wine taster. The adjacent patio is fitted with a wood-burning pizza oven for weekend picnics and special events.

In 2018, the Rooster Hill estate was purchased by Philadelphia physicians Paul Curcillo and Stephanie King, adding to their CK Cellars roster of enterprises (see page 72). Paul and Stephanie have injected new energy into Rooster Hill, placing Sadie Lewis squarely in charge of winemaking and expanding offerings to include bottles from other CK brands.

Favorites here include Silver Pencil, a blend of Riesling, Vidal Blanc, and Cayuga White, its name inspired by a breed of English hen, and Bubbly Bantam, a Prosecco-inspired blend of Riesling, Seyval Blanc, and Cayuga White named for the miniature Tuscan chicken. Bring out a bottle of this charming wine, and serve it as a dinner party aperitif.

The motto at Rooster Hill reads, "*Un esperienza di vino*" ("An experience in wine").

BARRINGTON CELLARS
2794 Gray Road
Penn Yan, NY 14527
www.barringtoncellars.com

Tucked against the side of a steep, almost breathtaking slope that rises above Keuka Lake, the Farnan family property has a fascinating story. In 1971, Ken and Eileen Farnan quit corporate jobs; purchased the original thirty-five-acre parcel, including a ten-acre vineyard; and became artisan farmers, growing Concord, Delaware, and Niagara grapes. Fruit that wasn't sold to the Taylor Wine conglomerate became homemade wine, a skill Eileen learned from her grandfather. And buzzards that ride currents over the lake gave the vineyard, Buzzard Crest Vineyard, its name.

It was in 1986, just as Taylor began reducing prices offered to growers, when the Farnans discovered an opportunity to sell table grapes and grape juices at the Union Square Greenmarket in Manhattan and the Grand Army Plaza Greenmarket in Brooklyn. It was the beginning of the big city's love affair with the wondrous assortment of fruit from Buzzard Crest, delivered downstate weekly from August to November and sought after by restaurants, including Blue Hill and Gramercy Tavern, as well as specialty foods icon Baldor.

Then, in 1995, armed with a farm winery license, the Farnans' first wines were released under the Barrington Cellars label, named for the vineyard's homestead in the village of Barrington. Today there are twelve acres of seedless and seeded table grapes and twenty-four acres of juice and wine grapes harvested from vinifera, hybrid, and native varieties. White wine grapes include Aurore, Catawba, Cayuga, Delaware, Diamond, Niagara, Riesling, Vidal, and Traminette. Reds include Baco Noir, Cabernet Franc, De Chaunac, and inky-black Vincent.

While Barrington wines are not organic, the vineyard is managed with organic farming techniques, and the grapes are certified organic, all under the careful supervision of Eileen, Ken, and the extended Farnan family. One of the benefits of visiting here is you're likely to meet one of the owners, learn about their passion and history, and taste wines that are not readily available elsewhere.

MCGREGOR VINEYARD

5503 Dutch Street
Dundee, NY 14837
www.mcgregorwinery.com

It's worth taking the long and winding drive out from the edge of the lake and up the glacier-carved hillside just for the views from the sunny, wine-tasting terrace. On a clear day, it's a jaw-dropping sight.

One of Keuka Lake's most venerable producers is indisputably the McGregor family enterprise, practicing the art of winemaking here since 1979. The rustic winery home, vineyards, and adjoining picnic grounds attract a year-round flow of visitors to this 1,200-foot perch overlooking Bluff Point at the widest expanse of the lake. The combination of cool temperatures and significant lake-effect winds on the steep, north-facing slope stresses the vines, producing smaller yields, which results in mature, concentrated flavors in the grapes that grow here.

Bob McGregor, Eastman Kodak physicist-turned-gentleman-grower, made his mark on Finger Lakes viticulture with much publicized plantings of Saperavi and Sereksiya Charni wine grapes, propagated from a mother lode of cuttings that originated in the former Soviet Republic of Georgia. Few Finger Lakes wines were more iconic than Black Russian, the original name for the unique blend of the two. The finished wine was always dominated by the Saperavi component, and in 2017, the winery released its first varietal Saperavi, encouraging other winemakers to follow the lead.

For more than two decades, Jeff Dencenberg has crafted this extraordinary wine for the McGregor clan. No other Finger Lakes winemaker knows Saperavi better than Dencenberg, and his barrel aging is deliberate and artistic. Following a traditional Georgian three-tiered aging system, he rests the wine in wood for one year before release, a Saperavi Reserve for two years, and the Grand Reserve for three or more years. Besides the grand experiment with the eccentric Eastern European variety, Jeff shows a steady hand in the crafting of a range of vinifera wines from grapes grown exclusively on the estate.

The pioneering winery and vineyards are now under the careful supervision of John McGregor, who continues the legacy handed down by his father.

RAVINES WINE CELLARS
14630 Route 54
Hammondsport, NY 14840
www.ravineswine.com

The winery takes its name from the numerous narrow gorges formed by small tributary streams that break up the declivities along Keuka Lake. In fact, the seventeen-acre vineyard landscape is bordered by two such ravines.

Danish-born enologist/winemaker Morten Hallgren was raised among the casks and vines of Domaine de Castel Roubine, his family's 170-acre vineyard and estate winery in the Côtes de Provence region of France. After stints at Cordier Estates in West Texas and the Biltmore Estate in North Carolina, in 1998 he became head winemaker at the Dr. Konstantin Frank Winery (see page 32). In 2001, Morten set out on his own path. He and his wife, Lisa, purchased this hillside parcel of land, determined to model his venture, in Morten's words, "in the spirit of those I have seen and loved in Provence." Two years later Ravines Dry Riesling was named best dry Riesling at the World Riesling Cup.

In 2012, the Hallgrens expanded Ravines to include 130 acres of prime estate vineyards, a state-of-the-art winemaking facility, and a neorustic tasting room in Geneva (see Ravines Wine Cellars, page 62).

This Keuka Lake location, the original vineyard and winery, now serves as a tasting room and wine shop. Swirl and sip on the patio while you take in the awe-inspiring views.

WEIS VINEYARDS
10014 Day Road (off Route 54)
Hammondsport, NY 14840
www.weisvineyards.com

Hans Peter Weis grew up in the vineyards and cellar of his family winery in Zell, a German town overlooking the Mosel River, where Riesling grapes have been cultivated and extraordinary wines have been produced for hundreds of years. After earning his winemaking and viticulture degree in Germany, Peter took his first job in the United States in 2005 at Schug Winery in the Carneros appellation of Sonoma County, California. A year later, he landed in the Finger Lakes, managing German varieties at the Dr. Konstantin Frank Winery (see page 32). In 2016, Peter purchased the former Lime Berry Wine Estates property—an eight-acre property with a house, barn, one-room schoolhouse, storage facility, and tasting room, where visitors sip wine facing a stunning view of the lake. A subsequent acquisition of 110 off-site land has become the source for estate-grown fruit.

Handcrafted Rieslings are clearly the center of attention here, each inspired by the styles and traditions of Germany. The Winzer (German for "winemaker") series includes Select Riesling K, produced in the light style of a classic Kabinett, and Select Riesling A, in reference to a late-harvest, Auslese-inspired wine.

While Riesling grapes are well suited to the cool climate of the Finger Lakes, the unpredictable weather presents challenges. The lakes help moderate temperatures yet not always enough to prevent frost damage. In 2013, Cornell AgriTech released Aravelle (from the Latin *Arabella*, which means "grace" or "favor"), a unique hybrid of Riesling and Cayuga, productive and more cold hardy than its Riesling parent.

As a curious and creative winemaker, Peter's four acres of Aravelle served as an incubator for Aravelle, growing the vines and producing wines for tasting by the research team. A visit to Weis Vineyards will provide an opportunity to taste the fledgling Aravelle, the sole grape in a wine called Heart of the Lake, reminiscent of a semi-dry Riesling yet a distinctive varietal of its own.

DOMAINE LESEURRE WINERY
13920 Route 54
Hammondsport, NY 14840
www.dlwinery.com

A husband-and-wife winemaking team, Sébastien and Céline LeSeurre raised the winemaking bar in this region with their combined French heritage and breadth of experience. Sébastien grew up in the Champagne region, where his family has been growing grapes and producing wines for six generations and where he studied viticulture and enology. Céline was raised next to her grandparents' vineyard in the foothills of the Pyrenees. Her first job was at Le Cellier des Templiers in the Languedoc-Roussillon region. The couple met while working at the Clos Henri Vineyard in New Zealand, then worked together again for De Bortoli wines in Australia before arriving in the Finger Lakes.

Sébastien became assistant winemaker at Dr. Konstantin Frank Winery (see page 32), while Céline served as US brand ambassador for the prestigious French winemaker Michel Chapoutier. In 2012, the couple purchased a favored property overlooking the lake while producing wine at an off-site winery. For their first vintage, Sébastien selected Chardonnay, Riesling, Gewürztraminer, Pinot Noir, and Cabernet Franc grapes after tastings at multiple vineyards.

The dynamic duo craft each wine and make decisions as a team—from picking the fruit through stages of fermentation, as well as bottling, labeling, and marketing. Without their own vineyard, they lease rows of vines from selected terroirs, monitoring the grapevines throughout the season for their growth, health, and ripeness and deciding the optimal time to harvest.

In French, the word *domaine* is defined as an "area of control," and in connection with wine, the word refers to a parcel of land under the primacy of a winemaker. Sébastien and Céline are passionate about creating wines that reflect their origin, wines that show the distinctive characteristics of the place where they are grown and made. They are preparing the soil on eight acres of nearby land for estate plantings in the next couple of years.

Small-batch wines are produced with an artistic approach that marries Old World traditions with New World advancements to produce the winery's limited production portfolio of profoundly expressive wines. Borrowing from tradition, they determine ripeness by taste, not by measuring brix, and the cellar is filled with the sound of batons stirring the lees inside French oak barrels filled with Chardonnay. For more modern management of fermentations, they employ temperature-controlled wine tanks.

Your greeting here begins with a message that reads, "Bonjour!" The tasting room reflects the home country of the LeSeurres, with signage in both French and English, as the French flag flutters on the front deck.

LIVING ROOTS WINE & CO.
8560 County Road 87
Hammondsport, NY 14840
www.livingrootswine.com

His great-great-great-grandfather Thomas Hardy started a company that grew to become Australia's largest wine producer. Sebastian Hardy grew up in the family business and earned a degree in viticulture and enology from the University of Adelaide.

Colleen Hurley grew up in Rochester; earned a degree in marketing from Michigan State; and, after three years, left a marketing research career for a five-month internship at the Hardy Company's Tintara Winery in the McLaren Vale wine region of South Australia.

It happened at Tintara during the harvest of 2014. Boy meets girl. Boy and girl fall in love. Three years later, boy and girl launch their own winery, housed in a refurbished warehouse on University Avenue in Rochester. Since 2017, Living

Roots Wine & Co. has been making wines with fruit from coveted sources, both the Finger Lakes region and South Australia. Many of the wines produced from Finger Lakes grapes derive from Shale Creek Vineyard owned by Mike Hurley, Colleen's father, a business partner in Living Roots. In 2023, the couple built a state-of-the-art tasting room, an extraordinary showcase for their wines, far above the east side of Keuka with a picturesque view of the lake and vineyards.

The couple's youthful energy brings a fresh appeal to the offerings, including Session Rizz (Australian slang for "Riesling"), made from Finger Lakes fruit, wild yeast fermented and unfined, and Red Rizza, Finger Lakes Riesling juice fermented wild on Cabernet Franc skins, then aged ten months in French oak. Australian bottles include Grenache, Shiraz, and a Cabernet Sauvignon–Tannat blend.

An experience in the tasting room follows two formats: curated flights including four wines or six-ounce pours by the glass. Snacks include tinned fish with sourdough, marinated Australian sheep cheese, and kangaroo jerky.

BREWERIES

LAURENTIDE BEER COMPANY
12 Maiden Lane
Penn Yan, NY 14527
www.laurentidebeer.com

A massive ice sheet called Laurentide moved across northern North America a half-million years ago and, among other effects, gouged out what became the Finger Lakes. Tracey and Marla Hedworth chose the name to reflect the geographic history of the region. In 2018, a village landmark, once the private residence of lieutenant governor of New York and later US state senator and congressman William Morrison Oliver, became the Laurentide Inn, an elegantly appointed, five-room bed and breakfast—the first part of the couple's ambitious plan. Two years later, Tracey and Marla converted the estate's carriage house into the home of the Laurentide Beer Company. Choose from a dozen beers on tap; sip inside or outside on a patio lined with Adirondack chairs.

Brewer Brett Driscoll sources regional malts and hops to craft Penn Yan Light Lager, a popular low-ABV-style, all-day sipper and the brewery's best-seller. If you're here in the fall, pay special attention to his Oktoberfest, a German-style Märzen. Beers are poured in five-ounce tasters, ten-ounce glasses, or traditional pints.

As a final piece in the Laurentide puzzle, the Hedworths purchased a former restaurant property behind the brewery and joined forces with local chef Ben Comstock and partner Jim Coriale of True Roots Catering to establish True Roots Kitchen at LBC. The charming café offers an ambitious gastropub-inspired menu with pampered dishes to complement the fresh brews.

FINGER LAKES BEER COMPANY
8462 Route 54
Hammondsport, NY 14840
www.fingerlakesbeercompany.com

Sometimes going against the grain is a good thing. In 2009, partners led by Mark Goodwin established this microbrewery just outside the wine-centric village of Hammondsport. Yet both locals and tourists have proved equally gregarious beer drinkers, keeping the pub-inspired taproom hopping as the range of offerings evolves and becomes more sophisticated. Goodwin, who holds a degree in brewing science from Chicago's Siebel Institute of Technology, alongside son Eric, who earned his stripes at Southern Tier Brewing Company in Lakewood, operate a seven-barrel brewhouse to craft a wide range of styles and flavor profiles, all offered in tasting flights, half-pints, pints, and pitchers.

Standbys include Copperline, an easy-drinking amber ale; sessionable Beach Blonde Ale; and Hammonds-Porter, well-hopped and dark, brewed with chocolate malt and fermented with Madagascar vanilla beans. During the summer months, attention turns to Watermelon Wheat, a German Weizenbier-style brew made with fresh local watermelons.

Master rollers at the Santiago Cigar Factory in Rochester ferment their wrappers in Finger Lakes Beer Company porters and stouts. The cigars are for sale at the bar.

CIDERIES

SYLVAN FARM & CIDERY

8080 Van Amburg Road
Hammondsport, NY 14840
www.sylvanfarmandcidery.com

Sally and Don Schmitt opened the famed French Laundry in Yountville, California, in 1978, and after selling the restaurant to Thomas Keller in 1994, they operated the Apple Farm, a cooking school and orchard in the Mendocino County town of Philo. Joshua Jenkins, former art teacher, and Charles Treichler, former theologian, met while working for the Schmitts as farmhands and learning farming skills.

There's an old saying about the lucky man who can eat the fruits of the trees his grandfather planted. Charles is that lucky man. His grandfather planted apple and pear trees on a three-hundred-acre farm just outside of Hammondsport. Charles and Joshua, partners in life, returned to the family farm as partners in a fruit-growing and cider-producing venture. While Charles interned at Eve's Cidery (see page 206), Joshua added plantings with a number of traditional cider apples, including Frequin Rouge, Harrison, Porter's Perfection, and others, supplementing the orchard's historic wild apples and pears.

Early ciders produced in small lots at Sylvan Farm include both apple and pear ciders (perries), crafted from wild fruit. Tastings are available by appointment.

DISTILLERIES

KROOKID LEYK DISTILLING
14322 Route 54
Hammondsport, NY 14840
www.krookidleyk.com

The seemingly misspelled name of this enterprise was actually inspired by local pronunciation of Crooked Lake, the nickname for Keuka's odd shape. The route to becoming a distiller is rarely ever a straight line. Patrick Rosno, a fourth-generation farm boy, was inspired by his grandfather, who (rumor has it) made moonshine during the dry days of Prohibition. In 2019, following in family footsteps, Patrick used his background in engineering and construction to design and build the handsome facility housing Krookid Leyk Distilling's production space and tasting room.

The distillery employs a copper still imported from China to produce Whitecap, a multiple-botanical gin, a cinnamon-infused whiskey, vodkas made from locally sourced wheat and corn, and a distinctly provincial rum crafted with maple syrup tapped from sixty-five maple trees on family property and locally sourced molasses.

Each spirit is bottled and labeled by hand before making it to the tasting room and retail shop.

SENECA LAKE (WEST)

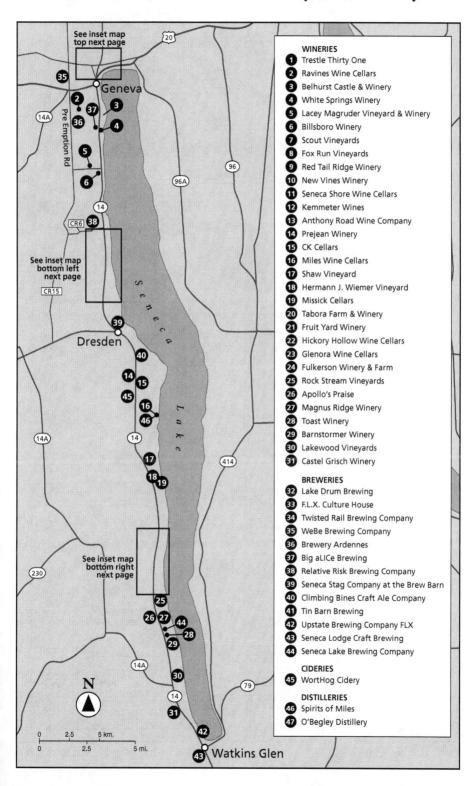

WINERIES
1. Trestle Thirty One
2. Ravines Wine Cellars
3. Belhurst Castle & Winery
4. White Springs Winery
5. Lacey Magruder Vineyard & Winery
6. Billsboro Winery
7. Scout Vineyards
8. Fox Run Vineyards
9. Red Tail Ridge Winery
10. New Vines Winery
11. Seneca Shore Wine Cellars
12. Kemmeter Wines
13. Anthony Road Wine Company
14. Prejean Winery
15. CK Cellars
16. Miles Wine Cellars
17. Shaw Vineyard
18. Hermann J. Wiemer Vineyard
19. Missick Cellars
20. Tabora Farm & Winery
21. Fruit Yard Winery
22. Hickory Hollow Wine Cellars
23. Glenora Wine Cellars
24. Fulkerson Winery & Farm
25. Rock Stream Vineyards
26. Apollo's Praise
27. Magnus Ridge Winery
28. Toast Winery
29. Barnstormer Winery
30. Lakewood Vineyards
31. Castel Grisch Winery

BREWERIES
32. Lake Drum Brewing
33. F.L.X. Culture House
34. Twisted Rail Brewing Company
35. WeBe Brewing Company
36. Brewery Ardennes
37. Big aLICe Brewing
38. Relative Risk Brewing Company
39. Seneca Stag Company at the Brew Barn
40. Climbing Bines Craft Ale Company
41. Tin Barn Brewing
42. Upstate Brewing Company FLX
43. Seneca Lodge Craft Brewing
44. Seneca Lake Brewing Company

CIDERIES
45. WortHog Cidery

DISTILLERIES
46. Spirits of Miles
47. O'Begley Distillery

See inset map top next page

Geneva

Pre Emption Rd

See inset map bottom left next page

Seneca Lake

Dresden

See inset map bottom right next page

N

0   2.5   5 km.
0   2.5   5 mi.

Watkins Glen

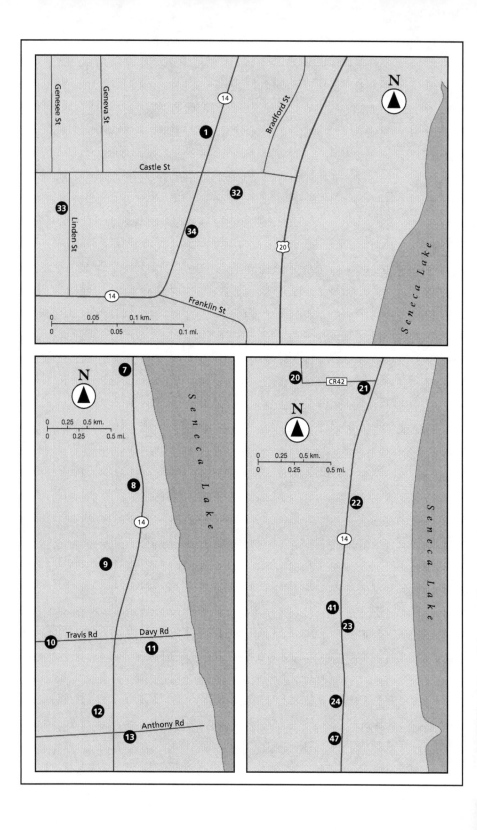

WINERIES

TRESTLE THIRTY ONE
436 Exchange Street
Geneva, NY 14456
www.trestle31.com

In 2016, Nova Cadamentre became one of the first graduates of Cornell's Viticulture and Enology Program, and a year later, she earned the master-of-wine certification. Her career has taken her to California as winemaker at Chateau Souverain and Asti Winery and as senior director of winemaking at Robert Mondavi Winery. She then came back to the Finger Lakes, where she became director of winemaking at Constellation Brands, developing the boutique 240 Days wine brand. Over the course of nearly two decades, Nova has become one of the most versatile and experienced winemakers and consultants in the industry.

In 2015, Nova and husband Brian purchased twelve acres of farmland on Seneca Lake, the beginning of a small-scale winemaking venture called Trestle Thirty One. The first part of the name comes from the railroad trestle prominent from the top of the property. The second part refers to the land's original deed number, part of the military tract that dates to the Revolutionary War.

Until the vineyard matures, fruit is sourced from other local growers. Keep an eye out for their distinctive Riesling, made from grapes from four carefully curated rows at nearby Zugibe Vineyards (see page 100), and Cabernet Franc, made from fruit picked at Simmons Vineyard on the Keuka Bluff and aged in French oak for eighteen months. The ultraboutique winery produces a mere six hundred cases of exceptional wines each year.

The stunning labels on each variety feature the work of distinguished artist Linda Williams McCune, who just happens to be Nova's mother. The Study Sketch series, featuring snippets from the artist's journal, is intended for experimental lots and creative styles, different with each vintage.

An Exchange Street storefront that formerly housed a tattoo parlor provides separate, well-appointed lounges for small gatherings. This isn't the kind of place you pop into and jostle for a spot at the tasting bar. Reservations are required for private tutored tastings.

RAVINES WINE CELLARS

400 Barracks Road
Geneva, NY 14456
www.ravineswine.com

The winery takes its name from the numerous narrow gorges formed by small tributary streams that break up the declivities along the winery's first home on Keuka Lake (see page 50). In fact, the seventeen-acre vineyard landscape is bordered by two such ravines.

Danish-born enologist/winemaker Morten Hallgren was raised among the casks and vines of Domaine de Castel Roubine, his family's 170-acre vineyard and estate winery in the Côtes de Provence region of France. After stints at Cordier Estates in West Texas and the Biltmore Estate in North Carolina, in 1998 he became head winemaker at Dr. Konstantin Frank Winery (see page 32). Beginning in 2001, Morten set out to produce the next great American Riesling. Two years later, Ravines Dry Riesling was named best dry Riesling at the World Riesling Cup.

In 2012, he and wife Lisa purchased the fifty-nine-acre vineyard of the White Springs Estate, its state-of-the-art winemaking facility, and sophisticated irrigation system. Turn onto unpaved Barracks Road and drive along what seem like endless rows of vines to the rustic tasting room housed in a century-old barn.

Although his work with a range of varieties is exceptional, one might say that Morten is to the Riesling grape what Yo-Yo Ma is to the cello. For the Ravines signature Riesling, prized fruit is sourced from the Argetsinger Vineyard on the east side of Seneca Lake. Its steep slope and loam and gravel soils over limestone provide one of the most remarkable terroirs of the Finger Lakes, lending a distinct minerality to the wines. *Decanter* magazine called this single-vineyard wine "perhaps America's preeminent Riesling." Not surprisingly, *Wine Spectator* named Ravines among the one hundred best wineries in the world.

This is an ideal stop for combining a wine tasting across the board with Lisa Hallgren's menu of small plates. Her focus firmly rests on developing and executing seasonal dishes that complement her husband's wines.

BELHURST CASTLE & WINERY

4069 West Lake Road
Geneva, NY 14456
www.belhurst.com

Carrie Harron Collins was a direct descendent of Henry Clay, the senator from Kentucky, speaker of the House, and secretary of state under President John Quincy Adams. In 1885, Mrs. Collins hired an architect and a crew of fifty laborers to begin work on a fairy-tale castle set amid twenty acres of forest on the shore of Seneca Lake. Four years later, Belhurst, meaning "beautiful forest," the three-story, turreted, red-stone curiosity, was completed.

In the years since, Belhurst Castle has been at various times a private home, casino, speakeasy, guesthouse, and restaurant, but it was not until 1992 that the property came into the hands of a developer whose vision was on a scale worthy of its history. In addition to restoring fourteen period bed chambers, six dining rooms, and a spacious ballroom, Duane Reeder constructed the Vinifera Inn, an adjacent twenty-room luxury hotel with meeting and banquet facilities and a tasting room and gift shop.

Now in the hands of Kevin Reeder, Cornell Hotel School grad, the resort includes a portfolio of contract wines produced from grapes sourced around the state and bottled under the Belhurst label. Pay special attention to the Riesling offerings, made from Finger Lakes fruit.

Adorned with an antique carriage and warmed with a stone fireplace, the spacious gift shop is easily a spot to take your time browsing accessories geared to the wine lover's lifestyle.

WHITE SPRINGS WINERY

4200 Route 14
Geneva, NY 14456
www.whitespringswinery.com

The White Springs name originates from one of the Native American villages who called the springs "clear waters" or "white-water springs." White Springs Farm was first established in 1801, and over its agricultural history, it has been used to grow grain crops, to raise sheep, to raise cattle, and as one of the largest orchards in the state. Between 1898 and the 1940s, White Springs was the home of Agnes Bevan Slosson Lewis, a suffragist and social activist.

In 2003, Carl Fribolin, seed grower and founder of Seedway, planted thirteen acres of grapes, and White Springs Winery was born. The vineyard subsequently expanded to forty acres of principally vinifera grapes, along with a few hybrids developed by the New York State Agricultural Experiment Station and Cornell University. In 2012, Morten Hallgren, owner and winemaker of Ravines Wine Cellars (see page 50), purchased the vineyard and production facility, while Fribolin sold the White Springs brand to Jody Earle and David DeMarco.

For the Chardonnay lover, a visit here is like being a kid in a candy store, an opportunity to compare several interpretations crafted from fruit grown on the estate's thirty-acre Dresden vineyard. Styles include New World, fermented in stainless steel and aged in oak; Traditional, both fermented and aged in oak; No Oak, the purest expression of the varietal; Row House series, a blend of Chardonnay and Cayuga; and (yikes!) a sweet Chardonnay.

But one bottle in particular steals the White Springs show. It's Portrait of a Native Grape, a blend of native varieties fortified in the style of a Port wine. The fascinating story of "born-here" grapes is told on the back label.

If you can be momentarily tempted away from the wines, the tasting room includes a hard cider produced from estate-grown apples.

LACEY MAGRUDER VINEYARD AND WINERY
462 Armstrong Road
Geneva, NY 14456
www.laceymagrudervineyardandwinery.com

Jim and Ruth Hundertmark quit their jobs, packed their bags, and left Baltimore with the romantic notion of living and working in wine country. They settled on a farm property with a two-hundred-year-old barn, and after a three-year apprenticeship at Lamoreaux Landing Wine Cellars (see page 103), Jim made his first wines. The Hundertmarks then opened a winery called Lacey Magruder. The winery's name is derived from the surnames of the couple's Irish grandmothers, and the barn was refurbished to resemble Jim's former Irish pub in the Fell's Point neighborhood of Baltimore.

Locals jokingly refer to vineyards near the deepest part of Seneca Lake as the "banana belt" because its temperatures run a few degrees warmer than other parts of the region. The term provides inspiration for the winery's Bad Monkey series of red wines, including Blaufränkisch, Pinot Noir, Cabernet Franc, and a Meritage-style blend.

There's none of the glitz and hustle here, just friendly folks and some interesting wines to try. Among the whites, a proprietary multiblend called Lot No.1 Cuvee combines Riesling, Chardonnay, Gewürztraminer, Grüner Veltliner, and Muscat Ottonel.

An endearing boutique winery, Lacey Magruder wines are produced in small quantities, typically seventy or so cases per vintage.

BILLSBORO WINERY
4760 West Lake Road
Geneva, NY 14456
www.billsborowinery.com

On his path to a career in winemaking, Vinny Aliperti apprenticed at Wölffer Estate Vineyard on Long Island under Roman Roth, then in the Finger Lakes at Hermann J. Wiemer Vineyard (see page 75). In 2001, he joined start-up Atwater Vineyards (see page 116), graduating from assistant to head winemaker.

Billsboro Winery, named for the hamlet of Billsboro Corners, was the retirement project of Dr. Robert Pool, esteemed professor of viticulture at Cornell's New York State Agricultural Experiment Station in Geneva. With his passing, the estate was purchased by Vinny and his wife, Kim, in 2007.

The small-lot production at Billsboro provides Vinny an opportunity to work with some of the region's less common varietals, including Syrah, Pinot Gris, and Sauvignon Blanc. Perhaps most interesting is his work with Albariño, a wine grape sourced from a small planting at Sawmill Creek Vineyard but indigenous to the Iberian Peninsula of Spain and Portugal.

Visitors can expect to enjoy a rotating selection of new releases, including wines from the Andante series, inspired by musical compositions. One year it might be a blend of Cabernet Sauvignon and Cabernet Franc; the next year, Blaufränkisch and Merlot.

The century-old post-and-beam barn and newly constructed adjoining pavilion reside on sixty idyllic acres surrounded by stately walnut trees, terraced fields, a deep wooded ravine, and views of the lake.

SCOUT VINEYARDS
468 Route 14
Penn Yan, NY 14527
www.scoutvineyards.com

A vineyard scout is responsible for monitoring issues that could affect the health and growth of the vines, identifying pests and diseases, and keeping track of weather patterns and other environmental factors. After graduation from Hobart and William Smith Colleges in Geneva, Daniel and Olivia Budmen headed out to California wine country. Daniel worked for Constellation Brands; Olivia, at Whitehall Lane Winery. After serving as vineyard scouts in New Zealand, in 2016 the couple returned to the Finger Lakes, where Daniel became assistant winemaker at Kemmeter Wines (see page 69), and Olivia became a cellar master at Hermann J. Wiemer Vineyard (see page 75). In 2018, their two families purchased a sixteen-acre property that would become Budmen Todd Vineyards and home to the Scout winemaking venture. Until those vineyards mature, Daniel and Olivia purchase grapes from a range of local growers.

The focus here is on exceptional Chardonnays made into distinct styles dictated by terroir and winemaking preferences, and at Scout, the lineup comprises four wines: Cayuga Lake Chardonnay, made with grapes grown at Cayuga Ridge Estate Winery (see page 139); Stainless Steel Chardonnay, an unoaked benchmark with fruit sourced from Long Island; En Vie Chardonnay, grown at Nutt Road Vineyard on Seneca Lake and aged for twenty-four months in French oak barrels; and Vive L'Amitie (French for "long live the friendship"), a Burgundy-inspired blend of Chardonnay and Pinot Blanc.

FOX RUN VINEYARDS
670 Route 14
Penn Yan, NY 14527
www.foxrunvineyards.com

At first sniff and sip, you will know you are onto something good here. For more than a century, Fox Run was a dairy farm. The first grapes were planted in 1984, and the barn, erected shortly after the Civil War, was restored and opened as a winery in 1990 by Larry and Adele Wildrick. Three years later it was sold to Scott Osborn and Andy Hale, who were drawn to the property for its promise of fine wine growing. With sixty acres of vines in production, the winery is one of the region's most influential enterprises, a testament to the tenure of Peter Bell, who, during his twenty-seven years as head winemaker, led Fox Run to place among the top one hundred wineries in the world, according to *Wine & Spirits* magazine. He was instrumental in helping define not only Fox Run's groove but also, in many ways, the direction the entire region has taken.

Following Peter's retirement in 2022, Craig Hosbach was appointed to head the winemaking team. Craig apprenticed at Four Sisters Winery in Warren County, New Jersey; Thousand Islands Winery in Alexandria Bay, New York; and Tug Hill Vineyards in Lowville, New York, before serving as lead winemaker at Hunt Country Vineyards (see page 27) for five years, and then he joined Fox Run. Craig is assisted by Angelica Lawler, who comes to Fox Run from Dr. Konstantin Frank Winery (see page 32).

The winemaking team has sustained the Fox Run reputation for Rieslings, from dry to off-dry to single-vineyard bottlings to bubbly Brillante Riesling. Other varieties include Chardonnay, Traminette, Cabernet Franc, Lemberger, Merlot, and Pinot Noir. The perfect place to taste these intriguing wines is the sunny terrace with idyllic views of the lake.

Recognizing the complementary nature of food and wine, visitors are pampered with a café menu, including naan bread pizzas, sandwiches, mac and cheese, and tacos prepared by chef Brud Holland. And after lunch, join the guided walking tour of the vineyard and winemaking cellar.

RED TAIL RIDGE WINERY
846 Route 14
Penn Yan, NY 14527
www.redtailridgewinery.com

A dynamic woman winemaker with a PhD in grape genetics in the UC Davis Viticulture and Enology Department and a decade-long career at E&J Gallo as vice president of viticulture and enology research and development, Nancy Irelan headed east to establish Red Tail Ridge in 2004. Twenty acres of grapevines fill the hillside of an enterprise she named for the pair of red-tailed hawks that live in the woods surrounding the vineyard.

The guest experience here was dramatically improved with the opening of a new tasting room, set among a sea of vines. Designed to be welcoming and educational, its open architecture is dramatically paneled with multiple wood varieties from the trees cut down to plant the vineyard. A separate, open-air pavilion provides a warm-weather alternative tasting venue, an excellent environment for sipping your way through an impressive lineup.

Working with her husband, Mike Schnelle, who manages the wisely planted vineyards, Nancy's focus is Riesling, with thoughtful crafting in styles from dry to late harvest (made from grapes afflicted with the "noble rot" of botrytized bunches), including a "spontaneously fermented" Riesling. A daring, progressive winemaker, Nancy was crafting semi-sparkling pét-nats before pét-nat was cool. Her Pétillant Naturel Riesling is a hallmark of the estate.

While Mike grows regionally popular Riesling, Chardonnay, and Gewürztraminer, his vineyard also includes a number of obscure grapes with underrated potential. Nancy enjoys showing off how exciting and delicious wines from unconventional and lesser-known varieties can be.

Red Tail Ridge is the only winery in New York (and possibly in the United States) that grows Lagrein and Teroldego, two red grape varietals from northern Italy. These wines are ready to drink now but built to age for decades.

NEW VINES WINERY
1138 Travis Road
Penn Yan, NY 14527
www.newvines.com

What started out as a wine-country bed and breakfast, the retirement homestead of Todd and Dani Eichas has evolved into a microwinery, with wines made from a vineyard planted in a single acre of vines, one of the smallest commercial estate vineyards and wineries in the Finger Lakes. The couple began gradually planting grapes in their backyard during the spring of 2007, and by 2014, they had filled the one-acre block with pristine rows of Riesling, Grüner Veltliner, Cabernet Franc, Lemberger, and Marquette.

New Vines is a labor of love for Todd, who refers to the vineyard as his garden and crafts wines from its fruit. His most intriguing offering, Fireside Marquette, is a fortified, Port-style wine made from estate-grown Marquette grapes, a winter-hardy, alternate variety developed at the University of Minnesota and, you guessed it, intended as a fireside sipper.

The limited, handmade production means that most wines are only available to members of the wine club.

SENECA SHORE WINE CELLARS

929 Davy Road
Penn Yan, NY 14527
www.senecawine.com

During the Middle Ages, kings and feudal lords owned vineyards, and at fall harvest, the citizens of each village joined in picking and processing the locally grown grapes. David DeMarco, a former software engineer, was inspired by medieval wine heritage when he created the theme for his winery and tasting room, decorated with swords, shields, helmets, axes, and other collectables. A huge sculpture of the legendary roc, a bird of prey popularized in Arabian fairy tales, greets visitors at the entrance. This is the perfect place to get in touch with your inner knight or lady-in-waiting.

The estate's eighty-five-acre vineyard was first planted in 1979 with twenty-three acres of a Chardonnay clone from Colmar in Alsace, France. Over the years, DeMarco diversified with plantings of Gewürztraminer, Merlot, Cabernet Franc, Pinot Noir, and Lemberger, grapes initially sold to surrounding wineries. Then in 1999, Seneca Shore was licensed as a farm winery, and he began the commercial production of wine.

Flagship offerings are Chardonnays, layered in French-oak-fermented and stainless-steel-fermented dry versions and a semidry varietal. Rieslings range from dry to semidry to semisweet. But the jewel in the medieval crown is undoubtedly Cabernet Franc Cask #58, aged for a minimum of eighteen months in a neutral French oak barrel to soften tannins. It rivals some of the best Cab Francs from Loire Valley in France, a style whose proper place would be in a carafe alongside steak and potatoes.

KEMMETER WINES

1030 Larzelere Road
Penn Yan, NY 14527
www.kemmeterwines.com

Johannes Reinhardt was born in the sleepy German village of Franconia, near Würzburg, where his family has tended vineyards and produced native *Frankenwein* since 1438. Groundwork at the side of his father and grandfather led to formal schooling in viticulture and enology. After making wines in his own village for two years, he worked at Estate Kistenmacher-Hengerer, then at Hartmann Dippon Castle Estate, before coming to America as an intern at Dr. Konstantin

Frank Winery (see page 32) in Hammondsport. After an impressive fourteen-year tenure as head winemaker at Anthony Road Wine Company (see below), he stepped down to focus on his own vineyard, determined to follow his own muse at Kemmeter, the name of his maternal grandmother.

You can take the man out of his German wine cellar, but you can't take the German influences out of his wines. Johannes makes his Rieslings with the confidence of Leonard Bernstein conducting the Meistersinger Overture, and the spirit of innovation and inquiry that punctuates every aspect of his winemaking is evident in Sonero, a stand-out off-dry beauty and SanSan, a reserve label for special vintages and in the artistic Kemmeter series with musical notes identifying each style.

A far cry from the din of busy commercial wineries along the wine route, Kemmeter is modestly under the radar. The spartan tasting room allows for a very limited number of visitors at a time, requiring advance reservations for tastings conducted by either Johannes or his wife, Imelda. It would be a mistake to miss a visit to what might just be one of the most personalized and memorable experiences in the region.

ANTHONY ROAD WINE COMPANY
1020 Anthony Road
Penn Yan, NY 14527
www.anthonyroadwine.com

John and Ann Martini settled on one hundred acres of farmland on this Seneca Lake address in 1973, where they planted grapes and raised a family. But selling grapes to the Taylor Wine Company didn't provide a livelihood, so in addition to his work in the vineyard, John held a research position at the New York State Agricultural Experiment Station.

In the late 1980s, John and Ann joined with Derek and Donna Wilburn to form the Anthony Road Wine Company, and the venture's first bottle of wine was released in 1990. A decade later, when Derek left to become winemaker at Swedish Hill Winery (see page 134), the Martinis persuaded a young German winemaker by the name of Johannes Reinhardt to accept a position.

Johannes, whose family has a long history of wine growing in Germany, first arrived in the Finger Lakes to work at Dr. Konstantin Frank Winery (see page 32). Taking charge of the Anthony Road cellar in 2000, his wines, well-made across the board over the years, have earned a place among the best in the region.

An accomplished artist with a background in fashion photography and a degree in sculpture, Peter Becraft joined Anthony Road as an apprentice in

2006. Two years later, he became associate winemaker, and by 2014, he was well prepared to head the winemaking team when Johannes left to open Kemmeter Wines (see page 69).

Peter keeps the region's signature Riesling at the core of the Anthony Road portfolio, the excellence best expressed in dry, semidry, and sparkling versions. Most notable is the Art Series Riesling, spontaneously fermented by the grape's indigenous yeast populations. The label is a reproduction of original artwork by Ann Martini, painted during her student days at Nazareth College in Rochester.

Anthony Road has been a pacesetter in the Finger Lakes for its carefully cultivated grapevines and its integrated use of technology alongside good old-fashioned winemaking. The next generation of Martinis, Peter, Sarah, Maeve, and Elizabeth, are now full-time employees and co-owners of the Anthony Road Wine Company.

PREJEAN WINERY
2634 Route 14
Penn Yan, NY 14527
www.prejeanwinery.com

In 1978, James and Elizabeth Prejean settled down on a farm near Seneca Lake, where they planted nine acres of grapes and eventually established what would become an important winery. More vineyards were added through the years, to a total of thirty-seven acres planted in both classical European vinifera and French-American hybrid varieties. Tom Prejean, who has assumed management of the winery, credits Cornell and the Geneva Experiment Station for their research and development programs and for making technical information available to the industry. He points to advancements in vineyard management, varietal selection, and winemaking technology that has helped raise the bar for Finger Lakes wine.

Tom is particularly proud of his finely executed Rieslings. In 2023, Prejean Dry Riesling was awarded a medal at the San Francisco Chronicle Wine Competition, and the winery's second label, Goldfinch Dry Riesling, earned double gold and best of varietal at the 2023 American Wine Society Competition.

Along with consulting winemaker Steve DiFrancesco, Tom also produces top-notch red wines, including Cabernet Franc, Merlot, and Cabernet Sauvignon. Pay special attention to Marechal Foch, a hybrid variety developed in Alsace, France, and made from some of the oldest plantings on the Prejean estate.

For nearly forty years, this stalwart winery has never lost sight of its focus on producing wines of quality and consistency, never pushing volume or prices.

CK CELLARS

2770 Route 14
Penn Yan, NY 14527
www.ckcellars.com

When you're ready to discover more than the region's signature Rieslings, make your way to the grand campus of CK Cellars. It's a refreshing surprise to find a tasting room—actually twin tasting rooms—with multiple categories and so many options to choose from. The story begins with a beekeeper named John Earle and his wife, Esther. In 1996, the couple purchased and remodeled a former restaurant property along Route 14 as a place to start selling meads made with nectar produced from their hives. This was the beginning of a venture that would grow beyond their wildest dreams. Over the next two decades, they added grape wines, branded as Torrey Ridge Winery, and hard ciders, branded as WortHog Cidery, while expanding venues to accommodate the scale of a growing business.

The story continues with two other dreamers. Paul Curcillo and Stephanie King, husband and wife Philadelphia-based surgeons, started making wines as a hobby, buying grapes and making home wines to serve at local fundraising events. With a growing passion for wine culture, their journey led to the Finger Lakes, just as the Earles were planning retirement. In 2015, Paul and Stephanie became owners of the estate and the collection of brands—lock, stock, and wine barrels.

Meadery, winery, and cidery now fall under the CK Cellars umbrella, and production across the board is in the capable hands of Sadie Lewis. While studying viticulture and enology at Finger Lakes Community College, Sadie interned with Derek Wilbur, winemaker at Swedish Hill Winery (see page 134), and after graduation, she started working for the Earles. With the change in ownership, she was named head winemaker, in charge of reinvigorating the portfolio.

Signature products remain, including the range of traditional honey meads, fruit and grape wines, and nearly a dozen ciders. But the newest focus is on a series called CuKi Wines, a distinctive approach showcasing expressions of native and hybrid varieties, wines that Paul and Stephanie believe best define the identity of the Finger Lakes as a wine region. Sadie's work shows that the sky's the limit on what these wine styles can be.

In 2018, Paul and Stephanie added Rooster Hill Vineyards (see page 47) on Keuka Lake to the CK Cellars roster of enterprises.

MILES WINE CELLARS
168 Randall Crossing Road
Himrod, NY 14842
www.mileswinecellars.com

No winery property in the Finger Lakes has a more interesting history than Miles Wine Cellars. Originally a land grant from the king of England to the Rapalee family, its dock on Seneca Lake provided area farmers with access to the barges that moved their produce to the cities. An imposing house built in 1802 was originally federal style in design but was converted to Greek revival fifty years later by the Rapalees. It became a stop on the Underground Railroad, a shelter for runaway slaves as they made their way north and into Canada, where they could live as free citizens.

In 1978, the Miles family purchased the old Rapalee estate, including its remaining 115 acres of land; the twenty-room mansion, nearly in ruins since it was abandoned in 1929; and the Rapalee family cemetery. Doug Miles switched his studies from architecture to viticulture, intent on developing a vineyard on what promised to be a nearly perfect site. Ties to Glenora provided his first market for the grapes, and as the vineyard expanded, as many as seventeen wineries came to depend on the vineyard's exceptional fruit.

This is a vineyard-driven enterprise. As an experienced and respected grower, Doug devotes full time to the grapevines and relinquishes winemaking to neighboring facilities. At harvest, he delivers his prime fruit to Fox Run Vineyards (see page 66) for custom winemaking in separate tanks and barrels designated for Miles Wine Cellars.

Noteworthy here are Cabernet Franc, Cabernet Sauvignon, and Lemberger, aged in Hungarian oak barrels, distinctive from French and American oak, imparting a richer sensation of weight and texture to the wines.

If you were looking for ghosts, you would probably start your search in a cemetery or in an old mansion. Because this place has both, folks have claimed it's haunted. An easy-drinking, semidry Chardonnay, one of the most popular wines here, is called Ghost, its label designed with the apparition of a woman whose spirit wanders around here.

Now for the stiffer stuff. Spirits of Miles is the boutique distilling project of Evan Miles, who handcrafts and hand-numbers bottles of well-aged bourbon, brandy, raspberry liqueur, and a black walnut amaro. At the end of your visit, don't leave without a bottle of Navy Strength Gin, infused with farm-foraged botanicals.

The unique sense of place and history makes this an important stop on any serious exploration of the Seneca Lake province. It's not only a picture-book setting, but you also can taste handcrafted wines and spirits in a haunted lakeside mansion.

SHAW VINEYARD
3901 Route 14
Himrod, NY 14842
www.shawvineyard.com

Steven Shaw is a highly respected figure in the recent history of Finger Lakes wine growing. Inspired by Dr. Konstantin Frank (see Dr. Konstantin Frank Winery, page 32) and Hermann Wiemer (see Hermann J. Wiemer Vineyard, page 75) and their successes growing vinifera varieties, in 1981 Steve began planting his first vineyard with European varieties when most of the region's growers were still focused on natives and hybrids. In 1999, Steve purchased fifty acres on Seneca Lake as the site for a new estate vineyard. The construction of a post-and-beam tasting room and underground cellar was followed in 2002 by a small, inaugural release of his first wines.

As both grower and winemaker, Steve is endlessly curious. He will tell you that the quality of a wine begins in the vineyard. It's the way in which a variety is grown that has the most profound effect on the wine. He employs a trellis system called *Pendelbogen*, most popular in Germany's Rhine Valley, the birthplace of Riesling. Bending the vines in the shape of an umbrella promotes sap distribution, producing more fruit. In the cellar, his focus is on long, gentle extraction, fermenting grapes on their skins and producing aromatic, fruit-forward wines without harsh tannins. Reds are often cellar-aged five years or more before bottling.

This is the place to go for a quiet tasting of Keuka Hill Reserve, a Bordeaux-style blend, its fruit sourced from the original Shaw vinifera vineyard, and Riesling, aged to bring out depth and complexity. The proof is in the glass.

Collectible wines are available in individually numbered magnums.

HERMANN J. WIEMER VINEYARD

3962 Route 14
Dundee, NY 14837
www.wiemer.com

When folks start talking about winemakers who changed the history of the Finger Lakes and who put Rieslings from this region on the world map, one of the first names that come to mind is Hermann Wiemer. If Riesling were a religion, Hermann would be a high priest. He is a native of Germany, descended from a long line of winemakers in a Riesling-producing region, so it was quite natural that he made his reputation with prize-winning wines from Germany's "noble grape." Perhaps no other wine region is so driven by a single grape as Germany is by Riesling, and it was Hermann's passion for this hearty variety that defined this place. He brought a strong sense of classical decorum to his operation and a remarkable measure of finesse and sophistication to the region. He was passionately and romantically involved in the life of his vineyard. The portrait that emerges from the winery that bears his name is of an impeccable artisan with a deep respect for his profession and his heritage.

Hermann retired in 2017, handing over the keys to the winery to Fred Merwarth, his longtime winemaking assistant. In perhaps the quintessential Finger Lakes wine story, Fred partnered with Swedish agronomist Oskar Bynke not only to protect the venture's legacy but also to expand on Hermann's approach to viticulture and winemaking, The new team takes notions from organic and biodynamic practices in the vineyard and has set even more ambitious standards for the already impressive range of wines.

Making wine at the very highest level continues to be at the core of the Hermann J. Wiemer enterprise. Through the estate's "blessed plots"—HJW, Josef, and Magdalena Vineyards—the aim is nothing less than to reach the pinnacle of Finger Lakes wine growing. That expertise shows in the Field White, a delightful everyday wine comprised of young-vine Grüner Veltliner, Riesling, and Chardonnay—and a bargain to boot.

This is, of course, among the places not to miss on a visit to Finger Lakes wine country. Don't expect any frills or breathtaking lake views. It's simply about great wine here.

MISSICK CELLARS
150 Poplar Point Road
Dundee, NY 14837
www.missickcellars.com

The historic twelve-acre parcel is the site of the oldest vineyard in Yates County, planted by Dr. Byron Spence in 1866, and some of the original vines can be viewed along the winding road into the property. The winery was first named Squaw Point by David Miles. Then in 2002, it was sold to Michael Litterio, who changed the name to Villa Bellangelo, intent on making Italian-style wines in the Finger Lakes. Litterio was among the first in the region to produce varietal wines from Valvin Muscat, a hybrid grape developed in 2006 by breeder Bruce Reisch at Cornell's Agricultural Experiment Station in Geneva.

In 2011, the winery was acquired by the Missick family, whose range of offerings include flowery Dry Muscat and a Finger Lakes version of the Italian Moscato, a semisweet sparkling wine inspired by the Asti wines of the Piedmont region of Italy.

The Bellangelo label represents everyday blends of hybrid and vinifera grapes. The 1866 Wine Cellars series commemorates the historic plantings on the property, small-production wines made from grapes sourced from single vineyards.

TABORA FARM & WINERY
4978 Lakemont Himrod Road
Dundee, NY 14837
www.taborafarmandwinery.com

Every traveler finds little gems now and then. For wine lovers, these are usually small family-run estates that are barely represented in tourist guides. Tabora is such a gem. In 1989, Jane and Roger Eatherton purchased a ten-acre orchard in Bucks County, Pennsylvania, where they operated a farm market and country store called Tabora, the name inspired by Jane's childhood home in Cape Town, South Africa. Twenty years later, the Eathertons moved to the Finger Lakes for a second act, this time a bakery, deli, and market housed in a renovated barn and a tasting bar, barrel room, and production space in a half-moon-shaped Quonset hut, both redesigned in Cape Dutch architecture, a hat tip to her South African heritage.

A minor detour off Route 14 and a wonderful distraction, the setting is a one-hundred-year-old farm property with a 250-acre vineyard, mostly planted in native and hybrid varieties. While most of the grapes are sold to other wineries and juice producers, a portion of each harvest is reserved for a range of house wines. Pay special attention to Heritage Noir, a blend of De Chaunac, Baco Noir, Marechal Foch, and Léon Millot, hybrid styles that thrive in the region's cool climate, handcrafted by winemaker Matthew Butts and aged in French oak barrels. This is small-production winemaking at its most authentic.

Tabora provides visitors with a complete wine-and-food experience. Stop here for an informational tasting across the portfolio. Walk over to the market and choose from soups, salads, sandwiches, and quiches at the deli counter. During the summer months, have lunch on a picnic table next to the grapevines. And don't leave without a few fresh treats from the bakery.

FRUIT YARD WINERY
5060 Route 14
Dundee, NY 14837
www.fruityardwinery.com

You can't miss the bright red building as you drive along Route 14. In an earlier life, it was a farmer's fruit stand, and in 2008, it became a winery tasting room. The grape is not the only fruit capable of making wine, of course, and a visit here is a journey into the world of fruit wines. After sourcing fresh, hand-picked fruit from regional orchards and farms, this sister winery to Seneca Shore Wine Cellars (see page 69) turns fresh blueberries, strawberries, peaches, and plums into small-batch fruit wines that remain true to the fruit. Because fruits contain relatively little sugar, the wines are made by adding cane sugar, so although predominantly sweet in taste, these are pure fruit wines, not blended with grape wines.

One wine attracts the most attention here: Chocolate Covered Strawberry is a blend of strawberry wine with rich chocolate flavors, bringing to mind chocolate-dipped red berries.

The wines are undeniably eclectic, and while the emphasis is primarily on fruit wines, there are a few grape wines to round out the offerings.

HICKORY HOLLOW WINE CELLARS

5289 Route 14
Dundee, NY 14837
www.facebook.com/hickoryhollowwines

Born and raised in Dundee, Nathan Kendall grew up at family-owned Hickory Hollow Wine Cellars, and after earning a business degree at SUNY Brockport, he set out to learn the craft of winemaking around the world. His five-year adventure included apprenticeships at Cline Cellars in the Carneros District of Sonoma County, California; Coopers Creek in Auckland and Waipara Springs in the South Island of New Zealand; Bird in Hand in the Adelaide Hills of Australia; Adelsheim in the Willamette Valley of Oregon; and S. A. Prüm in the Mosel region of Germany, one of the country's winemaking dynasties. Returning to his roots in the Finger Lakes, he worked with Morten Hallgren of Ravines Wine Cellars (see pages 50 and 62) and Steven Shaw of Shaw Vineyard (see page 74).

In 2011, Nathan launched his namesake N. Kendall brand (now Nathan K), a lineup of spontaneously fermented Riesling, Chardonnay, Pinot Noir, and Cabernet Franc, harnessing the unique traits of fruit from mature vineyards. He turns those grapes into wine with as little interference as possible, never correcting with fining agents, and only gently filtering before bottling. He takes a personal, hands-on approach to his craft, controlling the process from picking to bottling, making less than two thousand cases a year.

In 2016, Nathan partnered with Pascaline Lepeltier, master sommelier and evangelist of natural wines for, in Lepeltier's words, an "ecological and political project." They created Chëpìka, the Lenape word for "roots" in the language spoken by the Delaware tribe of Native Americans.

The project is a return to traditional, indigenous grape varieties and local winemaking techniques, producing small lots of still and pét-nat wines from organically grown Delaware, Catawba, and Concord grapes and a blend of all three varieties called Buzzard Crest, with fruit sourced from the Farnum family's Buzzard Crest Vineyard (see Barrington Cellars on page 48) on Keuka Lake.

Along your wine odyssey, if you're looking for something rare and wonderful to take home, something few others even know about.

GLENORA WINE CELLARS
5435 Route 14
Dundee, NY 14837
www.glenora.com

A foundational estate for the modern Finger Lakes, Glenora was the brainchild of three eminent grape growers led by Gene Pierce, who, as a young man, studied agricultural economics at Cornell. In 1977, when passage of the Farm Winery Act handed grape growers incentives to become vintners, Gene and his pals Ed Dalrymple and Eastman Beers, relying on fruit from their own vineyards, started Glenora, making them visionaries well before there was a lot of glamour in the Finger Lakes wine business.

One of the first hires was John Williams. His master's degree in enology and viticulture from UC Davis and an apprenticeship at Stag's Leap Wine Cellars in Napa Valley gave him a leg up over other candidates for the winemaking position. Glenora's founding fathers reasoned that a California-trained winemaker was essential to the start-up of an important venture. (Williams eventually returned to California and opened Frog's Leap Winery.)

Another California winemaker, Jim Gifford of Domaine Mumm, who would join the merry band ten years later, made significant contributions to Glenora. His 1988 production of Blanc de Blancs captured a double gold award at the San Francisco Fair Wine Competition, establishing the winery as one of the top sparkling-wine producers in the country.

A credentialed technician by the name of Steve DiFrancesco headed winemaking operations here for nearly three decades. Following in his footsteps, Edward Miller, former assistant winemaker at Merry Edwards Winery in Sonoma Valley, California, leads the new team, along with Emily Doi, former assistant at Hunt Country Vineyards (see page 27).

While Chardonnay and Pinot Noir grapes are cherished for the sparkling wines, Riesling has become especially important here. In fact, to fans of Riesling, the Glenora offertory is cause for celebration. In particular, Glenora's FLX Dry Riesling, sourced from multiple vineyard sites, is a textbook example of the noble variety, earning multiple awards in competitions, and ounce for ounce is a real bargain. A key player in the revival of the Finger Lakes as a wine-growing region, Glenora produces a wide range of good-to-terrific, humanely priced wines.

Towering above Seneca Lake and carpeted in meticulous vineyards, the complex has expanded over a quarter-century and now includes a thirty-room inn and a 125-seat restaurant, both commanding a spectacular view of Seneca Lake. Versaisons is the winery restaurant, its name inspired by the time in the vineyard season when grapes change color.

FULKERSON WINERY & FARM
5576 Route 14
Dundee, NY 14837
www.fulkersonwinery.com/

Steeped in history, the Fulkerson farm is comprised of vineyards, pastures, and ancient oak trees on rolling land that has been in the hearts and hands of the same family for two hundred years. The property was purchased in 1805 by Caleb Fulkerson, a veteran of the Revolutionary War, and was passed down to Samuel, then to Harlan, Harlan Jr., Roger, Sayre, and now Steven, the seventh generation of Fulkersons charged with preservation of the family farm as an agricultural enterprise. The winery is the culmination of the family's history of farming on a site that was cleared by Native Americans and planted with black raspberries by the early settlers. The first grapevines appeared around the time of the Civil War, intended not for wine but for table fruit.

Besides the usual suspects, offerings here provide an opportunity to try a few oddities. Fulkerson's Diamond, a rarely seen native American grape, perfectly expresses the nature of this varietal. Taking a sip is like biting into a fresh-picked grape. St. Vincent of Saragossa, the patron saint of winegrowers, inspired a hybrid grape variety that bears his name, suggesting a rustic Chianti. The Fulkerson vineyard has been growing Dornfelder, a robust grape from the German Rheinhessen, since the 1990s. Notice hints of agave in Tequila Barrel–Aged Riesling. And the winery makes a brave effort with botanical Albariño, the grape of Portuguese Vinho Verde.

A clever blend of two other varieties at Fulkerson's results in a wine that has probably given second thoughts to grape growers who've been busy uprooting their plantings of Catawba. The addition of flavorful Rougeon to Catawba moderates the telltale muskiness of the native grape, and attaching the name Red Zeppelin assures that this wine will not be mistaken for anything other than a sweetly refreshing quaff.

Besides these eccentricities, the winery crushes an impressive complement of other grapes, with nearly half the juice sold to amateur winemakers, the remainder turned into about ten thousand cases of wine each year. During fall harvest, customers place their orders at least one day in advance, then bring containers to fill with freshly pressed juice. To assist with home winemaking, Fulkerson's stocks a full range of supplies, equipment, and yeasts appropriate to each variety.

ROCK STREAM VINEYARDS
162 Fir Tree Point Road
Rock Stream, NY 14878
www.rockstreamvineyards.com

A retired army lieutenant colonel with a doctorate in chemistry, Mark Karasz founded Rock Stream Vineyards in 2005, producing wines from Riesling, Chardonnay, Cabernet Franc, as well as native and hybrid varieties. The "sweet-tooth" wine drinker will find a lot to like here. With whimsical names like Make Me Blush, Queen of DeNile, and Poolside Pink, you already know what to expect.

The tasting room is relaxed and welcoming. What catches the attention is Niagara, the indigenous variety named for Niagara County, where the grapes were first grown. While most Niagara wines are fruity, grapey, and sweet, Mark's Dry Niagara is an unorthodox style, with all the flavor of the grape but very little sugar.

During a three-year tour in Italy, Mark fell in love with grappa, and he uses an alembic pot still from Portugal to distill a grape-based brandy awarded a double gold medal at the New York Wine Classic.

APOLLO'S PRAISE
6085 Old Lake Road
Rock Stream, NY 14878
www.apollospraise.com

The winery's name is inspired by "Glorious Apollo," a song Kelby James Russell performed as a member of the Harvard Glee Club during his undergraduate years, highlighting his twin passions—wine and music—"each social pleasure giving and partaking." At Harvard, Kelby studied government and economics, but as a high tenor in America's oldest collegiate choir, he planned a career in orchestra management. During a fellowship program in Italy between his junior and senior years, he labored in a Tuscan vineyard for room and board, an experience that sparked another of his creative juices, this time a passion for wine. After graduation in 2009, it was a passion he would follow up on at Fox Run Vineyards (see page 66), eventually spending winters in New Zealand or Australia to double his experience but returning each autumn to Fox Run.

He started his first year-round salaried job in spring 2012, as assistant winemaker at Red Newt Cellars (see page 112). By year's end, he was promoted to head winemaker, and over the following eleven years, the Rieslings he produced there were among the region's most sought-after bottlings.

In 2022, Kelby and his wife, Julia Hoyle, head winemaker at Hosmer Winery (see page 141), purchased Lahoma Vineyard from grower Ken Fulkerson, including twenty acres of quintessential Finger Lakes Riesling vines. He built his reputation as a winemaker with fruit from this site, and now he owns it. Possessing one of the great terroirs of the region, Lahoma features Alsace-like, sandstone-derived soils that lend themselves to an opulent and seductive expression of Riesling.

The first vintage of Apollo's Praise wines includes three styles of Riesling; Chardonnay; Grüner Veltliner; Cabernet Franc; a dry rosé of Cabernet Franc; and Scheurebe, an Austro-German variety rare in the Finger Lakes.

He may have left music as a career, but Kelby still finds time to sing with the Eastman Rochester Chorus, and his wine labels suggest musical pairings instead of food pairings. Listen to a jazz organ piece by Joey DeFrancesco with one of Kelby's Rieslings.

MAGNUS RIDGE VINEYARD AND WINERY
6148 Route 14
Rock Stream, NY 14878
www.magnusridge.com

In 1992, Matt and Sandy Downey, engineers by profession, began making wine in their home kitchen with juice purchased from Fulkerson Winery (see page 80). When it turned out they had a knack for making quality wines, in 2002 they purchased fifty-seven acres of land and began planting grapevines—including Riesling, Pinot Gris, Gewürztraminer, Traminette, and Cabernet Franc. An initial vintage from estate-grown grapes was produced in 2007.

In 2011, the Downeys erected a movie-set version of a sprawling French countryside estate, designed by acclaimed Skaneateles architect Andy Ramsgard, aspiring to capture the same character, feel, and aesthetics found in those architectural gems. An exclamation point along Route 14, Magnus Ridge houses a bar surrounded by an assortment of wine-related gifts and accessories for folks who pop in for a tasting and multiple private tasting rooms that resemble rustic wine cellars for groups who arrive with advance reservations.

A visit here provides an opportunity to taste Gewürztraminer and Traminette (a hybrid of Gewürztraminer) side by side. And Magnus Ridge earns its grandiose name with the aromatically intense and palate-refreshing Pinot Gris, an estate-grown white wine that feels at home here, probably because the grape variety was originally from the countryside vineyards of Alsace, France.

The open-air porch and parklike patio area in the rear of the building is surrounded by ponds, trails, and waterfalls that will beckon you for a stroll.

TOAST WINERY
4499 Route 14
Rock Stream, NY 14878
www.toastwineryflx.com

In 2020, award-winning amateur winemaker Michael Gibbs left the corporate world and along with his wife, Jayne, moved into the building formerly occupied by Michael Lucent's Pompous Ass Winery, the name long considered an embarrassment in the wine community. The new name, Toast Winery, refers to the tradition of toasting. When a wine barrel is being constructed, the barrel maker heats, or toasts, the inside planks of the barrels to curve them into a barrel shape, a process that also imparts different aromas and flavors into the finished wines. Toasting can be light, medium, medium-plus, or heavy—even charred.

This is the perfect place to study the influence of wood on both red and white varieties, an opportunity to taste wines with varying levels of toast: Cabernet Franc and Riesling are fermented and aged in lightly toasted French oak barrels; Pinot Noir and Zweigelt (pronounced *TSVYE-gelt*), in medium-toasted oak. The tasting room is agreeable but not elaborate. Individual barrel staves reflecting the various degrees of wood toasting adorn the wall above the tasting bars, and a shelf of vintage home kitchen toasters brings a smile.

BARNSTORMER WINERY
4814 Route 14
Rock Stream, NY 14878
www.barnstormerwinery.com

After earning a BA in marketing at the University at Buffalo, Scott Bronstein developed events and hospitality for Castello di Amorosa Winery, housed in a Tuscan-inspired castle on a hillside above Calistoga, Napa Valley, California. The experience led to Scott's dream of owning his own winery, and in 2013, he opened Barnstormer Winery in a restored eighteenth-century barn on a sixteen-acre estate property. Inside resembles a mountain cabin in all its rusticity.

Armed with a degree in viticulture and enology from UC Davis, Taylor Stember honed her skills in cellars from California to Italy before arriving in the Finger Lakes. In 2020, she joined the winemaking team at Red Newt Cellars (see page 112), then became assistant winemaker at Anthony Road Wine Company (see page 70), before joining Barnstormer in 2023. Taylor works with estate-grown Blaufränkisch, Cabernet Franc, and Riesling and sources other fruit from as many as seven regional growers within a thirty-mile radius of the winery. The grapes for Barnstormer's single-vineyard Cabernet Franc, Cabernet Sauvignon, and Merlot are grown at Sawmill Creek. You'll learn how these varieties express the particular character of this legendary vineyard.

LAKEWOOD VINEYARDS
4024 Route 14
Watkins Glen, NY 14891
www.lakewoodvineyards.com

Lakewood Vineyards is recognized as one of the region's preeminent family-run wineries. The story begins in April 1951. Frank Stamp packed his wife and their three kids into the family Hudson and drove from Maryland to the patch of lakeside property he had purchased with his life savings. Within a year they had planted five acres of grapes in the fertile soil, and the Stamps have been faithful stewards of these vineyards ever since.

Monty Stamp, the oldest son, enrolled at Morrisville College to study agricultural science, then returned to run the farm. After growing and selling grapes to the Taylor Wine Company for thirty-six years, Lakewood Vineyards became a winery in 1988. Since then, the estate has been synonymous with the identity of this part of the Finger Lakes.

Chris, first-born of the third generation, earned a food science degree from Cornell, cut his winemaking teeth at Glenora Wine Cellars (see page 79), then served as winemaker at Plane's Cayuga Vineyard before joining the family enterprise. Now assisted by his daughter Abigail and son Benjamin, both graduates of Cornell's Viticulture and Enology Program, family craft shines through in the broad Lakewood catalog of estate wines.

The hillside Riesling vineyards exhibit a variety of microterroirs on the property, divided into five specialized blocks, with each specific location chosen according to soil-mapping for the depth, structure, and composition in order to achieve optimum expressions, the final brushstrokes for these masterworks from bone-dry to semisweet styles.

Lakewood is best known for those Rieslings, but there are so many good choices here, perhaps most interesting, a lush, creatively crafted Reserve Cabernet Franc and a Port-style blend of Baco Noir and Frontenac. Don't leave without a few cans of Bubbly Candeo, a Prosecco-style Cayuga, for your next picnic.

CASTEL GRISCH WINERY
3380 County Road 28
Watkins Glen, NY 14891
www.castelgrisch.com

Lush vineyards literally cling to the steep hillside, fanned by lively lake breezes; visitors enjoy a breathtaking view from the chalet while sipping estate-grown wines. If this sounds like a travelogue of Switzerland, then Castel Grisch has succeeded in bringing a bit of Alpine ambiance to Seneca Lake. The winery was founded in 1982 by Aloise Baggenstoss, a chemist by profession, and his wife, Michelle, both natives of Switzerland. They fell in love with this property, it is said, because, when viewed from here, the lake resembles the Rhine River Valley. The vineyard's first plantings of Riesling were, in fact, inspired by wines of the Rheingau. Besides estate-grown Rieslings, the Castel Grisch portfolio includes wines crafted from hybrid varieties, including Cayuga, Traminette, Chancellor, and Baco Noir.

The winery has changed hands more than once, now owned by entrepreneur Daniel Lai, who has created a fairy-tale experience surrounding the property. Once you're done swilling, visit the Festival of Lights, a visually spectacular installation, made up of more than a thousand silk, porcelain, and steel light sculptures. Wander along a mile-long wooded path with scenes of adventure, dinosaurs, tropical animals, and cultural traditions illuminated by thousands of LED-lit lanterns.

BREWERIES

LAKE DRUM BREWING
16 East Castle Street
Geneva, NY 14456
www.lakedrumbrewing.com

If the beloved sitcom *Cheers* took place in the twenty-first century, it would be set at Lake Drum. This is a place where the bartender remembers your name and favorite beverage and where you can sip among the local agriculturalists and artists crowding Tom Fish's handmade live-edge bar top, artfully supported by a poplar tree stump, or outside on a parklet that offers the only lake view from any brewery or restaurant in town.

Lake Drum's name comes from the Seneca Native American folklore about a young man who overfished and was banished as a frog to the bottom of the lake, and God makes a loud booming sound warning him to stay away every time he tries to surface. Owners Victor and Jenna Pultinas, along with resident brewer Rick Morse, have created Geneva's closest thing to a public living room, thanks to abstractly painted wall art, a bookcase overflowing with vinyl albums, and book exchange. Rick produces a rotation of ten reliable beers, including Bad Dog IPA, named after his dart-league alter ego. His showcase Buckwheat Stout is made with roasted grain from historic Birkett Mills in Penn Yan.

Victor and Jenna (also a winemaker at nearby Zugibe Vineyards; see page 100) produce inventive hard ciders, including easy-drinking herbal tea–infused versions with lavender, elderberry, staghorn sumac, and tulsi basil. Pay special attention to French Connection, a field-blend cider, barrel-aged in French oak for three years. This millennial-founded fairy tale of ferments is deeply rooted in the craft community, with a five-barrel beer system and roughly five thousand gallons of cider in barrels on their Waterloo farm after harvest season.

F.L.X. CULTURE HOUSE
22 Linden Street
Geneva, NY 14456
https://flx-culturehouse.com

This is an experimental, nanoscale project by Christopher Bates and Isabel Bogadtke, the indefatigable husband-and-wife team behind multiple food and wine ventures in the region. With his background as a sommelier and winemaker (see Element Winery, page 192), Bates places his focus on long fermentation methods, solera-inspired blending, and extended barrel-aging. The actual brewing takes place at nearby Lake Drum Brewing (see page 86).

TWISTED RAIL BREWING COMPANY
499 Exchange Street
Geneva, NY 14456
www.twistedrailbrewing.com

With two dozen different beers on tap, this is the epitome of a kid in a candy store for beer nerds or, you could say, kid in a movie theater. The enterprise began in 2013 as a humble three-barrel microbrewery housed in part of an old railroad depot in Canandaigua. Efforts of the beer-mad trio of Ian Boni, John McMullen, and Rich Russ have paid off, and over recent years, Twisted Rail has established outpost tasting rooms in Honeoye, Macedon, and the original Canandaigua location (see page 18), with the mothership brewhouse now headquartered here in the former 1920s-era Regent Theater building. There is still abundant evidence of the theater's past life: a massive chandelier in the lobby, an ornate balcony, and movie posters in vintage frames. But now the twenty-barrel brewhouse is center stage, and beers are the feature attraction.

Begin your visit here with a pour of easy-drinking Lake to Lake Lager. Follow that up with Spike Driver, the flagship IPA. In winter, the Chocolate Espresso Stout, with its roasted-coffee aroma, is as good a way as any to keep the cold at bay.

The ambitious kitchen turns out a full menu, including salads, handhelds, beer-battered fish fry, and brick-oven pizza to stoke your taste buds.

WEBE BREWING COMPANY

796 Pre Emption Road
Geneva, NY 14456
www.webebrewing.com

Follow beer tourists and local regulars to this craft brewery, west of town and just off Route 20. Everyone is welcome. In 2018, the husband-and-wife team of Colleen and Dan Lieberg added to Geneva's flourishing beer scene, making the leap from home brewers to brewery owners after converting a former car-repair shop into a combination brewery and taproom. Barley, the golden-doodle brewery dog, greets whomever walks through the door. Grab a seat at the ninety-foot sandstone-top bar illuminated with Edison bulbs or at one of the handmade tables, order a fresh pint, and catch a glimpse of the ten-barrel brewhouse in action.

WeBe is a chill place to sip Colleen's competition medal earners, including the Golden Peel, an aromatic hefeweizen, and S.O.S., a boozy Scotch ale. Cream of the Crop is an homage to those classic Upstate cream ales that go down so easy. And with nearly two dozen or so other beers on tap, you won't go thirsty.

Nibble popcorn, snack on pretzel bites, or feast on salty-bread pizza. Fill up a growler and continue sipping at home.

BREWERY ARDENNES

570 Snell Road
Geneva, NY 14456
www.breweryardennes.com

Born into a wealthy Upstate family, Katherine Bell was part of the women's suffrage movement, donating $10,000 to the cause in 1908. An astute busi-nesswoman, she purchased a 350-acre farm in Geneva and became a successful sheep breeder. The historic sheep barn on part of the former Bell estate now houses Brewery Ardennes, the Belgian-inspired farm brewery developed by Cor-nell grads Derek and Stacey Edinger. The talents of an engineer-turned-brewer and a sales and marketing professional have combined to create an extraordinary addition to the regional craft-beer landscape. The name comes from the region in southeastern Belgium whose forests, lakes, and rolling hills reminded the Eding-ers of the Finger Lakes. The atmosphere is warm, cozy, and "Belgian-rustic," a place that beckons you to stay awhile.

Offerings range from fruited sours to spicy tripels to hefty stouts, but most notable are the *bière de garde*—lager, wheat, and blonde—whose heritage can be traced to farmhouse breweries in the Hainaut Province of Belgium. The trick here is to order a flight of tiny sample glasses to discover your favorite—just be sure to include the award-winning Winter Farm Ale.

A dining as well as drinking destination, CIA-trained chef Jayden White's menu ranges from steaming bowls of savory beer-steamed mussels with twice-fried Belgian frites to Brewmaster's Bratwurst made with Scotch ale, each dish with a suggested beer pairing to complete the sensory experience.

BIG ALICE BREWING
4180 Route 14
Geneva, NY 14456
www.bigalicebrewing.com

The skyline of the New York City borough of Queens is marked by four tall generator stacks. In 1965, the largest of these generators, built by the Milwaukee-based Allis-Chalmers, became known as "Big Allis." In 2013, city boys Kyle Hurst and Scott Berger opened Big aLICe Brewing, honoring the Queens landmark and its home in Long Island City (the *LIC* in caps). On a ten-gallon pilot system, they brewed and bottled one-off batches with local, fresh, and organic ingredients from the neighborhood community-shared agriculture (CSA) program. Two years later, Big aLICe was voted New York City's favorite brewery and awarded the Ruppert's Cup at the conclusion of New York City's Beer Week. In 2019, they opened the Barrel Room, a dedicated barrel-aging facility and taproom within Industry City, Brooklyn's creative hub along the Sunset Park waterfront. The brewery's ambitious barrel-aging program imparts beers with the unique character of the wood for greater depth of expression.

No one pushes boundaries as well as head brewer Peter Achilles. One case in point, Long Way Home is a wild farmhouse ale made with native yeast and aged in French oak Blaufränkisch barrels from Keuka Lake Vineyards (see page 34). Another is Valley of Ashes, a barleywine (despite the name, actually a beer) aged for more than one year in bourbon barrels.

In 2021, production was shifted to the former Gael Brewing Company location outside of Geneva, where they produce flagships Queensbridge IPA and Lemongrass Kölsch and other rotational offerings on a fifteen-barrel brewhouse, opened a tasting room, and established a fervent fan base.

RELATIVE RISK BREWING COMPANY
1166 Earls Hill Road
Penn Yan, NY 14527
www.relativeriskbrewing.com

It's said that the biggest risk is not taking any risk. Here you're likely to bump into risk-taking brewer Andrew "AJ" Silvent, who has been innovating and perfecting his beers for years while working at his day job as a diesel mechanic. After picking up a handful of amateur awards, in 2021 he launched Relative Risk Brewing Company. While the brewery is perched on a sprawling twelve-acre hillside overlooking Seneca Lake, space is a premium inside, with beer making in a back room, a three-barrel workshop, and a no-frills bar/tasting room out front. This is a casual, no-nonsense, come-and-hang-out kind of place.

Saddle up to the bar for Hazard Ratio, a New England–style IPA from the rotating hop series, or Double Blind, a dry-hopped imperial IPA among the offerings. You never know what's going to be pouring on your visit. The trick here is to order a flight of tiny sample glasses to discover your favorite—just be sure to include Dark Obsession, a robust oatmeal stout.

SENECA STAG COMPANY AT THE BREW BARN
1720 Route 14
Penn Yan, NY 14527
www.senecastagbrewing.com

In a region packed with beer-drinking spots, it's hard to stand out from the crowd, but for Seneca Stag, the secret to success lies with some of the most authentic German-style beers around. Since 2021, a trio of Smiths has welcomed thirsty travelers to their painstakingly renovated hay barn: inside, a brauhaus; outside, a biergarten. It takes a division of labor to successfully run a family-owned brewery, and the Smith clan has it all figured out. Bradley Smith makes the beer, Michelle Smith Berch runs the tasting room, and mom Darlene "Dar" Smith does the cooking.

Bradley's handcrafting in the seven-barrel brewhouse includes Hefeweizen; Marzen; Munich Dunkel; and Festbier, a pale German lager true to the country's traditional low-alcohol beers—all of which pair well with offerings from the kitchen.

Farmer's Hand Pies rank high on the list of beer-friendly edibles, including handmade beer pretzels, loaded potato chips, and Friday night fish fry.

CLIMBING BINES CRAFT ALE COMPANY

511 Hansen Point Road (off Route 14)
Penn Yan, NY 14527
www.climbingbineshopfarm.com

The stars have aligned at Climbing Bines, a hop farm and microbrewery named for the vining plant that climbs by its shoots and wraps clockwise around its trellis, anchored on a farmstead settled by Chris Hansen's great-grandfather in 1905. Although most breweries don't have the real estate for growing their own ingredients, Chris, along with brewer Brian Karweck, have developed a model farm-to-glass enterprise, using a 1.5-acre hop yard with a mix of seven cultivars to lend flavors and aromas to a range of ales as distinctive and varied as those that grapevines and soils give to wines.

The hardest part of visiting this place is deciding what to order. Try the very drinkable Pandemonium beers (referencing an old name for Penn Yan in its less civilized past), made with local ingredients—barley, wheat, and rye—grown on nearby Peter Martin Farm. The brewery's flagship Imperial IPA, made with earthy Cascade, Chinook, and Nugget hops, stays true to the IPA's historical roots. Beers are offered by the pint, in a flight, or in cans to take home.

Climbing Bines Wood Fired outpost is at 486 Exchange Street in downtown Geneva, where you can sip beers and chow down on hand-stretched pizzas.

TIN BARN BREWING

5428 Route 14
Dundee, NY 14837
www.tinbarn.com

Lauren Van Pamelen's story began with a one-gallon homebrew starter kit, turning a beer lover into a beer brewer. After earning a brewing certificate from the American Brewers Guild in Vermont, she apprenticed at Long Island's Oyster Bay Brewing. In 2019, the former optician partnered with her father, Dale, the entrepreneur behind New York's Dog Spa and Hotel, to turn a former auction house in the Orange County town of Chester into Tin Barn Brewing, a locally popular spot for beer geeks, foodies, hipsters, and tourists. In 2022, the father-daughter team purchased former Starkey's Lookout, a defunct winery and brewery, and introduced head brewer Lauren's unfiltered, high-octane New England–style IPAs (some above 9 percent ABV) to the Finger Lakes.

Attitude and humor are at the core of branding. Keep an eye out for thirst-quenchers, including an imperial IPA called I'm Not a Bad Dog; Take It Back; and a fruited sour called A Pineapple in Paradise.

Tin Barn has a spacious taproom with a breezy, wrap-around patio providing stunning views of Seneca Lake and the fruitful vineyards of Glenora Wine Cellars (see page 79) across Route 14. Pull up an Adirondack chair, order a plate of warm Bavarian pretzels or maybe Buffalo chicken nachos. If you're looking for a crafty alternative to low-strength session beers, welcome to the oasis.

UPSTATE BREWING COMPANY FLX
17 North Franklin Street
Watkins Glen, NY 14891
www.upstatebrewing.com

From 1946 until 1996, Joe's Service Station was a place where travelers would stop for gas and receive a check under the hood, fluid top off, and windshield wash. The space is now home to the lively tap house and beer garden of Upstate Brewing Company, offering beers made at the original Elmira location (see page 200).

Besides creative rotating seasonals and limited release beers, Common Sense is top dog here, the revival of a dark cream style of beer once popular in and around Louisville, Kentucky, from the 1850s until Prohibition.

And because nothing goes better with a cold brew than fresh air and sunshine, during the summer months, overhead doors roll up to an outdoor beer garden. Unwind, sip, and savor just a stone's throw from the lake.

SENECA LODGE CRAFT BREWING
3614 Walnut Road
Watkins Glen, NY 14891
www.senecalodge.com

This Adirondack-style lodge sits above Old Corning Hill near the upper entrance to one of the most popular Finger Lakes destinations. Watkins Glen State Park has a reputation for leaving visitors spellbound—within two miles, the glen's stream descends four hundred feet past two-hundred-foot cliffs, generating nineteen waterfalls along its course. Swing open the wide, creaking door and walk through a wood-paneled dining room. Pull up a stool at one of the most unusual bars you will ever see. Beginning in 1948, the Seneca Lodge Tavern Room was a post-race gathering place for the Grand Prix, the first post–World War II road race in America. Walls of the bar are loaded with memorabilia, including the winner's laurel wreaths presented to James Hunt, Jackie Stewart, and Emerson Fittipaldi following Formula One victories, which ran at the glen from 1961 to 1980, as well as hundreds of arrows shot into the wall by ace archers who frequent the lodge during archery championships.

House-brewed beers on tap include Blonde Ale, Amber Ale, Oatmeal Stout, and aggressively hopped Hoptane IPA. This is a place to drink beer, not just taste it.

Another oddity: In longstanding tradition, bartenders at Seneca Lodge hand your change back in $2 bills.

SENECA LAKE BREWING COMPANY
4520 Route 14
Rock Stream, NY 14878
www.senecalakebrewing.com

A longtime staple in British pubs, cask-conditioned ale is stored in the pub's cellar, developing character, or "condition," for up to a week, thanks to the presence of live yeast in the beer. The result is an ale that has gentler carbonation; a smoother mouthfeel; and, because it's unfiltered, a more complex flavor and aromatic profile.

A native of Cranleigh, a village southeast of Guildford in Surrey, England, Bradley Gillett served time behind the stick at a village pub called the Three Horseshoes. With his technology background, he was lured to the United States to develop business platforms, and in 2014, he made his way to the Finger Lakes, intent on introducing the region to his native brews by creating the kind of establishment he knew back home, where friends, neighbors, and strangers gather to unwind and share tales of the day.

When you arrive here, you're greeted with a sign that reads, "Beerocracy." It's the first indication that this is not your average brewery. SLB feels just like what it is: a faithful recreation of a British pub, in both product and spirit. Operating on an eight-barrel brewing system imported from Lancashire in Northwest England, Bradley crafts a range of cask and bottle-conditioned ales pulled through traditional, hand-pumped beer engines.

Stop in anytime for a "warm one." Brews, including Bertie's Brown Ale and Kill Kenny with Kindness Irish Red, are served at cellar temperature, 52°F to 57°F, a bit warmer than American counterparts, allowing hop aromas and malt flavors to perform at their peak, often lost when beer is served ice-cold.

CIDERIES

WORTHOG CIDERY
2770 Route 14
Penn Yan, NY 14527
www.worthogcidery.com

See CK Cellars, page 72.

DISTILLERIES

SPIRITS OF MILES
168 Randall Crossing Road
Himrod, NY 14842
www.mileswinecellars.com

See Miles Wine Cellars, page 73.

O'BEGLEY DISTILLERY
5700 Route 14
Dundee, NY 14837
www.obegley.com

In 2011, James and Adam of the American Begleys began producing proprietary Irish-style whiskeys, a nod to their Irish farm-family roots in Kilfountan, County Kerry, Ireland. The project employs a custom-built still repurposed from industrial materials in a production space in Pittsford. They use locally sourced grains to produce traditional Irish pot-still whiskeys, a cream liqueur, and traditional Poitín whiskey. The bright, minimalist tasting room in Dundee seems more like a laboratory, providing an ideal environment where visitors can better focus on the sensory experience.

Poitín (pronounced *puh-CHEEN*) is the moonshine of the Irish, deeply rooted in the island's history and traditionally served at important Irish occasions, from wake rituals to weddings. It can be substituted for almost any spirit, from vodka to tequila. Cocktail options here include a Poitín-spiked bloody Mary. Whiskeys are aged for two years in ten-gallon first-fill bourbon casks from Woodinville, Washington, and "honeycomb" cooperage from Black Swan in Park Rapids, Minnesota. Most noteworthy is ancestor-inspired Old Kilfountan, a versatile fine-grain whiskey similar in style to Jameson, the world's best-selling Irish whiskey, and the center of attention in an O'Begley's Irish Manhattan.

SENECA LAKE (EAST)

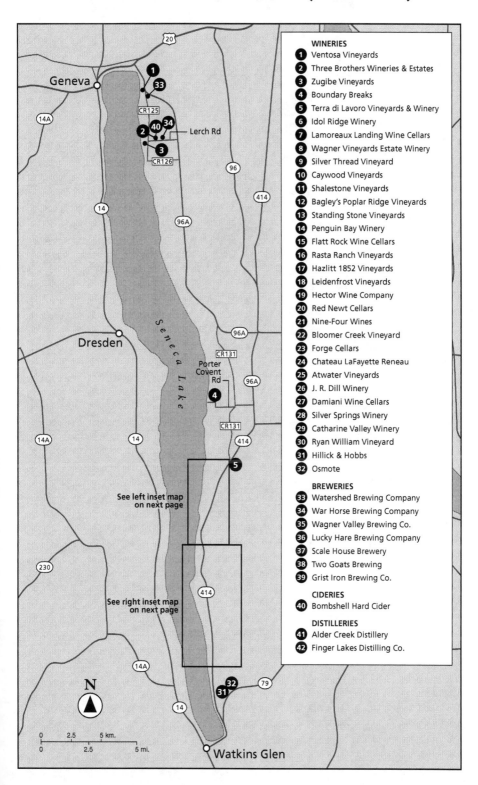

WINERIES

1. Ventosa Vineyards
2. Three Brothers Wineries & Estates
3. Zugibe Vineyards
4. Boundary Breaks
5. Terra di Lavoro Vineyards & Winery
6. Idol Ridge Winery
7. Lamoreaux Landing Wine Cellars
8. Wagner Vineyards Estate Winery
9. Silver Thread Vineyard
10. Caywood Vineyards
11. Shalestone Vineyards
12. Bagley's Poplar Ridge Vineyards
13. Standing Stone Vineyards
14. Penguin Bay Winery
15. Flatt Rock Wine Cellars
16. Rasta Ranch Vineyards
17. Hazlitt 1852 Vineyards
18. Leidenfrost Vineyards
19. Hector Wine Company
20. Red Newt Cellars
21. Nine-Four Wines
22. Bloomer Creek Vineyard
23. Forge Cellars
24. Chateau LaFayette Reneau
25. Atwater Vineyards
26. J. R. Dill Winery
27. Damiani Wine Cellars
28. Silver Springs Winery
29. Catharine Valley Winery
30. Ryan William Vineyard
31. Hillick & Hobbs
32. Osmote

BREWERIES

33. Watershed Brewing Company
34. War Horse Brewing Company
35. Wagner Valley Brewing Co.
36. Lucky Hare Brewing Company
37. Scale House Brewery
38. Two Goats Brewing
39. Grist Iron Brewing Co.

CIDERIES

40. Bombshell Hard Cider

DISTILLERIES

41. Alder Creek Distillery
42. Finger Lakes Distilling Co.

Geneva

CR125

Lerch Rd

CR126

20

14A

14

96

414

96A

Seneca Lake

Dresden

96A

CR131

Porter
Covent
Rd

96A

CR131

414

See left inset map
on next page

See right inset map
on next page

14A

14

14

230

414

79

Watkins Glen

14A

14

N

0   2.5   5 km.

0   2.5   5 mi.

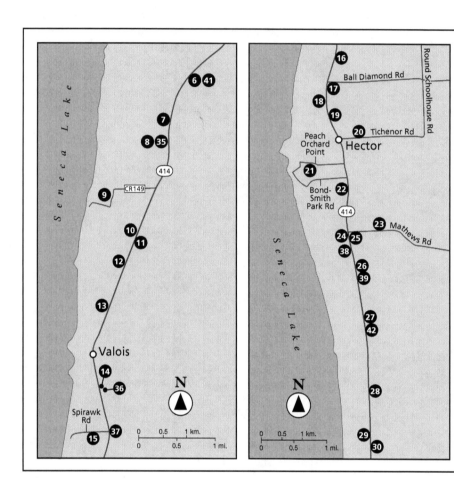

Seneca Lake

6 41

7

8 35

414

CR149

9

10

11

12

13

Valois

14

36

Spirawk
Rd

37

15

N

0   0.5   1 km.

0   0.5   1 mi.

16

Ball Diamond Rd

Round Schoolhouse Rd

17

18

19

20   Tichenor Rd

Peach
Orchard
Point

Hector

21

Bond-
Smith
Park Rd

22

414

23   Mathews Rd

24 25

38

26
39

27
42

Seneca Lake

28

N

29

30

0   0.5   1 km.

0   0.5   1 mi.

WINERIES

VENTOSA VINEYARDS
3440 Route 96
Geneva, NY 14456
www.ventosavineyards.com

His grandparents grew grapes in the wine region of southern Italy. Lenny Cecere made a fortune building theme parks and commercial swim and water parks around the world. Retired in 1997, he purchased a 107-year-old Geneva farm on a sixty-five-acre property on the northeast shore of Seneca Lake, turning the land into vineyards, creating a winemaking facility, and building a Tuscan-inspired tasting room.

Ventosa (Italian for "windy") offers several Old World–influenced, food-friendly wines fashioned from estate-grown grapes by winemaker Jeff Harvey. A graceful, everyday-sipping white blend, Vino Bianco maintains the body of a Chardonnay, complemented by Vidal and Riesling. Saggio (meaning "wisdom" in Italian) is a Bordeaux-inspired blend of Cabernet Sauvignon, Cabernet Franc, and Merlot. Ventosa reflects a powerful Italian presence, and there's no better place to taste Sangiovese, a rare varietal in the region, as well as the region's only plantings of Tocai Friulano, a northern Italian classic that locals call a "wine that makes friends easily."

Café Toscana, with dining options inside or alfresco on the terrace, offers cheese and charcuterie boards, paninis, pizza, homemade soups, antipasti, and biscotti with cappuccinos.

THREE BROTHERS WINERIES & ESTATES
623 Lerch Road
Geneva, NY 14456
www.3brotherswinery.com

Originally the modest estate of New Land Vineyards, the flamboyantly con-ceived venture is a theme park–inspired winery, brewery, and cidery. One of the region's most popular tourist destinations, the venue attracts 40,000 visitors annually. Purchased by Dave and Luanne Mansfield in 2006, Three Brothers Wineries & Estates opened in September 2007. The sprawling campus includes

Stoney Lonesome Wine, Passion Feet Wines, and Bagg Dare Wine, separate tasting venues. Heading the winemaking team for all three, Aaron Roisen comes to Three Brothers after stints at Hosmer Winery (see page 141) and Lamoreaux Landing Wine Cellars (see page 103). He produces four distinct "degrees" of Rieslings, from dry to sweet; a handful of serious varietals; and a range of sugary, suggestively named pop wines, including (gasp!) Skirt Lifter, Nearly Naked, Rider All Night, and 69 Ways to Have Fun.

In 2016, the Three Brothers complex added War Horse Brewing Company (see page 123), a 15-barrel on-site facility. If you can weave your way past the crowds at the wine slushie stand, sample head brewer Garrett Meakin's offerings, including Lieutenant Dan, a hazy IPA, the brewery's most popular beer, and Breakfast with Churchill, an oatmeal coffee stout, brewed with coffee from Monaco's Coffee in Geneva.

Most of the Bombshell Hard Ciders produced here are intended for the sweet tooth, with added fruit flavors—orange, pineapple, strawberry, tangerine, raspberry, lemon. A fee of $40 provides a "Tasting Experience Pass," good for one flight in each of the three wineries and the brewery. Ciders are available in the brewery.

ZUGIBE VINEYARDS
4277 East Lake Road
Geneva, NY 14456
www.zugibevineyards.com

This is a place to drink wines that reflect a sense of place, wines with a story from vineyards with a history. After retiring from his position as a research associate at the New York State Agricultural Experiment Station in Geneva, viticulturist Keith H. Kimball planted the original vineyard here, conducting rootstock trials and experimenting with innovative irrigation and grafting techniques while supplying small quantities of grapes to nearby wineries. In 2004, cardiologist Dr. Frederick Zugibe II purchased the property, and the following summer he planted twenty-three acres of Riesling (three different clones), Cabernet Franc, Pinot Gris, Gewürztraminer, Pinot Noir, Chardonnay, Cabernet Sauvignon, Merlot, and Sauvignon Blanc, totaling 122 rows of trellised vines. The following year he added Lemberger and Grüner Veltliner (the first planting of the variety in New York State). Today, the dedicated Zugibe family, Frederick III and brothers Brendan and Sean, follow in their father's footsteps, with work in the vineyards and cellar carried out in his memory, striving to produce wines with a deep connection to family heritage.

Named for the four generations in a row of Fredericks, 4 Freds Red is a blend of (you guessed it) four varieties: Cabernet Franc, Lemberger, Merlot, and Cabernet Sauvignon. Phoenician Red, a blend of Cabernet Franc and Lemberger, is a nod to the family's ancestral roots in Lebanon, a land of wine production since the ancient Phoenician civilization.

The bistro menu includes falafels, stuffed grape leaves, spinach pies, and other Middle Eastern dishes.

BOUNDARY BREAKS

1428 Porter Covert Road
Lodi, NY 14860
www.boundarybreaks.com

In 2007, Yale grad, former newspaperman, and media executive Bruce Murray and his wife, former high school science teacher Diana Lyttle, purchased 120 acres of land, convinced that they could harness the potential of a site originally farmed by multiple generations of the Covert family, also well-suited, it turned out, for growing grapes. With a creative-centric focus on "true Riesling," they began planting vines with four different German clones, all Riesling but genetically slightly different, a resolute experiment to determine which ones best express the terroir of this locale. The venture's name, Boundary Breaks, refers to the two deep gorges that lie along the northern and southern boundaries of the west-facing slope.

For the first harvest in 2011, Murray contracted with winemaker Peter Bell and the team at Fox Run Vineyards (see page 66) to turn his estate-grown Riesling grapes into wines. Since then, winemakers from several wineries around the lakes have produced wines for Boundary Breaks: the treasured Rieslings, of course, as well as Gewürztraminer, Cabernet Franc, Merlot, and Cabernet Sauvignon. The layered, complex Rieslings, each a liquid study in terroir, are wines that improve with age.

Murray's quest has earned critical acclaim. *Wine Enthusiast* named the 2012 Boundary Breaks Riesling Dry one of the top one hundred wines in the world. And in 2021, the 2019 Riesling Dry (#239) was named *Wine Spectator* magazine's list of top one hundred wines in the world.

The property itself is both grandiose and intimate. The grassy lawn beckons visitors to spread out a picnic blanket, open a bottle of wine, and stay awhile. It's hard to imagine a more signature experience of wine country than a visit to this destination estate and meeting the remarkable people who created it.

TERRA DI LAVORO VINEYARDS & WINERY

9013 Route 414
Lodi, NY 14860
www.terradilavoro.us

Terra di Lavoro means "land of work" in Italian, a name that has historical roots in southern Italy and one that honors Frank Vettese's heritage. Frank and his wife, Fumie Okubo, landed here from New York City, taking one of those leaps that wine country seems to inspire in city folks. The couple found their dream home in 2020 when they laid eyes on a charming farmhouse that locals will remember as a restaurant called Suzanne Fine Regional Cuisine. Two years later, it became Terra di Lavoro.

After a day of visiting the bustling wineries and breweries along Route 414, this is the perfect respite, a quiet place to sip Frank's small-batch wines in the quaint and intimate setting of a European-style café, a tasteful decor that exudes a sense of comfort and relaxation. There are a half-dozen wines to choose from, most notably Chiaretto Rosso, a red blend of local grapes reminiscent of a robust *vino da tavola*.

The kitchen offers a variety of dishes to complement the wines, including Pizza del Mezzogiorno, Polpette al Ragu, and Shrimp Arrabiata. It's easy to lose an hour or two here with a bottle of wine, plates of good food, and the warmth of wine-country hospitality.

IDOL RIDGE WINERY

9059 Route 414
Lodi, NY 14860
www.idolridge.com

Fossenvue was a lakeside summer campground founded on the eastern shore of Seneca Lake by suffragist Elizabeth Smith. The name Fossenvue is a rearrangement of the letters in *seven of us*, the number of visitors who landed at Fausett's Point that first summer. From 1875 to 1908, the camp became known for recreation, creative and artistic activity, and its association with elites from Cornell and Hobart and William Smith Colleges.

In 2013, the Martin family, owners of Montezuma Winery (see page 133), established Idol Ridge Winery near the site of Fossenvue, and winemaker Phil Plummer created a series of wines to commemorate the historic camp. Much like the Montezuma mothership, there are many wines, many styles, many choices here. While the Idol Ridge label varieties show bigger with more fruit intensity, Fossenvue wines take a more delicate, layered direction, both styles honoring winemaking tradition.

Perhaps even more interesting is Phil's work with the Local Culture wild-fermented series using a technique called *pied de cuve* ("foot of the tank"). A small volume of fermented musts prepared a few days before harvest is used to inoculate the subsequent batches of grape juice, helping to jump-start fermentation. These remarkable wines showcase individual vineyard and vintage, the most honest reflection of terroir.

Idol Ridge is also home to Alder Creek Distillery (see page 128), offering an array of spirits, including Single Barrel Wheat Whiskey, crafted from locally farmed wheat and aged for three years and fifty-five days, and Dropline Maple Bourbon Whiskey, made with locally sourced maple syrup.

The tasting room, rooted in Adirondack cabin vernacular, doubles as a gift shop, including an array of wine-related items, perfect for gifts or reminders of your trip to wine country.

LAMOREAUX LANDING WINE CELLARS
9224 Route 414
Lodi, NY 14860
www.lamoreauxwine.com/

Lamoreaux Landing Wine Cellars was founded in 1992 by Mark Wagner, a cousin of the Wagners of next-door Wagner Vineyards Estate Winery (see page 104). Mark grew up in the vineyards and, spurred by the Farm Winery Act, decided to make his own wine instead of solely supplying grapes to other wineries.

One of the most-respected growers in the region, Mark separates his vineyards into twenty unique, intensively managed blocks. Site-to-site comparison is interesting among the winery's single-vineyard Rieslings. And not to be overlooked, Lamoreaux Landing's dessert wines, Vidal Ice and Riesling Ice, mimic the legendary *eisweins* of Germany and Austria.

There are several novel aspects to this enterprise, not the least of which is the striking postmodern edifice designed by architect Bruce Corson and cited by the New York State chapter of the American Institute of Architects as one of sixty notable projects of the twentieth century. With a spectacular view of the vineyard hillside and lake, it suggests a cross between Greek revival architecture, common throughout the Finger Lakes, and one of the region's field barns.

Special mention should be made here of a wine that emerged from Mark's curiosity about how Cabernet Franc would do without oak age. Taking inspiration from a common practice in the French Loire, T23 Cabernet Franc matures in a specific stainless-steel tank.

Mark quietly continues his proud heritage and artisanal approach to grape growing and winemaking—making a connection between the land and the wine. His wines have an extremely loyal following and are sought by the region's best restaurants.

WAGNER VINEYARDS ESTATE WINERY

9322 Route 414
Lodi, NY 14860
www.wagnervineyards.com

The vineyards of Bill Wagner's youth were his playground. They would become his passion and his life's work. He returned home to the family farm from service in the navy at the end of World War II, planted a vineyard in Lodi, and became a grape wholesaler. Three decades later, he decided to turn his grapes into wine.

If the Finger Lakes were a dartboard, Wagner Vineyards would most likely be its bull's-eye, equidistant from all corners of the region—rather fitting because this enterprise played a central role in the early growth and development of the region's modern wine industry. Bill Wagner's vision was to create wines that belong in the company of the great wines of the world. By almost any measure, he succeeded in making that vision a reality.

The octagonal building that Bill conjured up to save space is a Finger Lakes landmark. The winery produces a total of three dozen wines, all from the estate's 240 acres of vineyards, all over the varietal map. Focus is on award-winning Rieslings—dry, semidry, sweet, ice, and Caywood East single-vineyard offering. Expect a few unusual bottles. Fathom 107 is an Alsatian-inspired blend of Riesling and Gewürztraminer, two aromatic grape varieties more commonly found in varietal form, named after the deepest point of Seneca Lake.

The winemaking team follows in the footsteps of celebrated alumni. Jess Johnson, former assistant winemaker at Standing Stone Vineyards (see page 107), worked with Ann Raffetto until her retirement, and Kevin Lee, Bill's grandson, stepped into his role after John Herbert's tenure.

Housed in a separate part of the octagon, Wagner Valley Brewing Co. (see page 124), established in 1997, was one of the earliest craft breweries in the region.

Stay for lunch. Head next door to the Ginny Lee Café overlooking the vineyards, and feast on soups, salads, sandwiches, and flatbreads.

SILVER THREAD VINEYARD

1401 Caywood Road
Lodi, NY 14860
www.silverthreadwine.com

Richard Figiel was a New York City journalist who, while reporting on breakthrough vintages in the 1970s, was drawn to the promise of greater wines in the Finger Lakes. He moved his family Upstate, where he planted grapes and worked as editor, first for *Eastern Grape Grower and Winery News*, then for *International Wine Review*, before setting out to make wines for a living. His pursuit became Silver Thread Vineyard, a small, ideologically driven winery named for a nearby waterfall and committed to natural farming and conservation. Silver Thread falls into the back-lane, select-pilgrimage category. Follow the narrow, unpaved end of Caywood Road heading down toward Seneca Lake to discover a hidden treasure.

In 2010, Paul and Shannon Brock, husband-and-wife team, became the new owners of Silver Thread. Paul earned a degree in enology and viticulture at Cornell and a BS in chemical engineering from RPI. Shannon served as wine director at the New York Wine and Culinary Center in Canandaigua. The Brocks have continued progressive pioneer Figiel's sustainable farming practices and handcrafted production of Chardonnay, Gewürztraminer, Pinot Noir, and exceptional estate-grown and outsourced single-vineyard Rieslings, working with some of the oldest, best-known vineyards in the region. They have injected Silver Thread with a sense of freshness and optimism, backed up by a series of exceptional vintages. Guided tastings provide an opportunity to compare flagship Rieslings alongside Doyle Fournier Vineyard and Gridley Bluff Point Vineyard Rieslings.

CAYWOOD VINEYARDS
9666 Route 414
Lodi, NY 14860
www.caywoodvineyards.com

Named for its location near Caywood Point, the only part of the Finger Lakes National Forest bordering Seneca Lake, Caywood is a satellite of the Pleasant Valley Wine Company (see page 36), a marketplace for the Doyle family roster of brands, including Great Western, Widmer, Gold Seal, Pleasant Valley, and Brickstone Cellars. Housed in a handsomely restored 1890s barn and packing house, the tasting-room bar was built with redwood and oak, handcrafted from recycled wine tanks. Sip wines next to a three-story fireplace made from native stone and gaze out over Chardonnay and Riesling vineyards planted by legendary Charles Fournier in the 1950s.

Don't leave without a bottle of the off-dry Gold Seal Riesling, crafted from the historic vineyards. The back label includes the story of pioneer winemaker Fournier.

SHALESTONE VINEYARDS
9681 Route 414
Lodi, NY 14860
www.shalestonevineyards.com

Here's a surprise: a highly respected Finger Lakes winery that doesn't sell a lick of white wine. It's by word of mouth that wine lovers discover the remarkable red wines produced by a gifted and, some would say, reclusive artisan named Rob Thomas. Rob started his career by tending vines at Rolling Vineyards, then honed his winemaking skills at Chateau LaFayette Reneau (see page 115), and in 1991 became head winemaker at Lamoreaux Landing Wine Cellars (see page 103). While still at Lamoreaux, he purchased a special plot of land, planted six acres of grapes, and built a low-tech cellar into the hillside.

In 1994, Rob released his first vintage of wines under the Shalestone label. The winery's name was inspired by a site where vine roots have barely twelve inches of soil above layers of fractured shale (or shale bedrock) deposited by ancient glaciers. He believed his vines would have to struggle mightily to survive here and that struggling would result in grapes of great intensity. History has proved him correct.

Too bad there are so few bottles for the world. Rob handcrafts less than one thousand cases of red wine varietals and creative blends each year, including the winemaker's "dream team," a Syrah–Merlot–Cabernet Sauvignon proprietary blend called Synergy. His human-scale production of rich, concentrated beauties are as close as we come to cult wines in the Finger Lakes.

BAGLEY'S POPLAR RIDGE VINEYARDS
9782 Route 414
Valois, NY 14841
www.bagleysprv.com

Dave Bagley was somewhat of a local legend. In the late 1970s, after passage of the New York Farm Winery Act, Dave taught many of the region's grape growers to make wine. Then, after working for several fledgling wineries, he purchased a farm near the lake, planted a twenty-acre vineyard, and in 1981 opened his own winery.

Wines are always a reflection of the people who make them, those who work day and night in the winery, transform grapes into wine, and create its image. And when it comes to reputation, Dave was the region's antisnob. He created wines with names like Busty Blanc and Pecker Head Red and invented the motto at Bagley's Poplar Ridge Vineyards, "Wine without Bull." Since 2008, it's been up to Dave's daughter Brittany to maintain the unpretentious spirit and laid-back vibe here.

STANDING STONE VINEYARDS
9934 Route 414
Hector, NY 14841
www.standingstonewines.com

The story here begins in a patch of earth with a fabled past. Fifty years ago, wine pioneers Charles Fournier and Guy DeVeaux of Gold Seal chose this site over a hundred others for their vinifera plantings, so when Tom and Marti Macinski acquired the property in 1991, they inherited vineyards of exalted pedigree. What was originally an old chicken farm overlooking Seneca Lake was planted with five acres of Riesling in 1972, then with eight acres of Chardonnay in 1974. The old, sadly neglected Gold Seal Area 13 was lovingly restored by the high-energy Macinskis as they added Gewürztraminer, Vidal, Pinot Noir, Cabernet Sauvignon, and Merlot.

The aura of the Finger Lakes and its winemaking traditions attracted the Binghamton natives to the project they named Standing Stone Vineyards, the name inspired by Indian legend. The earliest inhabitants of this region believed when you found the "standing stone," you found perfection. The goal, to grow and produce distinctive wines from this coveted site, was realized with the first vintage in 1993. Standing Stone came from out of nowhere to win a silver medal at the San Francisco International Wine Competition for Riesling and a gold medal at the New York Wine and Food Classic for Gewürztraminer. The following year, Cabernet Franc captured the New York State Governor's Cup as best in show.

After three decades and retirement on the horizon, the Macinskis sold their beloved Standing Stone Vineyards to Fred Merwarth and Oskar Bynke, owners of Hermann J. Wiemer Vineyard (see page 75), consummating a union of two of the region's most respected wineries.

The highlight here is undoubtedly Riesling Timeline Dry, a wine of breadth and complexity made with fruit from the vineyard's historic five-acre plot. And don't miss the "teinturier" wines made from Saperavi, whose flesh has color, unlike most red-berried varieties. Standing Stone rosés are made without skin contact, achieving a remarkably deep rosé hue purely from the flesh's pigment.

PENGUIN BAY WINERY
6075 Route 14
Hector, NY 14841
www.penguinbaywinery.com

The third jewel in the crown of Peterson family enterprises after Swedish Hill Winery (see page 134) and Goose Watch Winery (see page 136), Penguin Bay, launched in 2005, is a separate brand that maintains the Peterson philosophy of "something for everyone," types and styles, dry wine to dessert wines.

Artful blending is a hallmark of winemaker Zach Pegram's program, on display in Maroon Four, crafted with Corot Noir, Noiret (pronounced *nwahr-AY*), Lemberger, and Cabernet Franc, as well as a symbiotic Lemberger–Pinot Noir partnership. A visit here provides an opportunity to compare Gewürztraminer in dry and semisweet styles and Riesling as both still and sparkling wines.

The Petersons are longtime supporters of the Rosamond Gifford Zoo in Syracuse, home to a colony of Humboldt penguins, a vulnerable-to-extinction species that hails from the Humboldt current off the coast of Peru and Chile. A portion of every wine purchase at Goose Watch is donated to the Penguin Coast exhibit.

FLATT ROCK WINE CELLARS
5835 Spirawk Road (off Route 414)
Hector, NY 14841
www.flattrockwinecellars.com

In 2017, the retirement project of Dave and Darla Flatt blossomed into Flatt Rock Wine Cellars. Smitten by the *vin rouges* of Bordeaux during the years they spent in France, the couple arrived in the region intent on creating a venture focused on production of dry red wines.

The tasting room is a low-key, friendly experience. Offerings include Pinot Noir; Cabernet Franc; Cabernet Sauvignon; and proprietary Boulder Blend, a Bordeaux-style *ménage à trois*.

In France, there's a mandatory *l'heure de l'aperitif*, a time that ushers in dinner hour. Inspired by the French ritual and custom, Flatt Rock Brut Méthode Champenoise, a refreshing blend of Pinot Noir and Chardonnay, is a nod to European dining culture.

RASTA RANCH VINEYARDS
5882 Route 414
Hector, NY 14841
www.rastaranchvineyards.com

The hippie culture of the 1960s and the promotion of peace, love, and good times are alive and well at Rasta Ranch. Get into a groovy state of mind at Diane Buligion Mannion's curated treasure trove of quirky antiques, rock-and-roll memorabilia, vintage-style arts and crafts, racks of clothing, beads, bracelets, pictures of Bob Marley in every corner, and handmade wines, all stuffed into a den-like former hay barn with an unabashedly Rastafarian vibe. On a property that was originally a labrusca vineyard dating back to the late 1890s, Diane established a microwinery in 1993 and began planting vinifera varieties.

Besides the requisite sweet wines, including Uncle Homer's Red, made from the estate's Concord fruit, Diane's DryAnne series includes a blend of Grüner Veltliner and Seyval Blanc and a true-to-varietal rendition of Cabernet Franc crafted from grapes grown on Arlo Ringsmith's nearby vineyard.

HAZLITT 1852 VINEYARDS
5712 Route 414
Hector, NY 14841
www.hazlitt1852.com

The 153 acres of fruit trees and vineyards purchased by David Hazlitt in 1852 has been tended by the Hazlitt family for seven generations. The vineyards are situated on what's called Seneca Lake's "banana belt," consistently the warmest microclimate in the Finger Lakes as measured by Geneva Experiment Station thermometers planted throughout the region. From Peach Orchard Point north to Lodi Point on Seneca's eastern shore, the weather pattern keeps soil warmer into the fall. An extended growing season means the fruit has more time on the vine.

Jerry and Elaine Hazlitt founded the winery in 1985, its name marking the year the family first settled here. With century-old Catawba grapevines and eight acres of Baco Noir on the property, one of the first wines produced by the fledgling winery was a proprietary blend of the two. Combining both of these early-ripening, high-acid varieties proved much better than either one on its own, especially with added sugar for balance.

Red Cat (named for the *Cat* in *Catawba*) has become the best-selling wine in New York State, and its success in the growing low-price-point, sweet-wine category has spawned a line of products, including Red Cat Sangria, Red Cat Fizz, White Cat, and Pink Cat. In order to keep up with demand, the Hazlitts acquired the former Widmer Wine Cellars' large-scale production facilities in Naples (see Hazlitt Red Cat Cellars, page 14).

While Hazlitt 1852 Vineyards still calls itself "Home of the Red Cat" and fun-loving crowds who arrive by limo and pack the tasting room are here to party, the estate can hardly be defined by this one category. Rather, over three decades the Hazlitt family has developed an ambitious roster of serious wines, including Riesling, Chardonnay, Gewürztraminer, Pinot Gris, Cabernet Sauvignon, Cabernet Franc, and Merlot, all made with varietal fruit grown on the vineyard's remarkable terroir.

LEIDENFROST VINEYARDS
5677 Route 414
Hector, NY 14841
www.leidenfrostwine.com

John Leidenfrost qualifies as one of the region's modern-day adventurers in a quest of Pinot Noir, the "holy grail" of red wine. His vision and determination not only proved that the finicky varietal could prosper at his site, but he also established a touchstone with a style that bursts with ripe black cherry varietal character. Physically and temperamentally, the Leidenfrost property is a bit different from some of its neighbors. Steep slopes provide good drainage, and the soils assist ripening. Proximity to the lake provides a thermal advantage, especially on the eastern shore, where afternoon sun bathes the grapes while prevailing winds moderate temperatures. These conditions significantly extend the growing season, allowing grapes to hang on the vines longer and develop complex flavors.

Pinot Noir makes vastly different styles of wine on each plot of ground where it's grown, and, in nearly every respect, John's site appears to possess an ideal microclimate and soil structure for the capricious and sometimes elusive Pinot Noir; a Pinot Noir Rosé; and Tango (as in "two to tango"), a blend of Pinot Noir and Cabernet Franc. John, by the way, didn't end his pursuit of noble grapes with Pinot Noir. He also enjoys success with Cabernet Sauvignon, Cabernet Franc, Merlot, Sauvignon Blanc, Chardonnay, Riesling, and Gewürztraminer.

The estate remains entirely family run and managed. In 2010, Elizabeth Leidenfrost of the next generation joined her father in the vineyards and the cellar.

HECTOR WINE COMPANY
5610 Route 414
Hector, NY 14841
www.hectorwinecompany.com

Sawmill Creek is ground zero of Finger Lakes terroir, the vineyard against which all others are measured. During the modern era of wine production in the Finger Lakes, the Sawmill Creek Vineyard designation has graced wine labels of some of our most exceptional bottles. For years, the region's most revered winemakers have tripped over themselves trying to snag Sawmill Creek fruit.

The property, resting along the lake in what's affectionately known as the "banana belt," has steep slopes, shale soils, and a microclimate measurably warmer than most of the region—geographical advantages nearly unparalleled by any other locales. The Hazlitt family, once known for being the top peach farmers in all of the region, dove head first into growing grapes during the 1860s—and the rest is history.

In 2010, Jason Hazlitt, a seventh-generation family grower, teamed up with veteran winemaker Justin Boyette, who honed his winemaking skills at Atwater Vineyards (see page 116) and Red Newt Cellars (see below), to launch the Hector Wine Company, sourcing fruit from the iconic vineyard. Winemaking techniques include native yeast fermentations, unfined and unfiltered reds, and minimal intervention in the cellar. Sawmill Creek grows sixteen varieties on seventy acres, and Boyette has first pick of the fruit for his range of wines, most notably the Signature Series, including Chardonnay, Gewürztraminer, Riesling, Sauvignon Blanc, and Cabernet Sauvignon.

There are very serious wines being made here. Check out the attention-getting Soul Red, an exclusive red blend crafted from hand-harvested Chancellor, Cabernet Sauvignon, Syrah, Lemberger, and Merlot grapes.

Pull up a stool at the tasting bar and build a custom flight. Wines are priced per pour, depending on the type of wine and size of the pour.

RED NEWT CELLARS
3675 Tichenor Road (off Route 414)
Hector, NY 14841
www.rednewt.com

The enterprise began in 1999 as a husband-and-wife, wine-and-food collaboration, with David Whiting in the cellar and Debra Whiting in the kitchen. The couple's first home had a small pond that at springtime teemed with a local species of the red-spotted newt, inspiring the name for their dream venture.

Red Newt does not own its own vineyards and must purchase all its grapes. However, long-term contracts with dependable growers, including Fred Wickham of Tango Oaks Vineyard and John Santos of Curry Creek Vineyard, provide exceptional fruit to veteran winemaker Christina Zapel, who joined Red Newt in 2023. Christine's previous experience includes stints at Wölffer Estate in the Hamptons and Flowers Vineyards and Winery in Healdsburg, California, finally rising to winemaker at Foley Sonoma in Geyserville, California. Following in the footsteps of her predecessor, Kelby James Russell of Apollo's Praise (see page 81), she has assumed production here with the focus on as many as ten remarkable single-vineyard Rieslings.

If you could sum up Finger Lakes winemaking with a single bottle of wine, it would probably be Circle Riesling, a blend from several vineyard plots, with fermentation stopped at varying sugar levels, crafted to medium sweetness. It's considered a standard for the variety and is, by the way, one of the best bargains in the region. For wine geeks only, the Laboratory Series includes versions of Riesling, Gewürztraminer, and Merlot, each variety retaining sugars by muting fermentation and fortified with distilled grape spirits, meant to be drunk either as an aperitif, like Sherry, or as an after-dinner drink, like Port.

Red Newt provides a modest menu of "lite fare" fueled by local ingredients, to enjoy alongside an ambitious range of wine flights.

NINE-FOUR WINES
5281 Peach Orchard Road
Hector, NY 14841
www.facebook.com/ninefourwines

You might find the name curious. It can be chalked up to the shared birthdays of winemaker Phil Arras and sommelier Josh Carlsen, two men who began a postmodern winery project in 2016. Phil was head winemaker at Damiani Wine Cellars (see page 118), and Josh was beverage director at Stonecat Café. The pandemic disrupted their plans, and eventually Josh struck out on his own.

He began his career working in wine shops to gain extensive knowledge of great wines from around the world and developed affection for the white wines of Burgundy. The bootstrap enterprise captures the essence of making wine on a small scale, its focus on Burgundian-style Chardonnay, crafted with minimal intervention and restraint—wines that express every nuance of Finger Lakes terroir. Nine-Four produces three hundred to eight hundred cases of wine per year.

Josh sources hand-harvested fruit from Sawmill Creek Vineyard, where the steep slopes, shale soils, and exposure toward the long afternoon and evening sun have made it a prime grape-growing location for Chardonnay. Picked fruit that arrives at the Damiani facility is intensively sorted, then turned into wine in collaboration with winemaker Katey Larwood. The other wine produced here is a conversation piece. Sparkling Rosé is made from 80 percent Rougeon and 20 percent Vignoles, an attractive oddity in the region.

Nine-Four wines are available for tastings and purchase at F.L.X. Provisions in Geneva and Corning.

BLOOMER CREEK VINEYARD

5301 Route 414
Hector, NY 14841
www.bloomercreek.com

The winery takes its name after the rivulet that feeds Cayuga Lake from a spring at the old Bloomer farm. It cuts right through the center of a farm where Kim Engle and Deb Birmingham established Bloomer Creek Vineyard in 1999 from ten acres with two different vineyard designations—Auten Vineyard and Morehouse Road.

As one of the more idiosyncratic wineries in the region, the enterprise is meticulously farmed using low-impact, organic methods. They use hand-harvested, whole clusters; press gently; and ferment with ambient yeasts. If the wines take three or even six months to complete fermentation, the winemakers are happy to let them do their thing. Natural wine isn't just a trendy buzzword for Kim and Deb; it's a way of life.

Hard to imagine a more approachable tasting room, more like a living room housed in a quaint, Victorian-era carriage house, where you will likely sip some of the most experimental and innovative bottles in the Finger Lakes. Pay special attention to the Rieslings with the Auten Vineyard designation—Auten Dry Riesling, Skin-Fermented Auten Vineyard Riesling/Pétillant Wine, and Auten Vineyard Auslese.

Technically part of France, Alsace is often seen as culturally German, where the term *Edelzwicker* (which translates to "noble blend") is commonly used to designate any blending of white grape varieties, traditionally without any indication of percentage, a sort of a wine free-for-all. For Bloomer Creek's Edelzwicker Blue Cap, Kim combines Riesling, Gewürztraminer, Cayuga White, and other white varietals, replicating the Alsatian-inspired field blend, with grapes harvested and fermented together.

If you fancy art with your wine, then browse the original paintings by Ms. Birmingham, displayed in the tasting room.

Most of Bloomer Creek's wines are on measured allocation to the winery's cult following of consumers and restaurateurs. For this reason, the tasting room has very limited hours.

FORGE CELLARS
3775 Mathews Road
Burdett, NY 14818
www.forgecellars.com

For fifteen generations, Louis Barruol's family has produced wine at Château de Saint Cosme in the Gigondas winegrowing region of France, considered one of the southern Rhône's most exceptional appellations. After exploring several locations in search of the perfect location for a new winemaking adventure, Louis determined that the Finger Lakes had the greatest promise. In 2011, he established Forge Cellars along with partner Rick Rainey and winemaker Leana Godard.

This France–meets–Finger Lakes project focuses exclusively on bone-dry Riesling and Pinot Noir, wines that reflect the diverse, mineral-rich landscape of sixteen different vineyard sites, most located on an eight-mile stretch along southeast Seneca Lake. Grapes are vinified from those plots separately each year to produce single-vineyard-designated wines. The emphasis here is on exploring complexity in each site and crafting the ultimate expression of each terroir.

At the core of the Forge portfolio, Riesling fruit, sourced from multiple vineyards, contributes to blends that make up the foundational Classique series of wines. In 2020, the 2018 Forge Riesling Seneca Lake Dry Classique appeared on *Wine Spectator*'s "Top 100" list.

If you don't know where to look for Forge Cellars, you're quite likely to miss it. Take the drive up Mathews Road off Route 414, and find a row of barrels and only a name on the mailbox (there's no sign to identify the winery). Schedule in advance for tastings at the Summer House—elevated, personally guided flights that provide a solid introduction to the Forge portfolio. Or visit the Salon, a comfortable setting for glass and bottle service with optional food pairings of artisanal delicacies including baguettes, local cheeses, tinned fish, and imported ham.

CHATEAU LAFAYETTE RENEAU
5081 Route 414
Hector, NY 14841
www.clrwine.com

The Instagram-friendly setting is one of Seneca Lake's most beautiful landscapes, a hillside field adorned with grapevines. Following a career in the printing business, Richard Reno retired to an old dairy farm on Seneca Lake with nothing more ambitious in mind than keeping a rocking chair in motion. But soon he was out pruning, tying, and restoring the abandoned Concord, Catawba, and Niagara grapevines he found on a corner of the property. The success of neighboring wineries provided some needed assurance that this was, indeed, an ideal location to plant vinifera grapes. In 1985, he converted the cow barn into a winery and transformed his sixty-three acres of land into vineyards of Chardonnay, Riesling, Pinot Noir, Merlot, Cabernet Sauvignon, and Petit Verdot. By 1986, Chateau LaFayette Reneau had its first vintage, and the winery was open for business. Over the following years, the winery earned three Governor's Cups, four coveted Jefferson Cups, and a gold medal from Riesling du Monde.

Petit Verdot, most famously grown in Bordeaux, lends color and richness to blends of Cabernet Sauvignon, Cabernet Franc, and Merlot. Rarely seen in the Finger Lakes, a visit here is an opportunity to taste Petit Verdot as a stand-alone wine. As if to offset the snob appeal of its portfolio, LaFayette Reneau produces one of the region's best lighthearted quaffs. Seyval Chardonnay is a union of the French hybrid and the French classic, with Chardonnay adding structure and complexity to the bright citrus and subtle minerality of Seyval Blanc. This ingeniously blended table wine ought not to be overlooked.

The Inn at Chateau LaFayette Reneau, a craftsman-style house (circa 1911), is a fully restored five-bedroom farmhouse located on the property.

In 2013, the estate was purchased by Gene Pierce and Scott Welliver, owners of Glenora Wine Cellars (see page 79), and in 2019, it was sold to Ryan William of Ryan William Vineyard (see page 120).

ATWATER VINEYARDS
5055 Route 414
Burdett, NY 14818
www.atwatervineyards.com

In an earlier life, the property was called Rolling Vineyards Farm Winery, characterizing one of the most stunning landscapes along Seneca Lake's eastern shore. When Ted Marks, a Corning, New York, entrepreneur teamed up with Phil Hazlitt, scion of the legendary grape-growing family, to purchase the eighty-four-acre estate in 1999, they ushered in a new direction at the winery. Family ancestry inspired a new name for the venture, memorializing Rachel Atwater, who married James Hazlitt, the first in a lineage of pioneer vineyardists in the region. Phil is Rachel's great-great-great-grandson, and his expertise in wine growing was essential to the genesis of Atwater Vineyards.

While nurturing the property's original vines of Chardonnay, Riesling, and Gewürztraminer, Phil planted new acreage of Cabernet, Merlot, and Syrah on the hillside blessed with exceptional terroir. Excellent drainage on the slope means less vigorous vines, which produce smaller berries with more intense flavors.

The winery would take another step forward when Vinny Aliperti became head winemaker. His training included work with two disciplined German winemakers, first with Roman Roth at Long Island's Wölffer Estate Vineyard, then at Hermann J. Wiemer Vineyard (see page 75) across the lake. He adopted a European style of winemaking—that is, grapes processed with as little manipulation as possible and emphasis squarely on what goes on in the vineyard.

White wines include a Chablis-style Chardonnay and Rieslings in both off-dry and sparkling styles. Reds include Cabernet Franc from the estate's North Block Six and Symvolí (the Greek word for "confluence"), Atwater's signature red blend of Syrah, Cabernet Franc, Cabernet Sauvignon, Blaufränkisch, and Merlot. Reservations are suggested for the forty-five-minute enhanced tasting, guided by knowledgeable staff. Cheese and charcuterie plates are available to accompany each tasting.

In December 2020, the winery was acquired by Matt Russo and George Nosis, who has been Aliperti's assistant in the cellar since 2014. Aliperti has left to devote full time to Billsboro Winery (see page 65).

J. R. DILL WINERY
4922 Route 414
Burdett, NY 14818
www.jrdillwinery.com

In 2009, Jeffrey R. Dill escaped the world of commercial finance and joined the merry band of winemakers on the east side of the lake. You'll understand his calling to the wine industry when you visit the J. R. Dill Winery and browse a wall filled with vintage photos of bygone days around Seneca Lake. Take a close look, and you'll see one photo in particular: H. J. Dill, Jeffrey's great-grandfather in 1902, "working in the vineyards." The young man was destined to follow in his family's footsteps.

Jeffrey doesn't have vineyards of his own, so he sources all his grapes from neighboring growers, a number of excellent terroirs, and transports them by truck to the winery. The fruit for a particular wine might come from as many as three different vineyards, blending percentages determined with each vintage.

The cheerful, wood-paneled room has two bars: one for tastings, over an illuminated countertop filled with salvaged lake glass, and the other for more serious drinking, a vintage counter and backbar from a former Watkins Glen soda fountain. What at many places is relegated to the sidelines, wine production here is on view through a roll-up glass door.

Both 2014 and 2015 J. R. Dill Dry Rieslings earned double gold awards at the New York State Wine and Food Classic. Notable bottles include a French oak–aged DeChaunac, a 50/50 blend of Cabernet Sauvignon and Cabernet Franc, and a more traditional Bordeaux-style Three Barrel Blend of Cabernet Sauvignon, Cabernet Franc, and Merlot.

If the weather cooperates, there's a covered outside porch with picnic tables or a manicured lawn with Adirondack chairs, each a comfortable place to sip and pontificate over the subtleties of a wine. Round off your visit with a photo in front of the giant waiter's corkscrew.

DAMIANI WINE CELLARS

5281 Peach Orchard Road
Hector, NY 14841
www.damianiwinecellars.com

It was a turning point for the Finger Lakes in 1996, when Lou Damiani and Phil Davis founded Damiani Wine Cellars and set out to prove that exceptional red wines could be made here. Since then, the collaboration between the winemaker and the wine grower has made an impressive contribution toward firmly establishing the reputation of reds in the region. The sentiment "We make the wines we like to drink" has served Lou and Phil well on their unconventional path through the years. Damiani was the first winery in Finger Lakes to receive a 90+ point rating from *Wine Spectator* for a red wine, the 2010 Cabernet Sauvignon Reserve.

Phil grew up on family orchards and vineyards, the site of initial plantings of Pinot Noir, Merlot, and Cabernet Sauvignon. Lou served as head winemaker until 2011, when Phil Arras came onboard. Katey Larwood joined Phil for the 2021 harvest, and when Phil left to join the Nine-Four Wines project (see page 113), she was named head winemaker. A West Coast native, Katey studied viticulture and enology at California Polytechnic State University, San Luis Obispo, and held winemaking positions in California, New Zealand, Australia, France, and the Finger Lakes at Keuka Lake Vineyards (see page 34).

Yes, the Damiani portfolio includes a few white wines, but the passion for reds continues to dominate, with Merlot, Pinot Noir, Cabernet Franc, and Lemberger produced as varietals. Blends include a classic Meritage; Pn (Pinot Noir and Lemberger); Sole e Terra (Pinot Noir, Lemberger, and Saperavi); and Vino Rosso, made from 100 percent Marechal Foch, an homage to the village wines of Italy.

Damiani offers a range of tasting formats, including a custom-curated journey through five wines guided by trained staff. Weather permitting, memorable tastings are elevated on the balcony with a view of the lake.

SILVER SPRINGS WINERY
4408 Route 414
Burdett, NY 14818
www.silverspringswinery.com

A trifecta of good vibes provides the theme of this enterprise. In 2004, a serial entrepreneur and self-described renaissance man by the name of John Zuccarino created a microwinery with a message of peace, love, and wine. A visit here is the opportunity to meet the vineyardist, winemaker, alchemist, idealist, and all-around guru of Silver Springs Winery. He looks the part of an aging hippie; wears a colorful Rasta tam; sports a long, gray beard; and prefers to be called Don Giovanni to honor his Italian heritage. He'll tell you about helping his grandfather make wine when he was ten years old and how he traced his roots back hundreds of years to family winemaking in Italy. And he keeps his own proprietary yeast cultures in a locked vault.

With as many as twenty wines divided into two groupings, there's a good chance he will personally pour samples from among his whimsical Silver Springs label (sweet and fruity wines) and the more serious Don Giovanni label varietal wines. The Cognac barrel–aged Tri-dition, a Bordeaux-style blend, is his showpiece.

Don't pass up the chance to visit here. The iconoclastic winemaker has the ability to entertain, to charm, and to elevate the wine-tasting experience.

CATHARINE VALLEY WINERY
4201 Route 414
Burdett, NY 14818
www.catharinevalley.com

The name was inspired by nearby Catharine Creek, a major tributary to Seneca Lake. The thirty-five-acre property included eight acres of productive vineyards when Donald and Jessica Kilcoyne put down roots here in 2001. Don kickstarted his journey at Fulkerson Winery & Farm (see page 80), intent on learning the art and science of making wine. He then apprenticed under the wing of Dave Bagley at Bagley's Poplar Ridge Vineyards (see page 107), assisting with grunt work in the cellar. The Kilcoynes' dream winery became a reality with its first vintage in 2003. The property's refurbished horse barn earns its status as a cozy tasting room courtesy of rustic charm and warm wooden accents.

High on the list of staff favorites, Lost Irishman is a quaffable Catawba blush wine that leaves the impression of eating fresh, firm grapes. Be sure to arrive early in the season. The wine is produced in small lots, and once it's sold out, that's it for the year. Estate Riesling is called König (German for "king"), a reference to the grape's status in the region.

RYAN WILLIAM VINEYARD
4156 Route 414
Hector, NY 14841
www.ryanwilliam.com

In 2005, vineyardist Ryan William acquired an extraordinary forty-acre parcel on the eastern slope of Seneca Lake and began developing a vineyard. Then in 2010, after selling the fruit from his vineyard to neighboring wineries, he decided it was time to launch his own eponymous winery. In 2016, William created one of the region's destination tasting rooms, housed in a stylishly realized midnineteenth-century barn once used to stable horses and store hay and grain.

Winemaking is in the hands of Jacob Altmann, holder of a degree in viticulture and enology from Hochschule Geisenheim University and head of the winemaking team at neighboring Chateau LaFayette Reneau (see page 115), also owned by William. Altmann crafts Chardonnay, Riesling, Gewürztraminer, Grüner Veltliner, Merlot, Cabernet Franc, and Pinot Noir culled solely from grapes grown on the estate's lakeside vineyard. Red wines are fermented in open bins and aged in French oak barrels; white wines, fermented in stainless steel, with the exception of Chardonnay, which is partially fermented in oak. Most wines are bottle-aged for two to five years before release. Don't leave without sampling the Alsatian Blend Reserve, an Edelzwicker-style "noble blend" of Riesling and Gewürztraminer.

You can keep it simple with a mixed-flight tasting at the bar, or you can complete the experience with a food and wine pairing. The midday-fare menu, created by Samira William and fueled by local ingredients, ranges from brioche French toast to mussels steamed in Grüner Veltliner, with many of the culinary ingredients grown on the property.

HILLICK & HOBBS
3539 Route 79
Burdett, NY 14818
www.hillickandhobbs.com

An exacting winemaker and quality fanatic, *Forbes* magazine called him the "Steve Jobs of Wine." After earning a master's degree in viticulture and enology from UC Davis, Paul Hobbs began his winemaking career at the side of Robert Mondavi, who handpicked him for the inaugural Opus One team. He later served as winemaker at Simi Winery and consulted at Napa Valley's Peter Michael and Lewis Cellars and at Argentina's Bodegas Catena, where he was an early disciple of Malbec. In 1991, Hobbs established the eponymous Paul Hobbs Winery in Sebastopol, California, and went on to create international partnerships with Viña Cobos in Mendoza, Argentina; Crocus in Cahors, France; Yacoubian-Hobbs in Armenia; and Alvaredos-Hobbs in Galicia, Spain.

In 2013, Hobbs selected a seventy-eight-acre property on the southeastern shore of Seneca Lake, and he chose well. The winery holds a special meaning for Hobbs, named after his parents, Joan Hillick and Edward Hobbs. In a powerhouse collaboration with Johannes Selbach, owner and winemaker of Mosel Valley's Selbach-Oster, the two began planting twenty-five acres of Riesling vines purchased regionally and with rootlings brought from Germany by Selbach. The inaugural, much-praised 2019 vintage of Hillick & Hobbs Dry Riesling was released in 2021.

He bucked conventional wisdom by planting his vines vertically down the steep slope, east to west, instead of terracing horizontally, allowing for better airflow, a practice borrowed from Germany's Mosel region. Hobbs has trusted supervision of the cellar to winemaker Lynne Fahy and management of the vineyard to Samuel Pulis. If you want to learn about the complex intersection of terroir and winemaking, there is no better place to get a firsthand introduction. Guests sample wines in a sophisticated, Scandinavian-modern, cypress-wood-planked tasting room, the setting for vertical tastings and service by bottle or glass. A food-pairing menu is provided by Hazelnut Kitchen in Trumansburg.

OSMOTE

3879 Marcia Lane
Burdett, NY 14818
www.osmotewine.com

Armed with a degree in viticulture and enology from Cornell, native Ithacan Benjamin Riccardi began his journey to winemaking at Sheldrake Point Winery (see page 142), then worked his way around the world, crafting vintages in Chile, Australia, New Zealand, France, Sonoma Valley, and Long Island. After serving as assistant winemaker at City Winery in Manhattan, the well-traveled Mr. Riccardi returned to the Finger Lakes to establish Osmote (its name is a play on the word *osmosis*, the process of gradual assimilation of ideas), a small-scale venture fueled by a desire to push the limits of low-intervention winemaking.

He purchased a thirty-one-acre property overlooking Seneca Lake, complete with an old farmhouse and barn, and as he cultivates the land and plants rows of resilient Marquette and Aromella vines, he's on the cusp of realizing a long-held dream of creating a progressive estate winery. Until the vineyard matures, Ben sources fruit from both Seneca and Cayuga Lake vineyards for Chardonnay, Cabernet Franc, and his flirtation with both Cayuga White and mixed hybrids made as pét-nats.

A technical winemaker, his meticulously handcrafted Seneca Lake Chardonnay is fermented and aged in Dargaud et Jaegle oak from one of the world's oldest wine barrel cooperages. A wine with bright acids and rich texture, it's one of the region's most compelling examples of the variety.

BREWERIES

WATERSHED BREWING COMPANY
3543 East Lake Road
Geneva, NY 14456
www.watershedbrewingflx.com

In 2016, the 1950s-era Gothic-arch barn that once housed seventy-two cows and 750,000 pounds of hay was transformed into Bottomless Brewing by Carrie Fischer and Tom Thompson. In 2023, the old barn got a new name and new beers.

The Watershed Brewing Company story starts with Ken Greenwood, a card-carrying member of Upstate New York Homebrewers Association. Inspired by the culture of beer and the region's emerging craft-beer scene, Ken, an RIT-trained mechanical engineer and consultant, put his homebrewing to the test and turned a serious hobby into a full-fledged profession. Recipes are tested in a one-barrel pilot system, essentially small-batch brews that foster creativity and collaboration, develop new styles, and experiment with growing trends.

Begin your visit with a small pour of Tempting Fayetter Pilsner, an easy-sipping pale golden lager. Follow that up with Isn't It Ironic and Citmolicious, both hazy IPAs. But don't stop there. The fifteen-barrel brewhouse produces a range of brews for every palate.

As the new venture finds its footing, dining options are expanding, live-music nights are increasing, and indoor and outdoor spaces are improving.

WAR HORSE BREWING COMPANY
623 Lerch Road
Geneva, NY 14456
www.3brotherswinery.com

See Three Brothers Wineries & Estates, page 99.

WAGNER VALLEY BREWING CO.
9322 Route 414
Lodi, NY 14860
www.wagnerbrewing.com

Inside the iconic octagon at Wagner Vineyards Estate Winery (see page 104), wine and beer exist alongside each other in fermented harmony. The Wagner family produces a total of three dozen wines, all from the estate's 240 acres of vineyards and all over the varietal map, but wine is not the only intriguing product offered.

Established in 1997, Wagner Valley Brewing Co. was one of the earliest craft breweries in the Finger Lakes. Its twenty-barrel, steam-fired, four-vessel, German-style brewhouse follows the German Purity Law (or *Reinheitsgebot*), using only malt, hops, yeast, and water to make beer. Among a dozen or so brews on tap, mainstays include Sled Dog Doppelbock, an expressive, russet-hued, tan-headed, Bavarian-style double bock, and classically malty Dockside Vienna Lager. Most beers are available in twelve-ounce bottles and sixteen-ounce cans.

Head next door to the Ginny Lee Café for lunch overlooking the vineyards; feast on soups, salads, sandwiches, and flatbreads.

LUCKY HARE BREWING COMPANY
6085 Beckhorn Road (off Route 414)
Hector, NY 14841
www.luckyharebrewing.com

In 2015, marine-biologist-turned-brewmaster Ian Conboy and his partner Richard Thiel, a health-care professional, converted a one-hundred-year-old barn into a microbrewery and the adjacent farmhouse into a tasting room. The start-up was named Lucky Hare Brewing Company. Three years later, Lucky Hare had outgrown the on-site brewhouse, and production was relocated to the Schuyler County Business Park with the installation of a state-of-the-art beverage system outfitted by Deutsche Beverage Technology.

Here's a good beer with a good story. A fellow by the name of Benjamin Moreland Record opened Watkins Glen Brewery following the end of Prohibition in 1933, only to be wiped out by the flood of 1935. He reopened as the Glen Brewing Company in 1937, producing a malted corn beer called Glen Ale, an all-but-forgotten style, reimagined here by Conboy, who sources all ingredients locally. It's the kind of beer your granddad used to sip after work.

The convivial bar is a great place to hang out and sip on other superbly executed mainstays—Falcon Punch IPA, London Gentleman, and Milk Milk Stout. On the experimental side, Ian has developed the highly regarded Wild Hare Series, a rotating range of foeder-aged (pronounced *FOOD-er*) wild ales made with locally sourced fruits.

Lucky Hare operates a satellite taproom at 17 Lake Street in Owego.

SCALE HOUSE BREWERY
5930 Route 414
Hector, NY 14841
www.scalehousebrews.com

The enterprise began in 2006 as a microbrewery inside Steve Fazzary's Pizzeria in the Small Mall just outside of Ithaca. A dozen years later, Scale House took a giant leap, relocating to Hector, placed squarely among the wineries of Seneca Lake. There are breweries that serve food, and restaurants that serve beer. Scale House is the latter, a reliable stop for nourishment along the wine trail, now in the hands of Luke Fazzary.

Beers are house-made on a seven-barrel system by Dominic Sims, former brewer at Big aLICe Brewing (see page 89). Guests can chase a trio of IPAs, a light-bodied cream ale, or a fruited apricot-blueberry kettle sour with sixteen pizza varieties, quesadillas, meatballs, and calzones.

TWO GOATS BREWING
5027 Route 414
Burdett, NY 14818
(607) 546-2337
www.twogoatsbrewing.com

This converted nineteenth-century timber-frame barn just off the Seneca Lake wine trail is a convivial Finger Lakes version of a British pub, opened in 2010 but a place that feels like it's been here forever. While it's more of a local hangout that winemakers consider their special joint, traveling beer enthusiasts will find much to enjoy among the offerings. When you're ready to take a break along your wine-tasting jaunt, stop here for both brew and view. Sip in style on the wraparound porch and take in the picturesque lake and surrounding vineyards.

Sample a flight according to style—hoppy or malty or both—or just do as the locals do: Belly up to the bar and knock back a pint or two of honest, unfiltered beer handmade by owner-brewer Jon Rogers.

You can munch on fresh-popped popcorn, but the best thing to eat is the Buffalo-inspired beef on Weck, slow-roasted local beef on a Kimmelweck roll. It wants to be washed down with a Kellerbier-style lager called Hector Logger or a hazy IPA called Golden Crush.

GRIST IRON BREWING CO.
4889 Route 414
Burdett, NY 14818
www.gristironbrewing.com

At what must be one of the most scenic locations of any brewery anywhere, Grist Iron is perched over Seneca Lake's waters on a sprawling 150-acre property. Since 2015, this noisy and bustling enterprise has provided a beer lover's oasis along the Finger Lakes' most-traveled wine trail. The whole place has a giant, upscale warehouse vibe. Pull up a stool along the curving, seventy-foot-long bar, where you get up close and personal to the gleaming brewing vats, where the magic happens. There are two seating areas—the adjoining room (there's a warming fireplace in winter) and a sun-drenched patio. The kitchen churns out everything from Bavarian pretzels and Polish sausage bites to barbecue plates and pizzas.

Head brewer Patrick Palmer's mastery of the arts has propelled the brewery into one of the area's favorite gathering spots. As many as fifteen plucky brews made on-site include IPAs with oomph, creative ales, fruited sours, and a rotating series of barrel-aged beers. Start your enjoyment with Campfire Lite, an easy-sipping lager, and end with Strange Brew Coffee Cream Ale, an homage to the New York coffee-cart-classic "coffee regulah."

Stay late on weekends when Grist Iron hosts live music to accompany the refreshments. Grist Iron offers overnight accommodations at the neighboring nine-room lodge.

CIDERIES

BOMBSHELL HARD CIDER
623 Lerch Road
Geneva, NY 14456
www.3brotherswinery.com

See Three Brothers Wineries & Estates, page 99.

DISTILLERIES

ALDER CREEK DISTILLERY
9059 Route 414
Lodi, NY 14860
www.idolredge.com

Fossenvue was a lakeside summer campground founded on the eastern shore of Seneca Lake by suffragist Elizabeth Smith from 1875 to 1908, associated with elites from Cornell and Hobart and William Smith Colleges. In 2013, the Martin family, owners of Montezuma Winery (see page 133), established Idol Ridge Winery near the site of Fossenvue, which is also home to Alder Creek Distillery.

Alder Creek offers an array of spirits, including Single Barrel Wheat Whiskey, crafted from locally farmed wheat and aged for three years and fifty-five days, and Dropline Maple Bourbon Whiskey, made with locally sourced maple syrup.

The tasting room includes a gift shop, including an array of wine-related items.

FINGER LAKES DISTILLING CO.
4676 Route 414
Burdett, NY 14818
www.fingerlakesdistilling.com

It was a chance meeting between two McKenzies, Brian McKenzie and Thomas Earl McKenzie, that started it all. Unrelated but of like minds, Brian was vice president of Elmira Savings and Loan, and Thomas was a brewer and winemaker from Alabama, and they were both in Kentucky for a craft-distiller's conference in 2007. A venture that was made possible with the New York State Farm Distillery Act, Finger Lakes Distilling Co. opened in 2009, one of the state's first small-batch spirits start-ups sourcing the majority of farm products from the region.

Grapes are good for more than just wine. Reflecting the venture's presence in Finger Lakes wine country, master distiller Collin McConville, formerly of Rootstock Cider and Spirits in Williamson, transforms four acres of Concord and Niagara grapes grown on the distillery's property into Vintner's Vodka and Seneca Drums Gin (a truly elevated spirit, it's best sipped by itself to best appreciate the distinctive flavors of eleven carefully infused botanicals). Rye gets a final thirty-day rest in sherry casks before it's bottled, while bourbon finishes in barrels that once held local Chardonnay.

The structure is topped, Scottish-distillery style, with a black-trimmed, white stucco-peaked roof and pagoda. With a breeze coming off the lake, you might catch the scent of alcoholic vapor dispersing into the atmosphere, lost spirits called the "angel's share."

CAYUGA LAKE (WEST)

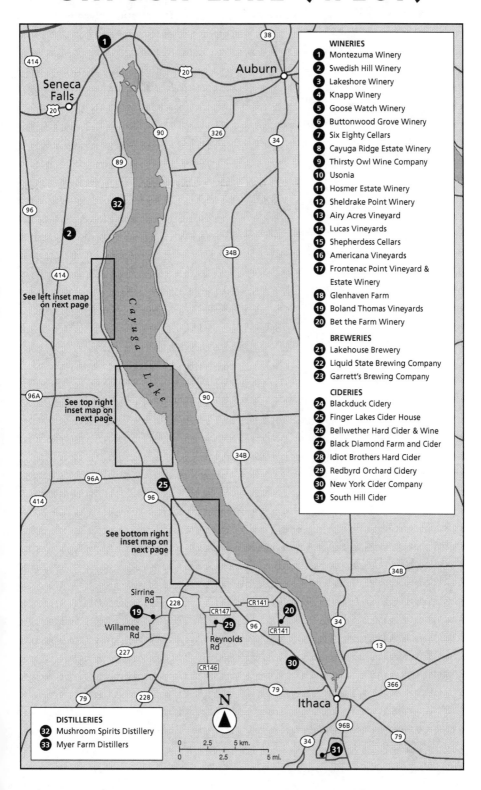

WINERIES
1. Montezuma Winery
2. Swedish Hill Winery
3. Lakeshore Winery
4. Knapp Winery
5. Goose Watch Winery
6. Buttonwood Grove Winery
7. Six Eighty Cellars
8. Cayuga Ridge Estate Winery
9. Thirsty Owl Wine Company
10. Usonia
11. Hosmer Estate Winery
12. Sheldrake Point Winery
13. Airy Acres Vineyard
14. Lucas Vineyards
15. Shepherdess Cellars
16. Americana Vineyards
17. Frontenac Point Vineyard & Estate Winery
18. Glenhaven Farm
19. Boland Thomas Vineyards
20. Bet the Farm Winery

BREWERIES
21. Lakehouse Brewery
22. Liquid State Brewing Company
23. Garrett's Brewing Company

CIDERIES
24. Blackduck Cidery
25. Finger Lakes Cider House
26. Bellwether Hard Cider & Wine
27. Black Diamond Farm and Cider
28. Idiot Brothers Hard Cider
29. Redbyrd Orchard Cidery
30. New York Cider Company
31. South Hill Cider

DISTILLERIES
32. Mushroom Spirits Distillery
33. Myer Farm Distillers

See left inset map on next page

See top right inset map on next page

See bottom right inset map on next page

Seneca Falls

Auburn

Cayuga Lake

Ithaca

Sirrine Rd

Willamee Rd

Reynolds Rd

N

0   2.5   5 km.
0   2.5   5 mi.

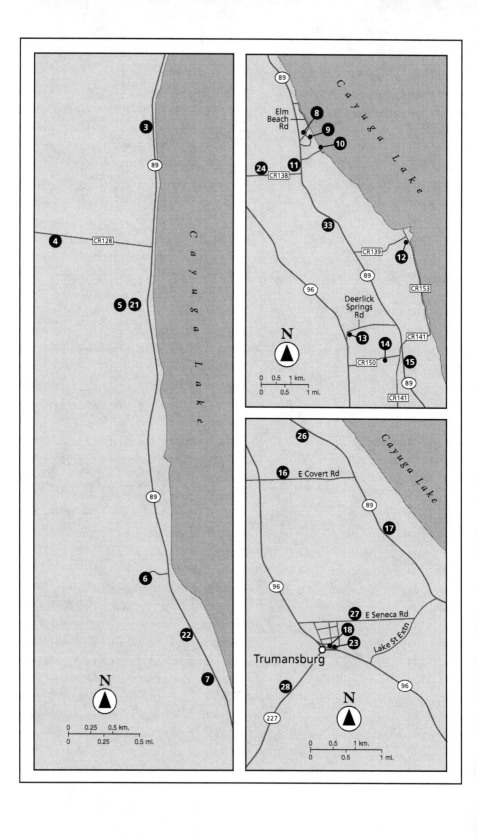

WINERIES

MONTEZUMA WINERY
2981 Auburn Road
Seneca Falls, NY 13148
www.montezumawinery.com

The extensive marshes at the north end of Cayuga Lake were left behind ten thousand years ago in the last retreat of the melting glaciers. With a mixture of nutrient-rich waters, lush and diverse vegetation, and rich invertebrate and insect life, the wetlands provide a resting, nesting, and feeding habitat for waterfowl and other migratory birds on their journeys to and from northeastern Canada. Montezuma was the name that New York City physician Peter Clark gave his marshland estate in the early 1800s, inspired by his trip to Mexico City and the site of the Aztec emperor's palace. Over the years, the marsh, the local hamlet, the wildlife refuge, and the Martin family winery all adopted the name.

George Martin, a commercial beekeeper by trade, established Montezuma Winery in 2001. While his initial focus was on the production of mead (honey wine) and fruit wines, over the years, sons Bill and Ed have expanded and diversified the family enterprise, the focus shifting to grape wines.

The cellar here is the personal fief of one of the region's most technically versatile winemakers. As an undergrad at RIT, Phil Plummer's summer job at Casa Larga Vineyards and Winery (see page 189) was his entry into the world of wine. Following an internship at Anyela's Vineyards (see page 184), he joined the Martin family at Montezuma, where by 2013 he ascended to head winemaker. During his tenure here, Phil has taken a leading role in the development and production of a wide-ranging portfolio of wines made from grapes, fruit, and honey and was instrumental in the launch of Montezuma's sister winery, Idol Ridge Winery (see page 102).

This is rock-and-roll winemaking, most obvious in the Voleur series. The name is French for "thief," reflecting the "theft" of time-honored techniques to produce wines with, in Phil's words, "reckless novelty." Back labels suggest elevating the sensory experience of drinking these art wines by connecting the spirit of each variety or blend to the theme of a specific book, film, and song.

For drinkers who may be more merry-go-round than roller coaster, Montezuma's options include a dozen different spirits, a project that started in 2007, branded as Hidden Marsh Distillery. Working from a four-hundred-liter

Christian Carl pot still custom built by coppersmiths in Germany, Phil produces a range of spirits, most notably Apple Brandy, made with locally grown Honey Crisp apples, and Bee Vodka, triple-distilled from local honey.

Montezuma has tasting room outposts at 3050 Route 28, across from Walt's Diner in Old Forge, and at 4841 Route 28, next door to Cooper's Barn ice cream shop in Cooperstown.

SWEDISH HILL WINERY
4565 Route 414
Romulus, NY 14541
www.swedishhill.com

In 1969, Dick and Cindy Peterson named their farm Swedish Hill and began growing and selling grapes to the big boys. In 1986, with a weakening market for local grapes, the Petersons decided to produce a small quantity of their own wines from Aurora, Catawba, Vignoles, and Chardonnay—and a farm winery was born.

David, the next-generation Peterson, is a highly respected figure in the recent history of Finger Lakes wine country. Armed with a PhD in viticulture from Penn State, he assumed management of the family enterprise in 1996, striking a balance between indigenous grape varieties and their more glamorous European counterparts. In the long run, that balance has proved to be a winning strategy.

Dave recruited an award-winning winemaking team led by Derek Wilbur, who earned three Governor's Cups, the highest award given to New York State wines. In 2021, Derek relinquished his duties to Zach Pegram, who earned a master's degree in enology from Cornell University, interned under Peter Bell at Fox Run Vineyards (see page 66), and served as assistant winemaker at Red Tail Ridge Winery (see page 67). Zach works side by side with associate winemaker Josh Kessler, another Cornell grad, making wines that pay homage to the region.

Winemakers typically make countless decisions when handcrafting a wine, all with the goal of creating the best wine possible. At Swedish Hill, their secret is the age-old practice of blending to produce a finished wine. The decision to add just a small percent of a second or third variety is often intuitive, and can change the whole sensation of a wine. Almost all wines in the Swedish Hill portfolio are blends of some sort with 100 percent Rieslings the exception.

The rustic tasting room is a bit like a country general store, very atmospheric, homey, and friendly. If you visit, be sure to ask about Doobie, the winery's pet miniature donkey.

LAKESHORE WINERY

5132 Route 89
Romulus, NY 14541
www.lakeshorewinery.com

Lakeshore Winery first opened to the public in 1982, making it one of the oldest producers on Cayuga Lake. In 1994, John and Annie Bachman purchased the estate from the winery's founders, Bill and Doris Brown. Since then, John and Annie have continued a tradition established by the Browns, essentially taking an intimate, personal approach to winemaking.

There are few places in the region where you'll feel more at home than in the rambling barn, situated on a farmstead that dates back to 1825 and has been transformed into a rustic winery. Chatty, informal wine tastings take place near the warmth of a working stone fireplace, where you're invited to pull up a rocking chair, relax, perform sensory evaluations, and speak your mind. It's like going to someone's home to learn about wine, a wonderfully intimate experience. Unlike many of their neighbors, the Bachmans' enterprise represents an alternative life-style choice, one they intend to keep on a very small scale.

Aunt Clara and Uncle Charlie are not relatives of the Bachmans, nor are they folks you should expect to meet in the tasting room. Rather, these are whimsical names attached to two versions of Catawba, made into compulsory picnic wines with grapes purchased from a nearby grower.

KNAPP WINERY

2770 County Road 128 (Ernsberger Road)
Romulus, NY 14541
www.knappwine.com

This important winery and one-hundred-acre estate was established by Doug and Suzie Knapp in 1978, sold to Glenora's Gene Pierce and Scott Welliver in 2000, then acquired by Cole and Karen Wilson in 2021. The newest owners are on a path to maintain and enhance the magic and charm of this wonderful place. Moving on from a successful career trading foreign currencies, Cole first dipped his toe into wine culture at Damiani Wine Cellars (see page 118), from toiling at harvest to directing operations, combining his business savvy with his love of wine.

For his objectives at Knapp, the right winemaker was the new owner's most important hire. Classically trained and credentialed, Vanessa Hoffman earned her master's degree in viticulture and enology in Italy prior to working in Piemonte and Chianti. Back home in California, she joined the winemaking team at Groth Vineyards & Winery in Napa Valley before joining the Duckhorn group as an assistant winemaker with Decoy Wines in Sonoma Valley. She was the perfect fit in the new culture here. Vanessa marches to her own muse. While most winemakers focus exclusively on developing the technical components of a wine, she also pays attention to the innate hedonism of the wine, the simple pleasure of drinking it.

An eclectic, something-for-everyone range of wines in her portfolio includes Saperavi and Blaufränkisch among the reds, Vignoles and Vidal among the whites, Black Cherry and Loganberry fruit wines, and even a couple native varietals. Knapp is among a very few to grow the somewhat obscure Austrian grape Siegerrebe (pronounced *zee-geh-RAY-buh*). Descended from Gewürztraminer, much like its ancestor, it's very aromatic. Saignée (pronounced *sohn-yay*) is a method that involves bleeding off a portion of red wine juice after it's been in contact with the skins to produce a rosé. Beginning as an experiment with Saperavi in the cellar and bolder and darker than other rosé wines, Knapp Saignée Rosé should please both red and white wine drinkers.

The Vineyard Restaurant at Knapp serves a range of dishes that highlight and elevate the wines produced here. Executive chef Benjamin Bird sources fresh, locally grown ingredients for every farm-to-table meal he prepares. A delicious oddity is the kitchen's Cayuga Caviar, a sweet and spicy marinated vegetable, bean, and corn relish served with house-made corn tortilla chips.

GOOSE WATCH WINERY

5480 Route 89
Romulus, NY 14541
www.goosewatch.com

When Ott Davis put his chestnut farm up for sale in 1996, the Peterson family seized the opportunity to expand the venture they began at Swedish Hill Winery (see page 134). An idyllic property set among the rows of chestnut trees, Goose Watch Winery has built a name for itself as a progressive albeit slightly eccentric winery. The motto here is "A path less traveled."

This enterprise is about exploration and innovation under the guidance of David Peterson, who has set the winery apart in philosophy from Swedish Hill. He has challenged his team, headed by winemaker Zach Pegram, to experiment with a range of wines, including Viognier (pronounced *VEE-own-yay*), a full-bodied white wine that originated in the Rhône region of southern France, and Zweigelt (pronounced *TSVYE-gelt*), a cousin of Blaufränkisch, widely plant-ed in Austria but rare in the Finger Lakes.

The art of blending begins with Dave and the winemaking team blind-tasting each varietal at 100 percent, then considering other options and adding just a small percent of a second or third variety to improve the finished wine and make the sum better than the individual pieces. The Zweigelt, for example, could in-clude Marquette (a grandson of Pinot Noir) as a component in one year, and a different option might bring something else to the table in another year.

The Goose Watch team collaborated with Cornell's grape-breeding program to produce the very first Aromella varietal wine. Peterson planted the vines of this granddaughter of Gewürztraminer in 2005, and it took eight more years to pro-duce the inaugural vintage. A lovely sipping wine, Aromella is marked by peach and tropical-fruit aromas with a bit of spice from its grandparent.

In 2019, the Petersons converted the estate's carriage house into Lakehouse Brewery (see page 150), offering private-label contract beers and a rotation of taps from other regional brewers.

BUTTONWOOD GROVE WINERY
5986 State Route 89
Romulus, NY 14541
www.buttonwoodgrove.com

White-bark buttonwood trees thrive in the ravines that border this Cayuga Lake hillside property, native symbols of the region's growing seasons. In winter, after all the leaves have fallen, one-inch fruit balls remain, swinging from flexible stems that are two to three inches long. In early spring, the balls burst and disgorge seeds that sail on the winds with tiny parachutes, putting on a show for visitors at Buttonwood Grove Winery.

In 1997, horticulturalist Ken Riemer began a methodical, seven-year plan to develop a vineyard and winery at this site, releasing his first vintage in 2004. After a decade of producing noteworthy wines, Riemer sold the estate to David Pittard, a Cornell Aggie who broke away from his family's Beak and Skiff Apple Farm en-terprise to pick up where Ken Riemer left off. Brimming with new ideas, David and his wife, Melissa, have expanded the vineyards and completed construction of a new winemaking facility.

Named head winemaker during ownership transition, Sue Passmore didn't take long to show her skill with Riesling. Buttonwood Grove was awarded the Governor's Cup, designating Sue's 2016 Riesling as that year's best wine in New York State.

While a remarkable range of wines succeed here, the continuing focus is on Riesling, from individual estate blocks—Frances Amelia, Big Hollow, Waterfall, and the Riemer Block, the oldest vines on the property—as well as Skaneateles Riesling, made with grapes grown in partnership with Hobbit Hollow Farms on Skaneateles Lake. Blends from multiple estate blocks are used to produce a force-carbonated Riesling Bubbly and méthode ancestrale–inspired Riesling Pét-Nat.

The tasting experience is hands-on and personalized, guided by a knowledgeable, professional staff.

SIX EIGHTY CELLARS
3050 Swick Road
Ovid, NY 14521
www.sixeightycellars.com

From the edge of Cayuga Lake to the uppermost point of the estate, the dramatic elevation rise of 680 feet gives the winery its name. By 2020, David and Melissa Pittard were already well-established winegrowers at Buttonwood Grove Winery (see page 137) when a neighboring vineyard came up for sale. To distinguish the new venture from Buttonwood, the Pittards determined that Six Eighty Cellars would be innovative and experimental, taking a hands-off, minimal-intervention approach in the cellars, including spontaneous fermentation with wild yeasts.

Head winemaker and crusader of the natural wine movement Ian Barry borrows from the roots of ancient culture, fermenting and aging small-batch wines in a variety of clay, stone, concrete, and terracotta amphorae, allowing the wines to better express their varietal characteristics and gain complexity due to the very slight micro-oxidation qualities of the vessels. Winemakers who have switched to amphorae insist the vessels produce the purest expression of their grapes and vineyard areas. Further courting the curious palate, for a few wines, Barry employs pét-nat (pétillant naturel), a winemaking technique in which the wine is bottled before primary fermentation is finished, and the end product is often unpredictable, surprising even the most expert taster. And if all that isn't enough to set the Six Eighty project apart, in addition to the more familiar Rieslings, Cabernet Francs, and Chardonnays of the region, the vineyard includes less common vinifera varieties, including Grüner Veltliner, Pinot Meunier, and Chenin Blanc.

You may have to plan ahead (reservations are required), but wow, is it ever worth it. You will have a formal sit-down and a one-on-one focused educational experience with an expertly trained guide.

CAYUGA RIDGE ESTATE WINERY
6800 Route 89
Ovid, NY 14521
www.cayugaridgewinery.com

Ovid, New York, was named for the Roman poet and vinophile who wrote, "It warms the blood, adds luster to the eyes; and wine and love have ever been allies." So Cayuga Ridge Estate Winery in the village of Ovid may have been destined to play a central role in the history of the Cayuga Lake wine region.

When Tom and Susie Challen purchased the winery from Robert and Mary Plane in 1991, the location was already well entrenched as one of the Finger Lakes' most influential properties. As Plane's Cayuga Vineyard, guided by the noted Cornell chemistry professor and his wife, it was the site of Cayuga Lake's first commercial planting of a fascinating variety, not only genetically designed specifically for this region, but also a grape that tells people where they are.

Cayuga White, a hybrid cross between Schuyler and Seyval Blanc named at the Agricultural Experiment Station in 1972, is one of the most productive and disease-resistant varieties grown in the eastern United States. The mother block of Cayuga White at Cayuga Estate, blankets eight acres of the vineyard with ripe clusters of greenish-gold, translucent grapes. Tom shepherds his "old-vine" Cayuga through fermentation, producing an easy-to-enjoy "sipping wine" reminiscent of a Pinot Grigio.

The grand old cavernous barn at the heart of picturesque Cayuga Ridge Estate provides a rustic surrounding for tasting not only the historic Cayuga White but also Chardonnay, Cabernet Franc, Chancellor, and assorted fruit wines.

THIRSTY OWL WINE COMPANY
6799 Elm Beach Road (off Route 89)
Ovid, NY 14521
www.thirstyowl.com

When Jonathan Cupp purchased a parcel of the former Plane family estate in 2001, he inherited the oldest Riesling vines on Cayuga Lake. Robert Plane, educator and viticulturalist, first planted experimental Rieslings on this site in 1972, and many of the original vines continue to thrive in the estate's sixteen acres. It should come as no surprise that Thirsty Owl bottles regularly capture prestigious medals in wine competitions.

Older vines have roots that find more abundant water and extract higher levels of mineral nutrients from the soil. The root systems, which have labored over the years to reach down as deep as eight or ten feet into the stony granite soil, pick up flavors of the earth unobtainable from younger counterparts. Although extremes of climate are tempered by the property's close proximity to the lake, the mature vines have come to terms with the unpredictability of seasons in the Finger Lakes.

While Jon is engaged in diplomatic chores at the estate, winemaking and vineyard management have long been assigned to Shawn Kime, Cornell grad and an early student of winemaker Nancy Newland. Some of his most challenging work is with cold-sensitive Malbec and Syrah, rarely seen varieties in the Finger Lakes. While the quality of red wines in the region is variable from year to year, Shawn explains that Syrah's consistency is a happy exception, especially valuable as a blending wine.

One of the oddest things about Thirsty Owl is the winery's name. Jon explains that it was inspired by the tale of his father's sighting of a huge horned owl in the family's backyard. He suspects that the elder Cupp's wine consumption may have been responsible for exaggerating the bird's proportions, so when it came to selecting a name, Jon couldn't resist making an owl the symbol of his winery.

Just off the tasting room, the seasonal bistro menu offers a range of well-prepared, wine-friendly small plates, salads, mac and cheese, and sandwiches.

USONIA
6935 Route 89
Ovid, NY 14521
www.usoniawine.com

The Finger Lakes winescape is changing, as a growing contingent of adventurous vintners arrive here, unbound by the shackles of convention and attuned to the desires of millennial consumers. Julia and Alex Alvarez-Perez are among that next generation. The couple met in 2012 while working at Terroir, a progressive wine bar in Manhattan. With growing attachments to wine culture, they headed west, where they managed wine programs at fine dining restaurants in San Francisco. Sommeliers-turned-aspiring-winemakers, they cut their teeth in the cellars of Austria's Burgenland and Australia's Adelaide Hills before moving back to their native East Coast. Attracted by the promise of the Finger Lakes, the couple found jobs here: Julia, at Forge Cellars (see page 115); Alex, at Bloomer Creek Vineyard (see page 114).

Their first wines were made in 2019, using the facilities at Shaw Vineyard (see page 74). The big leap came in 2022 with the purchase of the former Randolph

O'Neill Vineyard, a thirty-five-acre property with three "active" acres of Riesling and Cabernet Franc grapes. The venture would be called Usonia, a term coined by architect Frank Lloyd Wright to reference unrestrained potential, pushing the conceptual and technological frontiers of his field. With this notion as their mantra, Julia and Alex have embarked on a journey into the world of unfiltered, untamed wines made with wild, native yeasts, focusing on terroir and the natural attributes of its fruit.

Much of the vineyard is being replanted, this time with Cinderella vines, varieties that are not classics but are becoming increasingly fashionable in the Finger Lakes. Aravelle is a cross between Riesling and Cayuga White; and Noiret (pronounced *nwahr-AY*), an amalgam of native and vinifera varieties. Their hardiness, particularly in our region's cold winters and humid summers, means the growers can use far fewer synthetic sprays like herbicides and insecticides. With these varieties at the heart of the enterprise, an enlightened conversion is underway at Usonia to transition to fully organic practices by 2025.

HOSMER WINERY
6999 Route 89
Ovid, NY 14521
www.hosmerwinery.com

Since 1972, the Hosmer family has been farming grapes on a 250-acre tree-clad property near Cayuga Lake. The first estate wines were produced in 1985, and the rustic tasting room emerged from a refurbished barn in 1990—the same year as the vineyard's first planting of Cabernet Franc.

Many Finger Lakes wineries buy grapes from dozens of small growers, but not Cameron "Tunker" Hosmer. He owns every inch of the vineyards that supply his wines. Hosmer was one of the region's earliest believers in Cabernet Franc as a varietal. His adventure with Cab Franc began with a visit by a delegation of French winemakers who wondered why no one was growing the winter-hearty wine grapes in the region. The Hosmer estate's historic Patrician Verona Vineyard is the site of the variety's first plantings.

A red wine most often used as a minor component in Bordeaux blends, Cabernet Franc is a fruitier and less tannic relation of Cabernet Sauvignon. It buds and matures earlier than its sister grape; produces larger, juicier fruit; and needs less heat to ripen fully. It thrives in the French Loire, especially in Chinon, where cooler growing conditions serve to accentuate the grape's herbaceous, grassy aromas.

Winemaker Julia Hoyle, who honed her craft at Yalumba Winery, Australia's oldest family winery, arrived at Hosmer in 2017 after stints at Atwater Vineyards (see page 116), Fox Run Vineyards (see page 66), and Sheldrake Point Winery (see below). Julia, by the way, is the wife and "co-conspirator" with Kelby James Russell of Apollo's Praise (see page 81). While she works with ten different varieties grown at Hosmer, she has an extraordinary dedication to those compact clusters of Cab Franc grapes, producing a vineyard-driven varietal, a Cabernet Franc–Lemberger blend, and a dry rosé of Cabernet Franc. The precocious variety has become the flagship red wine here and the winery boasts some of the best bottles in the region; some say the finest in America.

SHELDRAKE POINT WINERY
7448 County Road 153 (off Route 89)
Ovid, NY 14521
www.sheldrakepoint.com

The prominent point at Sheldrake-on-Cayuga is a hamlet of summer cottages and gracious lakefront estates, over the years providing summer homes for such notables as George Westinghouse and Rod Serling. Just a stone's throw from the lake, this is one of wine country's most charming finds.

After earning a graduate degree from the Cornell Hotel School, Chuck Tauck joined sommelier Bob Madill, intent on converting one of the Point's old dairy farms into a winery and determined to take full advantage of the temperature-moderating "Sheldrake effect." Vineyards now hug the shore at the lake's deepest point, where the microclimate lengthens the growing season more than two weeks over many other areas in the Finger Lakes. In addition, the east-facing slope warms up faster in the morning hours than west-facing slopes, and deep gorges on both sides of the vineyard promote effective air drainage, inhibiting both frost and disease.

Although the average depth of Cayuga Lake is 179 feet, just off the beach at Sheldrake, it plunges to 435 feet. Because deep water heats and cools more slowly, it delays both the onset of warm temperatures in spring and the first frost in fall. Cold air masses are warmed significantly as they cross the lake, and clouds formed by the exchange of heat and moisture moderate surrounding temperatures.

While tasting-room offerings include the usual suspects, including a remarkable range of Rieslings, Provençal-style Dry Rosé, a pale pink, minerally, dry, yet delicately fruity wine from 100 percent Cabernet Franc, has become the cornerstone of the Sheldrake portfolio, with 2,500 to 3,000 cases comprising fully one-third of total annual production.

Devoting a prime section of Cabernet Franc estate vineyards exclusively to its annual creation, grapes are crushed and destemmed, allowing the mixture of juice, skins, and seeds to soak overnight. This contact between the juice and skins is what gives the wine its salmon pink hue. A style of wine that goes deliciously with everything, it's what you bring to dinner when you don't know what's cooking.

AIRY ACRES VINEYARD
8011 Footes Corners Road
Interlaken, NY 14847
www.airyacresvineyard.com

This is a tale of a family with deep roots in the village of Interlaken and how the Bassette farm evolved across multiple generations, planting the property's first vines in 2015 and producing the first vintage of wines in 2020. Fred Bassette is the great-great-great-grandson of Lemuel Bassette, who moved to this sublime setting from Connecticut in 1810, first in a succession of gentleman farmers. With Fred at the helm of the heirloom estate and with help from his son Noah and the extended family, the winery venture, while still in its infancy by the region's standards, is poised to create its own history.

Airy Acres is named for the functional private airstrip on the property, built by Fred's dad in 1957, and yes, that's the image of an aircraft propeller on the labels. Two separate vineyard sites, totaling twenty-one acres, are currently planted in Chardonnay, Riesling, Gewürztraminer, Cabernet Sauvignon, Cabernet Franc, Lemberger, and Saperavi. While production facilities are in the planning stage, winemaking is contracted out to a local production site and a consultant winemaker.

Noah, who served apprenticeships at nearby Buttonwood Grove Winery (see page 137), is focused on developing blends that make the most of what the vineyards have to offer. Crosswind, a crisp white named for breezes from the lake that keep vineyard temperatures moderate, combines Gewürztraminer and Riesling. Osprey, named for a hawk's nest on the property, unites oak-aged Cabernet Franc and Lemberger. Pay special attention to Glide, the name for an unexpected sparkling Gewürztraminer. The bubbles are small and smooth but plenty, an enticing introduction to the varietal.

LUCAS VINEYARDS

3862 County Road 150 (off Route 89)
Interlaken, NY 14847
www.lucasvineyards.com

Ruth and Bill Lucas uprooted their family in 1975, moved out of the Bronx, and resettled here in order to grow grapes on a patch of land overlooking Cayuga Lake. For Bill it was a stark contrast to his job as a tugboat captain in New York Harbor, but he was married to a remarkable partner. Ruth's enthusiasm and optimism set an example for her family as she mastered the economic and agricultural basics of the winegrowing business.

At first, the family supplied grapes to a number of wineries, including Taylor and Glenora. Then, with the 1980 harvest, the Lucas clan seized the opportunity to make their own wines. Starting with production of just four hundred cases of Cayuga and De Chaunac, they carefully expanded the fledgling operation. The dictionary definition of a family business, Ruth, now sole owner of the estate, is the mother hen of the winery; daughters Ruthie and Stephanie manage day-to-day operation and oversee the tasting room; and Stephanie's husband, Jeff Houck, is the winemaker (trained by Ruth), crafting a balanced mix of hybrid and vinifera grapes and producing some of the most reasonably priced wines in the region.

The star performer here is Cayuga White, a prodigious French-American hybrid varietal that once might have defined the region. It is historically at the heart of the Lucas white wine program, with "museum vines" still producing in the original nursery block. Besides the Germanic-style still wine, this early-harvested grape is crafted into an extra-dry sparkling wine.

The bustling tasting room offers fifteen different wines, including dependable Chardonnay, Cabernet Franc, and consistently excellent Rieslings. The Tug Boat series of wines (inspired by family history) and the Nautie series (inspired by the Lucas women), perhaps less serious than the European varietals, speak to the heart of this remarkable enterprise.

SHEPHERDESS CELLARS

8189 Route 89
Interlaken, NY 14847
www.shepherdesscellars.com

In 2016, father and son Bruce and Mark Radloff took a leap of faith with the intention of making great wine representative of the Finger Lakes region. A Cornell Hotel School grad, Mark's path to winemaking began at Red Newt Cellars (see page 112), and his first wines were produced at the Hector Wine Company (see page 111).

Mark sources his grapes from local growers, concentrating on the personality of each harvest to craft as much wine as he can give his personal attention to. He is constantly touching, tasting, and smelling each fermenter and barrel, making sure the wines meet his personal style preference. His portfolio includes regional essentials Cabernet Franc, Pinot Noir, Chardonnay, and Dry Riesling. But his skill as a winemaker shines in an enticing blend called White Forager, marrying Chardonnay, Vidal Blanc, and Riesling, a harmonious composite with layers of depth on the palate, more indulgent than any of the wines separately on their own. Red wines are matured in once-used French oak barrels acquired from California wineries. Mark's Cabernet Franc is resting in barrels that once held Opus One.

AMERICANA VINEYARDS

4367 East Covert Road
Interlaken, NY 14847
www.americanavineyards.com

Established by James and Mary Anne Treble in 1981, Americana Vineyards was purchased by Joseph Gober in 1997. The tasting room is housed in an early-nineteenth-century barn rescued from demolition, meticulously dismantled, and moved piece by piece five miles to the winery property. With an array of wine accessories, gourmet gifts, locally made arts and crafts, souvenirs, geegaws, and knickknacks, it's like the inside of a Cracker Barrel. The next-door Crystal Lake Café serves soups, salads, sandwiches, cheeses, and chocolates.

At one time, Baco Noir was widely grown in Burgundy and the Loire, but while the hybrid grape has since fallen out of favor in the Old World, it has been embraced by some North American vintners, including Mr. Gober. As the signature variety at Americana, Baco Noir is offered as a varietal and appears in several blends, including Barn Raisin' Red, a Red Cat wannabe mix of Baco Noir and Catawba. Even the café's brownies are spiked with Baco Noir.

FRONTENAC POINT VINEYARD & ESTATE WINERY
9501 Route 89
Trumansburg, NY 14886
www.frontenacpoint.com

Nearly five decades ago, Jim Doolittle's desk job at the Department of Ag and Markets in Albany included guiding development of the New York State Farm Winery Bill. That piece of legislation would eventually allow independent grape growers to operate small-scale wineries and sell wines directly from their farms. Among the unsung heroes of the modern Finger Lakes wine industry, Jim, along with his wife, Carol, purchased a nineteen-acre apple orchard, replaced apple trees with grapevines, and became winegrowers. Its name taken from *Frontenac*, the legendary steamboat that once ferried passengers across Cayuga Lake, the estate is home to a boutique-size winery, with Jim's idiosyncratic wines focusing on quality over quantity.

Bred in France, Chambourcin was at one time widely grown in the Loire Valley. It's still used as a blender in many wines but seldom receives any credit on labels. A hearty French-American hybrid, the grape was a favorite of Jim's mentor at Cornell for its resistance to disease and its ability to produce dark pigment even in cold growing seasons. While some hybrid flavors, especially among the reds, will challenge a palate accustomed to viniferas, in the right hands, Chambourcin is an exception. It dominates the Frontenac Point portfolio with no less than five wines produced from the versatile grape: a varietal Chambourcin, aged up to nine years; Stay Sail Red (a blend of Chambourcin, Pinot Noir, Zweigelt, Chelois, and Marechal Foch); Proprietor's Reserve (a blend of Chambourcin, Zweigelt, Chelois, and Marechal Foch); and two styles of rosé, Stay Sail Rosé (dry) and Clos Frontenac (semisweet).

For a glimpse of the Finger Lakes before things got precious, visit Frontenac Point, an intentionally low-tech and old-school winery. Don't miss the ten-foot-tall, wind-driven sound sculpture installed on the bow of the tasting deck, the perfect setting to sip, chill, and soak up the view overlooking Cayuga Lake.

GLENHAVEN FARM
6121 Sirrine Road
Trumansburg, NY 14886
www.glenhavenfarm.com

For more than four decades, John Tamburello has been perfecting the art of growing blueberries. The story begins with John's purchase of an idyllic and historic farm property, a dream supported by his close-knit Italian family. A graduate of the Ag School at Cornell, he was on a path to become a fruit grower, and in 1979, that dream ripened into a u-pick blueberry farm. By 1985, with six thousand plants flourishing on eleven acres of the estate, Glenhaven Farm's harvest was sizable enough for John to join the Ithaca Farmers Market, where he introduced local shoppers to plump, sweet fruit sold by the pint. His mainstay northern highbush variety Bluecrop was selected to yield large, bright blue berries by midsummer, and a smaller yield of late-ripening, slightly tart Elliots extended offerings at the market into September.

The grape, despite its reputation, is not indispensable to winemaking, and in 2008, John squashed his first batch of blueberries to produce wine to utilize excess fruit at the end of the season—and curious, of course, to see how the berries would portray themselves in wine form. Today, he handcrafts raspberry, blackberry, and rhubarb wines that reflect his favored terroir and the personality of each, but John makes his mark in three styles of his beloved blueberries, each with distinct profiles and sensory characteristics.

The first is a sweet wine; the second, a semidry style; and the third, an exceptional dry version. Serious wine drinkers who are hesitant to stray from tradition might actually be surprised when a fruit wine they quaff tastes more like a young Cabernet Sauvignon or Syrah.

Blueberries are picked by hand in August; lightly crushed; fermented; and stored in separate small batches, both stainless-steel and French oak, in the cellar of the estate's 1873 farmhouse. After judicious blending, wine is ready for sale by the following summer. John is passionate about his fruit, his wines, and the way of life it provides.

BOLAND THOMAS VINEYARDS

30 Main Street
Trumansburg, NY 14886
www.btvineyards.com

For his services in the Revolutionary War, Abner Treman received six hundred acres of land, now in part occupied by the village of Trumansburg. It was once known as Shin Hollow because, legend says, folks bumped their shins on tree stumps as they made their way home from the local tavern. The village was later renamed for the Treman family but misspelled as Trumansburg by the postmaster (perhaps after visiting the same tavern), and so it has remained.

Today's Trumansburg is still basically a one-road town, an old-fashioned Main Street with shops, professional offices, distinctive homes of unique architectural designs, and the homey tasting room of Kimbly Boland and Mark Thomas and the couple's microfarm winery. Since 1998, Kimbly and Mark have nurtured two precious acres of grapevines, one of Riesling, the other of Cabernet Franc and Cabernet Sauvignon. At harvest, grapes are hand-picked, hand-sorted, and carried in early morning to nearby Hosmer Winery (see page 141), where winemaker Julia Hoyle oversees the limited production.

Riesling is crafted in both dry and sparkling versions, as well as the primary component in a lovely rosé. The vineyard's full yield of the two Cabernets at harvest becomes Field Blended Red Wine. Kimbly guides tasters through multiple vintages in vertical flights to showcase the same varietal from the same vineyard in sequential vintages. You'll note subtle differences made by the year's weather in the vineyard and judge how each wine matures over time.

The owners' passion for fishing and Cayuga Lake's bountiful supply of trout, walleye, and northern pike provides a theme for the winery and inspires Kimbly's graphic imagery on the labels. Ask to see the couple's collection of antique lures. This might be the region's most idiosyncratic winery. Visit here to sip wines on a porch overlooking the village and watch the world go by.

BET THE FARM WINERY
4204 Krums Corners Road
Trumansburg, NY 14886
www.btfwines.com

Attracted to the region and the prospect of winemaking, biology postdoc Nancy Tisch tutored under Lou Damiani at Damiani Wine Cellars (see page 118). As she developed skills in the cellar, lab, and vineyards, she decided to "bet the farm" on a venture of her own. Her first wines, made from purchased grapes, were sold in a small shop in the village of Aurora. By 2018, Nancy and her husband, Kit Kalfs, began planting a vineyard and building a winemaking facility on a patch of land between Trumansburg and Ithaca.

The couple's big blue barn and the estate's Jacob Thomas Vineyard, named in honor of Kit's father, overlooks Cayuga Valley, beckoning visitors to discover some lesser-known Finger Lakes varietals, including Dornfelder and Traminette. Nancy has mastered Traminette, the Cornell hybrid of Gewürztraminer and Seyval Blanc. Her bottles are better balanced and more aromatically pure than many of the region's labored attempts at mother Gewürz.

There's magic happening at Bet the Farm, and it's because of Nancy's work with Gamay Noir, a cousin of Pinot Noir and the grape variety responsible for the red wines grown in its spiritual home of Beaujolais, sandwiched between Burgundy to the north and the Rhône Valley to the south. Nancy has had a longtime flirtation with Gamay, produced from two precious acres on the estate, both as a crowd-pleasing still table wine and as a sparkling brut Gamay. Her passion and personal attention reflect a sense of place in every bottle. If you're lucky, Nancy will be around to talk about her wines (she loves to).

BREWERIES

LAKEHOUSE BREWERY
5480 Route 89
Romulus, NY 14541
www.lakehousebrew.com

See Goose Watch Winery, page 136.

LIQUID STATE BREWING COMPANY
6128 Route 89
Romulus, NY 14541
www.liquidstatebeer.com

The seasonal outlet of Liquid State Brewing Company (see page 172), midway between Ithaca and Geneva, is a beer lover's oasis among the wineries of Cayuga Lake. Open from May through October, the sprawling complex has ten glass overhead doors that open up to a one-hundred-foot-long covered patio. Enjoy live music and, weather permitting, an alfresco game of cornhole. Sip beers crafted at the mothership brewery in Ithaca, along with ciders and wines, and feast on wood-fired pizzas, warm Bavarian soft pretzels, and other snacks.

GARRETT'S BREWING COMPANY
1 West Main Street
Trumansburg, NY 14886
www.garrettsbrewing.com

There's something mythical about this space. In 1973, Alex Brooks and Vivian Bridaham, Cornell Hotel School grads, converted a local card and gift shop into what would become the "living room of Trumansburg." You can still see a few remnants from the Rongovian Embassy to the USA, the legendary local watering hole lovingly called the Rongo, in Greg Garrett's taproom.

A former military police officer, Greg worked as a builder and playground installer, and in his spare time, he began brewing batches of beer in his kitchen. As home brewing became an obsession, the beers kept getting better and better. Friends and family encouraged him to go pro, and after taking an introductory beer-making course with Randy Lacey of Hopshire Farm & Brewery (see page 171), that avocation blossomed into a full-fledged business.

Standards here include #Almost, an easy-drinking pale ale; American Whigs, a New England–style IPA; and Jenny's Cream Ale, Greg's homage to the Genesee Brewing Company original. Friends and neighbors provide other beverage choices—ciders from Black Diamond Farm and Cider (see page 154) and wines from Bet the Farm Winery (see page 149).

The popularity of this establishment may be due to the beers, but food is anything but an afterthought at Garrett's. The kitchen offers a full menu of Mexican-style staples, from nachos to tacos. Ground beef is sourced from a local farm, its cows fed on spent grain from the beer-brewing process.

CIDERIES

BLACKDUCK CIDERY
3046 County Road 138
Ovid, NY 14521
www.blackduckcidery.com

John Reynolds studied plant genetics at Cornell, worked at the Agricultural Experiment Station in Geneva, made wine at Sheldrake Point Winery (see page 142), and began working full time at his own family farm between Cayuga and Seneca Lakes. Over the years, John and his wife, Shannon O'Connor, built out Daring Drake Farm by hand, slowly filling thirty-six acres between Seneca and Cayuga Lakes with an amazing diversity of crops—apples, pears, quince, currants, cherries, grapes, gooseberries, and elderberries—and a roving brace of ducks, adding personality to the farm and inspiring a brand. In Native American culture, the black duck symbolizes adaptability and resourcefulness, and with eighty varieties of apples grown on two orchards three miles apart in Ovid, the resourceful couple launched Blackduck Cidery.

To produce ciders that speak of his specific locale, John pushes the boundaries of his craft using wild native yeast for fermentation. His unfiltered, unfined ciders are crafted from more than forty different heirloom and modern apple varieties. Blackduck's Bankers Blend (named for Ovid's historic John Banker Farm) is a tannic English-style cider that includes, among others, Harry Masters Jersey, Kingston Black, and Somerset Redstreak varieties. This is just one example from one of the most baffling, unconventional, and intriguing cidermakers in the region.

The barn/tasting room is a modest affair, with just enough room for a personal and educational experience. Or visit the Blackduck stand at the Ithaca Farmers Market, where John and Shannon have been regulars since 2008.

FINGER LAKES CIDER HOUSE

4017 Hickok Road
Interlaken, NY 14847
www.fingerlakesciderhouse.com

In 2008, Melissa Madden and Garrett Miller purchased a sixty-nine-acre corn and soybean field and reworked the land into Good Life Farm, the name representing what Garrett calls a "wildly diverse ecosystem of fruits, animals, microbes and ideas." By 2012, they embarked on cider production, filling the pasture with cider apple trees in American heirloom, English, and other European varieties. And by 2015, they had transformed the old barn into a charmingly provincial tasting room and bottle shop that opens up to a deck where you can sip ciders and gaze at acres of bucolic farmland at its feet and a view of Cayuga Lake in the distance.

Offerings run the gamut from still to sparkling, from crisp, dry Pioneer Pippin to earthy, barrel-aged Funkhouse. FLCH offers a rare opportunity to taste single-varietal ciders. Northern Spy, Golden Russett, and Baldwin are all made entirely from one variety of apple. Honeycrisp Ice is a sweet dessert cider made from the cultivar developed at the Minnesota Agricultural Experiment Station. It's no surprise that Finger Lakes Cider House was voted the best cider establishment in the East by the United States Association of Cider Makers.

In keeping with the terroir-focused approach, locally sourced delicacies are available to try alongside the ciders. An open kitchen prepares cheese boards and soups, a biodynamic field greens salad, pasture-raised pulled pork, and cast-iron grilled cheddar cheese on Wide Awake Bakery sourdough. Almost everything is "insanely local," sourced from local farms, with some ingredients grown right here on Good Life Farm.

You can extend your visit to this atmospheric spot with a stay at the Yurt, a rustic studio alongside a creek that runs through the property, or at the Loft, an Airbnb rental above the tasting room.

BELLWETHER HARD CIDER & WINE

9070 Route 89
Trumansburg, NY 14886
www.cidery.com

The term *bellwether* comes from an age-old practice in sheepherding of putting a bell on the sheep that leads the flock. *Bellwethers* now refer to people who take the lead, stick their necks out, and start a movement. In 1996, after travels through the cider regions of France and groundwork as home cidermakers, Bill and Cheryl Barton became leading figures in the revival of cider culture in the region with an ambitious start-up they appropriately called Bellwether Hard Cider.

The wide choice of locally sourced apples provides Bellwether cidermaker Bill a lot to work with, and the results are exceptional varietals and blends. Many of his ciders are concocted from varieties usually considered eating apples. Liberty Spy has a hearty taste and succulent mouthfeel from the blend of Liberty and Northern Spy apples; the marriage of local Tompkins King and Baldwin produces a tart, refreshing quaff called King Baldwin. Bellwether's Rhode Island Greening is an artisanal triumph. The semidry sparkling cider is made from an old North American heirloom discovered in Rhode Island near Newport in the 1700s by an innkeeper/apple grower named Mr. Green.

Bill suggests drinking his ciders at the same temperature as white wine, about 55°F, and insists that hard cider's acidity and lower alcohol make it an even better match with food than many wines.

BLACK DIAMOND FARM AND CIDER
4675 East Seneca Road
Trumansburg, NY 14886
www.blackdiamondcider.com

Based on reputation alone, you might expect the tasting room to be a lot different from the modest Cider Shack on Black Diamond Farm. Disciples of Ian Merwin's ciders make pilgrimages here to meet the emeritus Cornell professor of pomology, apple hunter, orchardist, and one of the most influential mentors in the community of American cidermakers.

Don't blink as you drive along East Seneca Road, or you're likely to miss the small, weathered sign marking the entrance to a driveway along rows of fruit trees. The Merwin family grows more than 145 varieties of apples, many of them rare heirlooms and European varieties. These apples have much higher levels of bitter and astringent tannins than are found in market varieties and are selected especially for their cider-making qualities. Production here is limited to five thousand gallons, allowing Ian and his team hands-on control of the process from orchard to bottle.

Among the farm-crafted ciders, Porter's Perfection is a British bittersweet cider apple from the 1800s crafted into a varietal called Shin Hollow. The cider pays tribute to the old name of the village of Trumansburg and is supposedly a reference to men's legs bumped on their way home from the local tavern, a dangerous trip because one had to weave in and out among the tree stumps.

During the summer months, the Merwins also grow cherries, blueberries, peaches, plums, pears, grapes, and kiwi, and since 1998, the Black Diamond Farm stand has been a fixture at the Ithaca Farmers Market.

IDIOT BROTHERS HARD CIDER
8315 Route 227
Trumansburg, NY 14886
www.idiotbrothers.com

After Rob and Richie Kuhar brainstormed dozens of potential names for their fledgling hard cider company, a skeptical friend suggested Idiot Brothers. Case closed. Housed in a restored mid-nineteenth-century-era barn on Crow's Nest Farm, this is strictly a small-scale, word-of-mouth sort of place where you won't find balloons out front or signs that read, "Buses welcome." The amiable tasting room resembles an indoor flea market with shelves filled with antiques and novelties, and yes, everything's for sale.

Curious visitors find their way here for the small-batch ciders, intentionally crafted, in Rob's words, "not by the book" but in the way rustic ciders were made centuries ago. A variety of heirloom apples is sourced from nearby orchards, with the boys sometimes bartering skill and labor for fruit, supplemented with hand-picked, wild-foraged crab apples from old-growth trees, many discovered in abandoned local orchards.

The two brothers are enthusiastic about fermenting both apples and pears. Complex and funky, American Heritage is a faithful homage to the nearly forgotten past of American cider making. Gnarly Branch Rosé is fermented with wine yeast and Gamay Noir grape skins from Sheldrake Point Winery (see page 142). And Very Underrated Perry, an old-school, pear-based cider, is made with Bosc pears, a mix of orchard-grown and wild-harvested fruit.

Stop by to see what's pouring at the moment, and plan to spend some time here. A small bakery on the property provides freshly baked breads and pastries to accompany sipping and conversation. And the convivial setting includes overnight accommodations in the Bunker, as well as a glamping tent out back.

REDBYRD ORCHARD CIDERY
4491 Reynolds Road
Trumansburg, NY 14886
www.redbyrdorchardcider.com

In 1920s Austria, the concept of biodynamics was introduced by philosopher and esotericist Rudolf Steiner. His philosophy of agriculture was one of healing the earth and the soil rather than stripping away its life-giving properties. Steiner's ecological and holistic teachings provide the guiding principles at the Redbyrd enterprise. The result is exceptional fruit and a healthy orchard.

After earning a degree in agriculture and biology from New Mexico State, Eric Shatt made wines at Ventosa Vineyards (see page 99), managed vineyards at Hermann J. Wiemer Vineyard (see page 75), and supervised Cornell orchards and research farms. Deva Maas has a background in sustainable agriculture from Evergreen State College. In 2003, the husband-and-wife team began planting more than 150 varieties of heirloom, wild-seedling, and European cider apples in their four-acre orchard, cultivating trees propagated from the wild and then crossing them with others. In 2013, they began selling Redbyrd Orchard ciders.

As a progressive "young-gun" pommelier, Eric's practice includes manures and composts and excludes synthetic fertilizers, pesticides, and herbicides. His ciders can be cloudy and sometimes retain sediment from forgoing filtration and clarification. They can also be earthy, effervescent, wild, enjoyably unpredictable, and endlessly interesting. Workman Dry, the flagship barrel blend at Redbyrd, is made from twenty-five varieties of heirloom, bittersweet, bitter-sharp, and wild-seedling apples. Starblossom is a multiple-vintage cider made from nearly thirty varieties, including a distinct species grown from seeds collected in the 1980s in Kazakhstan, the apple's ancestral home.

Redbyrd ciders are available for purchase at the Ithaca Farmers Market.

NEW YORK CIDER COMPANY
245 Hayts Road
Ithaca, NY 14850
www.nyciderco.com

Every artisan cider has a story to tell, but partners Joe Steuer and Steve Daughetee have a favorite, the one about a customer who walked up to their stand at their Ithaca Farmers Market and asked if they might be interested in the old apple trees at his nudist colony, the Empire Haven Nudist Park in Moravia. It seems the property surrounding the colony contains the remnants of a large pre-Prohibition seedling cider orchard, and in 2020, New York Cider Company introduced Naturist, a full-bodied blend made with the distinctive apples gathered there.

Unlikely cider makers, Steuer was a journalist in New York City, with bylines in the likes of the *New York Daily News*, the *Hollywood Reporter*, and the *New York Post*'s Page Six. He arrived in Ithaca to sell real estate. Daughhetee remodeled houses in the region for many years before crafting ciders full time.

The enterprise, established in 2017, was born of their mutual passion for cider, and the partners have become full-time cider makers on Ithaca's West Hill using apples from their own Hayts Road orchard, donated apples, and pounds of apples foraged from nearby wild or abandoned orchards. An adjacent parcel once belonged to Moses Snook, a farmer and horse breeder who planted many of the trees on the property, estimated to be 150 years old.

Among the exclusively bone-dry ciders, Champagne-like Hedgerow is crafted with at least thirty varieties, a mix that includes heirloom American and English apples. The Newtown Pippin juice in Monarch is infused with grape skins from Sheldrake Point Winery (see page 142), and Firefly is made with the wild fermentation of Wickson Crab, Rhode Island Greening, and Tolman Sweet.

New York Cider Company ciders are sold at the Ithaca Farmers Market, the Union Square Greenmarket in New York City, and on weekends at the Hayts Road tasting room.

SOUTH HILL CIDER
550 Sandbank Road
Ithaca, NY 14850
www.southhillcider.com

If you're wondering about the connection between cider making and old-time fiddle music, Steve Selin is the perfect person to ask. As both cider maker and fiddler, he'll tell you the two are firmly grounded in American folk culture. Steve studied forest ecology at Virginia Tech, so while his educational background is more suited to growing trees than making cider, he became a passionate hobbyist who enjoyed bringing home-brew kegs to old-time music nights at winery gigs. While Steve fiddled, winemakers sipped his ciders. His collaboration with Dave Breeden, winemaker at Sheldrake Point Winery (see page 142), helped Steve to transition from a hobby to a business.

It was his homestead property on Ithaca's South Hill that provided a serendipitous location for both orchard (its slope orientation with air drainage and soils with nutrient-rich bedrock) and tasting room (its proximity to both Upper Buttermilk Park and downtown Ithaca). There are two thousand apple trees in twenty different varieties growing on his ten-acre domain. Among small-batch offerings, Old Time Cider, a sparkling, off-dry sipper, is the South Hill flagship. Steve calls it an "homage to old traditional cidermaking." For his Keeved cider, he instigates a long, slow, wild fermentation, which starves the yeast of nutrients before it can consume all the natural sugars. The process is time consuming and labor intensive. And while few American cider producers attempt this process, when Steve's efforts are successful, this blend of tannic cider apples retains much more of the apple's terroir than other methods.

Visit the tasting room, stroll the grounds, and enjoy sipping a favorite hard cider with wood-fired pizzas, smoked sausages, or charcuterie plates. Come on Thursday evenings to hear live music. If you're lucky, it will be a night when Steve brings his fiddle.

DISTILLERIES

HIDDEN MARSH DISTILLERY
2981 Auburn Road
Seneca Falls, NY 13148
www.montezumawinery.com

See Montezuma Winery, page 133.

MUSHROOM SPIRITS DISTILLERY
4055 Route 89
Seneca Falls, NY 13148
www.mushroomspiritsdistillery.com

In 2009, transplanted New York city couple Joe and Wendy Rizzo landed in Ithaca as mushroom growers, selling gourmet mushrooms at the local farmer's market every Saturday. They called their venture Blue Oyster Cultivation, named for the mushroom that starts out strikingly blue, then turns gray as it matures—with a wink to the heavy-metal demons of the 1970s. A decade later, the energetic entrepreneurs refined their art at the other end of Cayuga Lake, infusing corn-distilled vodkas with dried mushrooms, including Hen of the Woods, Enoki, Shiitake, Destroying Angel, Pleurotis, and Spore. Alcohol in the vodka extracts nuanced mushroom flavors and other compounds, showcasing the subtle, earthy nuances and umami of each different variety in the base spirit.

This part tavern, part tasting room provides an alternative stop along the wine trail, a place to sip and savor a range of curious spirits. A popular cocktail here is a mushroom-inspired version of the classic Moscow mule, made with Hen of the Woods Vodka. The mushroom character is subtle, cutting some of the vodka bite and adding savory and woodsy notes to the drink.

MYER FARM DISTILLERS

7350 Route 89
Ovid, NY 1452
www.myerfarmdistillers.com

The Myer family has a rich history in Ovid, dating back to 1810, when ancestors settled in the village and became not only the first to plow local farmland but also among the first to make liquor. A Cornell Aggie, John Myer, of the fifth generation on the original nine-hundred-acre homestead, grows winter and spring wheat, spelt, barley, rye, oats, clover, alfalfa, and soybeans on one of the largest and oldest operating organic farms in the Northeast United States. In 2012, John, along with brother Joe, drawing inspiration from family roots, learned the craft of distilling hands on and began producing small-batch spirits from the certified organic grains grown on the farm, establishing a true "field-to-flask" estate distillery. The Myers both plant the seeds and produce the spirits.

The enterprise is housed in a hip-roofed, pagoda-topped stone structure partly inspired by images of old distilleries of Scotland and outfitted with a 650-liter copper-pot still imported from Germany. Products include vodka, gin, bourbon, flavored whiskies, and specialty liqueurs. The small-scale production here translates into artistic interpretations and unique products, and a sampling of Myer Farm spirits all show a grain-forward flavor profile. Complete your expertly curated bar cart with a bottle of Cayuga Gold Barrel-Aged Gin, a robust hybrid of gin and dark spirit made from botanical-rich gin rested in emptied bourbon barrels from their own production.

The tasting room combines farmstead vibes with high-end spirits.

CAYUGA LAKE (EAST)

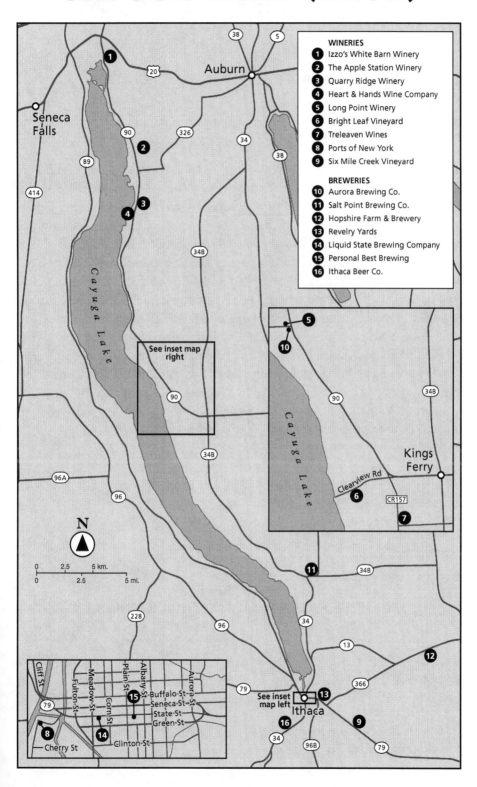

WINERIES
1. Izzo's White Barn Winery
2. The Apple Station Winery
3. Quarry Ridge Winery
4. Heart & Hands Wine Company
5. Long Point Winery
6. Bright Leaf Vineyard
7. Treleaven Wines
8. Ports of New York
9. Six Mile Creek Vineyard

BREWERIES
10. Aurora Brewing Co.
11. Salt Point Brewing Co.
12. Hopshire Farm & Brewery
13. Revelry Yards
14. Liquid State Brewing Company
15. Personal Best Brewing
16. Ithaca Beer Co.

Auburn

Seneca Falls

Cayuga Lake

Kings Ferry

Clearview Rd

CR157

Ithaca

See inset map right

See inset map left

N

0   2.5   5 km.
0   2.5   5 mi.

Cliff St
Meadow St
Fulton St
Corn St
Albany St
Plain St
Buffalo St
Aurora St
Seneca St
State St
Green St
Clinton St
Cherry St

WINERIES

IZZO'S WHITE BARN WINERY
6634 Cayuga Road
Cayuga, NY 13034
www.izzoswhitebarnwinery.com

The imposing, white-coated one-hundred-year-old hay barn provides the name for this artisan winery and rustic event space. The fourteen-acre abandoned farm property, purchased by John and Lorraine Izzo in 2009, has been transformed into three postage-stamp-size vineyards, a picturesque setting surrounded by manicured meadows with a pond lovingly called Lake Lorraine.

Housed in a building next to the barn is a small-production winery, but that means focused attention to some very special wines. While the Izzos purchase most of the fruit from nearby vineyards for more standard offerings, estate-grown wines are produced from four fascinating hybrid varieties: Aromella and Corot Noir, developed at the New York State Agricultural Experiment Station in Geneva, and La Cresent and Landot Noir, crossed varieties produced by the University of Minnesota grape-breeding program. The shallow northern end of Cayuga Lake lacks the beneficial warming lake effect enjoyed by more southerly vineyards, so winemaker John Izzo selected these hybrids for their cold-hardy tolerance and diverse characteristics. A visit here becomes an opportunity to try small-lot, single-vineyard wines you've never heard of before.

THE APPLE STATION WINERY
5279 Cross Road
Cayuga, NY 13043
www.theapplestation.com

Off the beaten path and on a winding road between the villages of Union Springs and Cayuga, this hidden gem looks and feels like an inviting country store, not only because of the vintage gas pumps out front and antique memorabilia inside, but also because of the friendly proprietors. Bob Wintamute, fruit farmer and apple grower, along with wife Kathy, embarked on this apple-centric venture in 1986. You can pick orchard-grown apples here in season or buy multiple varieties in the store along with other local fruits, cheeses, jams, jellies, and honeys.

To make the most out of a visit, come in the fall for apple cider doughnuts and join tourists and locals in the orchard for a wine-country picnic.

After obtaining a farm winery license in 2010, the Wintamutes began producing handcrafted apple wines, apple and fruit wine blends, and sweet ciders, all fermented in small batches. The Station's most popular refresher is called Moo Moo Blue, a flavorful diversion made from a variety of freshly pressed estate apples and blueberries from a neighboring grower. It's named for the winery dog, Moo Moo, a Jack Russell Terrier, and a reminder that wine doesn't have to be all serious.

QUARRY RIDGE WINERY
4242 Route 90
Union Springs, NY 13160
www.quarryridgewinery.com

Union Springs owes its name to the confluence of several mineral springs, the source of water not only to drive its early mills but also for their purported healing or healthful benefits. The village flourished as a spa resort and with the extraction of limestone from nearby limestone quarries.

Perched on a hillside just outside the village, Quarry Ridge Winery is a Cuthbert family enterprise, with Andrew Cuthbert as winemaker. After earning a degree in biochemistry from St. John Fisher University, followed by an online certificate in winemaking from UC Davis, Andrew apprenticed under Lindsay Stevens at nearby King Ferry Winery (see Treleaven Wines, page 166). In 2018, ten acres of grapes were planted on the thirty-acre former hayfield, including Pinot Noir, Cabernet Franc, Chardonnay, and Riesling varieties. By 2021, Andrew was brimming with new ideas.

The first released estate wine was the Cask Riesling, fermented in a vertical five-hundred-liter oak foeder (pronounced *FOOD-er*) made of a series of French oak staves held together by metal hoops crafted by Italian coopers. While oaked Rieslings are rare in the Finger Lakes, it remains common in wine regions of Germany, where gentle oxygenation that occurs in old wooden barrels softens the edges of the wine and adds complexity. After fermentation, the wine ages in wood for another three to four months.

On the other end of the spectrum, while it's common to find Cabernet Franc aged in oak for additional body and richness, Andrew's cheerful Cab Franc is fermented and rests in stainless steel, producing a light-bodied and more fruit-forward wine than more serious oak-aged reds. With its fortuitous location on a patch of limestone rock quarry at the shore of Cayuga Lake, Quarry Ridge takes an adventurous approach to winemaking.

HEART & HANDS WINE COMPANY

4162 Route 90
Union Springs, NY 13160
www.heartandhandswine.com

Here, heading south about a mile from the village of Union Springs, is where old quarries were operational for nearly one hundred years. Limestone mined from these open quarries was shipped by canal and used to pave Lower Manhattan, including Wall Street. Novelist and wine writer Jay McInerney asks, "Is it a gross abuse of poetic license to detect marine elements in a wine grown on limestone that was once a Jurassic seabed?" It so happens that Pinot Noir is most at home on the limestone soil of gentle slopes, with no better example than the wine-producing region of Burgundy, France.

Following his passion for Pinot Noir, aspiring winemaker Tom Higgins left a career in information technology and began training in France, then headed to California to work under Josh Jensen of Calera, a West Coast pioneer in the effort to craft Burgundian-style Pinot Noir in America. In 2006, Tom returned to his roots in the Finger Lakes with stints at the Thirsty Owl Wine Company (see page 139) and Atwater Vineyards (see page 116). Besides honing his wine-growing skills, he began planning his own wine venture.

Every decision made during the establishment and life of a vineyard is based on site selection, and Tom used Burgundy as a model for desirable terroir. After a two-year-long search for the "holy grail" location most conducive to growing the elusive Pinot Noir, Tom located a site, some would say in the middle of nowhere, yet along the Onondaga limestone escarpment. In 2007, Tom and his wife, Susan, purchased that six-acre plot across from the shoreline of Carr's Cove on Cayuga Lake and began planting Pinot Noir and Riesling grapevines. The winery officially opened in 2008, followed by a modest tasting room a year later.

The Heart & Hands roster includes Riesling and Chardonnay, but relentless focus is on crafting authentic Pinot Noir. The winemaker allows the soil to speak through the vine with careful placement on this sustainably farmed site, and the results are beautifully balanced wines characterized by tremendous energy and bright fruit. If you're seeking a taste of Pinot Noir inspired by Burgundy yet one that speaks clearly of its Finger Lakes origins, look no further than Mo Chuisle ("Pulse of My Heart") Estate Reserve Pinot Noir, the best expression of the Heart & Hands terroir.

LONG POINT WINERY

1485 Lake Road
Aurora, NY 13026
www.longpointwinery.com

Midway between the northern and southern ends of Cayuga Lake and just south of the village of Aurora, Long Point State Park provides a boat launch, playground, picnic area, fishing access, and four miles of hiking trails. The nearby vineyards overlooking the lake belong to Gary and Rosemary Barletta. Gary's passion for viticulture and enology started in his childhood, inspired by his Italian grandfather, who made Old World–inspired wines in his home cellar. His path to becoming a professional winemaker began in the cellars of King Ferry Winery (see Treleaven Wines, page 166) under the tutelage of Peter Saltonstall, before establishing Long Point Winery in 1999.

Eight acres are planted in Chardonnay, Riesling, Cabernet Franc, and Pinot Gris. Cabernet Franc excels in the estate's fertile, mineral-rich soil, and Pinot Gris (Pinot Grigio), more commonly grown in northern Italy than in the Finger Lakes, benefits from the lake's moderating air currents. Fans of Pinot Grigio can expect a very respectable, Italian-style wine at Long Point.

Long Point operates as a commercial winery, so unlike most of the region's farm wineries, the Barlettas are permitted to purchase grapes from out of state. At harvest time, a refrigerated truck arrives at Long Point filled with California-grown varieties, including Zinfandel, Merlot, Cabernet Sauvignon, Sangiovese, and Syrah. Gary's long-standing relationships with Mendocino County and Suisun Valley growers supplement his estate-grown offerings.

Winery dogs are unofficial mascots of the Finger Lakes. Long Point boasts a handsome canine greeter. Look for Lissy on the label of a sweet-style Riesling.

BRIGHT LEAF VINEYARD

1250 Clearview Road
King Ferry, NY 13081
www.brightleafvineyard.com

Set above rolling vineyards on a ninety-four-acre estate overlooking Cayuga Lake, this sophisticated wine-country enterprise is the fulfilled dream of Michael Wilson: his love of wine and pursuit of perfection. In 2013, Dr. Wilson, an orthopedic surgeon, and his wife, Donna, purchased what had been a cattle farm and planted fourteen acres of vinifera grapevines determined to create an important destination in Finger Lakes wine country.

Bright Leaf is really two vineyards, and the exceptional 100 percent estate-grown wines crafted by winemaker Colleen Lukas truly reflect this distinct location. An Ithaca native, Colleen studied chemistry at Hobart and William Smith and served as assistant winemaker under Lindsay Stevens at King Ferry Winery (see Treleaven Wines below). In 2016, she joined Bright Leaf as assistant and moved up to head winemaker for the 2018 vintage.

White varietals Riesling and Chardonnay grow in the loose, airy, gravel/shale soils on the cooler Hillside Vineyard, affording excellent drainage and higher acidity and encouraging the vines to send their roots down deep in search of nutrients. It warms up quickly, retains its heat well, and is responsible for many fine wines, most notably from the Mosel. Red varietals Pinot Noir, Cabernet Sauvignon, Merlot, Cabernet Franc, and Lemberger thrive on the Lakeside Vineyard in the heavier, richer, limestone/clay soil. World-renowned wines hail from such soils, including Tempranillos in Rioja and Pinot Noir in Vosne-Romanée, Bourgogne.

A handsome tasting room perfectly complements the stunning natural surroundings, and the hospitality offered by the eager-to-please staff is genuine. Casual fare of cheese and charcuterie is available both inside and, weather permitting, on the outdoor patio overlooking the picturesque lake, where the wines and the views cast a memorable spell.

TRELEAVEN WINES
658 Lake Road
King Ferry, NY 13081
www.treleavenwines.com

His grandfather was known on Capitol Hill as the "gentlemanly gentleman from Massachusetts." After serving three terms as governor and four terms in the US Senate, Leverett Saltonstall stepped down from public service to become a gentleman farmer. His oldest son, also named Leverett, eschewed politics and instead distinguished himself in agriculture as professor of agronomy at Cornell, cattle rancher, and seed producer on the four-hundred-acre Treleaven Farm bordering the eastern shore of Cayuga Lake.

You could say that Peter Saltonstall is more deeply rooted here than any of his vines. The remarkable wine-growing endeavor begun by Peter and his wife, Taci, has become one of the true institutions of Finger Lakes wine country, mentoring fellow winery start-ups and raising Treleaven Wines to the heights it has reached today. On a pasture where beef cattle once roamed, wine grapes now flourish. What started as a seven and a half acres of grapevines planted in 1984 now includes about a dozen wine varieties each year harvested from fruit grown on twenty-seven acres, annually producing 11,000 cases of wine.

The story had its beginning when Peter and Taci visited the Burgundy region of France. They were inspired by their love of the legendary wines of the region and returned home determined to emulate the Burgundian style of white wine with Finger Lakes Chardonnay. While the winery first made its name with those rich, rounded, oaky Chardonnays, in the last several years Treleaven has produced a full range of exceptional wines, in particular, terroir-driven Rieslings, consistently showing well in competitions.

An experienced winemaker, Matt Denci's career has spanned Burgundy, New Zealand, Australia, and California, with more local stints at Red Newt Cellars (see page 112) and Keuka Spring Vineyards (see page 46), before heading the team at Treleaven. Matt works with estate-grown grapes and judiciously sourced fruit from other parts of the region.

Today, Peter is active in the New York Wine Policy Institute, advocates of the state's wineries and grape growers, and watches over the family enterprise now in the safe hands of his son Leverett. Under Lev, the sprawling complex has grown to include Hangtime, an open-air pavilion, music venue, and event space. Visit the tasting room, sip a flight of wines, and stay for lunch in the rustic Barrel Room, home to Simply Cookie's Kitchen under the direction of executive chef Susanne "Cookie" Wheeler. Her smoked chicken wings are legendary.

PORTS OF NEW YORK
815 Taber Street
Ithaca, NY 14850
www.portsofnewyork.com

Finger Lakes winemaking has perhaps found its most unlikely location. This is not only the region's most eccentric winery but also a winery conceived as a work of art unto itself. Frédéric Bouché, owner and winemaker, comes from a long line of vintners in France. His great-great-grandfather owned vineyards in Bordeaux. His great-grandfather made wines at Maison Bouché in the Calvados appellation of Normandy. And growing up, Frédéric worked with his grandfather and was trained in family techniques that he uses at Ports of New York. In an earlier career, Frédéric was an artist known for large-scale installations, and Ithaca's urban winery is perhaps his most impressive creation.

Unlike producers who imitate Port wines with lesser-quality varietals, Frédéric contracts for premium local grapes and fortifies the wines with distilled spirits of native Catawba. The wines are made using a traditional solera system, blending from a series of French oak barrels holding wines that have been aged from four to seventeen years. While inspired by the venerable Portuguese originals, his buzz-worthy wines are truly singular products of the region.

Red Meleau, based on Cabernet Franc, stays true to varietal character, and White Meleau is made with fragrant Muscat Ottonel grapes purchased from local growers. The red version is most appropriately served at room temperature for consumption after a meal. (Tradition calls for Port being served at a formal dinner to be passed to the left, the bottle never touching the table on its way around.) Follow the French habit of chilling and serving the white version as an aperitif. While his company is called Ports of New York, Frédéric cannot use the word *Port* in the product name. International agreements limit its use to the wine made from grapes grown in the Douro region of Portugal.

Straying from Frédéric's signature bottles, a savory, Sancerre-style white and a Bordeaux-inspired red table wine are appropriately labeled Quotidian, meaning "everyday," because these are approachable everyday drinking wines. And for his Crémant-style, gently sparkling Riesling, he suggests chilling overnight, then ten minutes in an ice bath to get it as cold as possible before serving.

SIX MILE CREEK VINEYARD
1551 Slaterville Road (Route 79)
Ithaca, NY 14850
www.sixmilecreek.com

It's said that Six Mile Creek was named by an early settler, marking the distance between a Cayuga Nation crossing point over the stream and the trail's end at Cayuga Lake. Three miles or so east of downtown Ithaca and too far from the winter-moderating protection of the lake, Cornell professor Roger Battistella ignored conventional wisdom and bravely planted French-hybrid and vinifera grapes on a patch of land that slopes down to the creek. Taking extra care to ensure the health of the vines helps the plants to withstand temperature extremes, and as a happy consequence, the vineyard's lower yield of fruit results in greater concentration of varietal characters in the wines.

The vineyard overlooks the wooded, stone-walled creek gorge near Businessman's Lunch Falls, now capped with Van Natta's Dam to create a reservoir for Ithaca's drinking water. A pre–Civil War cemetery borders one end of the historic grounds; an old stagecoach stop marks the other. Winemaking takes place in a restored eighteenth-century Dutch colonial barn, moved in its entirety to the current foundation.

In 2015, former restaurateur Mark Renodin assumed the reins of the estate and, along with the winemaking skills of Paul King, has continued to produce exceptional wines that confound the experts. After working for Boyce Thompson Institute at Cornell as a plant research scientist, Paul came to Six Mile Creek Vineyard more than twenty-five years ago as a vineyard assistant. He now oversees the vineyard, winemaking, and distilling process.

The vineyard's flagship wine, appropriately named Ithaca White, is crafted from Cayuga White with a dollop of Chardonnay for a bit of finesse. Cabernet Franc became the new story here after winning the Governor's Cup, the top prize in the 2019 New York Wine Classic. But perhaps most interesting is the new emphasis on estate-grown Vignoles, an adaptable hybrid most often produced as a late-harvest dessert wine yet produced here in an attractive, cross-palate, near-dry style.

Small-batch spirits, crafted in a 150-gallon stripping still and a 25-gallon copper finishing still, are part of the Six Mile Creek portfolio, with offerings including gin, vodka, grappa, limoncello, orangecello, and amaretto.

The hospitality-driven tasting room, overlooking a picturesque pond, rolling fields, and meticulous vineyards, has become one of Ithaca's must-visit destinations. Even if they did not make very good wines, it would still be worth the detour to Six Mile Creek.

BREWERIES

AURORA BREWING CO.
1897 Route 90
King Ferry, NY 13081
www.brewaurora.com

Two pals, Mark Grimaldi and Joe Shelton, were in search of a business they could call their own, so in 2016, they set out to open a brewery. The Aurora Brewing taproom, a relaxed, comfortable, craft-beer setting, takes full advantage of its location in rural wine country, offering views of lush vineyards on the shore of Cayuga Lake from the breezy beer garden. The scene inside is more British style than American, a pubby, social place where everyone interacts.

The focus here is on small batches of IPA, lager, stout, barrel-aged, experimental brews, and curious styles. The undisputed flagship, Fresh to Death, is a dry-hopped, New England–style IPA, so popular that the five-barrel system can barely keep up with demand. No doubt, Grimaldi and Shelton are having fun making beers, perhaps best on display with a dessert-style called Supreme Peanut Butter Banana Laser-Beam Imperial Pastry Stout. This must-try, over-the-top, full-bodied brew is made with Nilla wafers cookies, real bananas, peanut butter, local maple syrup, Madagascar vanilla beans, and milk sugar.

Smoked and wood-fired chicken wings complement proper pints and rotating weekly flight offerings.

Besides the original brewery location, Aurora beers are available at both the Ithaca Farmers Market and a satellite tasting room at 604 Pittsford Victor Road in Pittsford.

SALT POINT BREWING CO.
6 Louise Bement Lane (off Route 34)
Lansing, NY 14882
www.saltpointbrewing.com

From 1891 to 1962, the Cayuga Lake Salt Company produced refined salt from brine pumped from wells drilled on land that juts into Cayuga Lake, spawning the name Salt Point. Not far from the historic site, two families, Chris and Sarah Hesse and Camilo Bohorquez and Dr. Alexandra Karnow, tossed all four of their hats into the Finger Lakes craft-brewery ring, creating a hoppy oasis for beer lovers in Lansing and attracting both thirsty locals and beer tourists. Beginning with a cramped space and a two-barrel system in 2018, Salt Point Brewing graduated to a seven-barrel operation in a new, expanded facility three years later, with the ability to produce more experimental and unique beers in larger batches.

The convivial taproom features eight rotating taps, some mainstay brews, and a few seasonal creations. At one end of the bar, chef Andrew Schneeberger prepares beer-friendly snacks and bakes sourdough-crust pizzas in a wood-burning oven.

In warm weather, roll-up, garage-style doors open to the lawn, making this an awesome place to hang out on a sunny day. Pull up an Adirondack chair and sip a hefeweizen; doppelbock; or the brewery's mainstay, Uncle Hazy IPA, a West Coast–New England–style hybrid. Sample a flight, and take home favorites in cans or growlers.

HOPSHIRE FARM & BREWERY
1771 Dryden Road (Route 13)
Freeville, NY 13068
www.hopshire.com

In a well-appointed taproom that more resembles a winery tasting room, Randy Lacey, a former mechanical engineer at Cornell who is passionate about the importance of local ingredients, crafts artfully minded beers in an on-site seven-barrel brewhouse.

The regional beer scene takes a giant leap forward with Lacey's eminently drinkable and true-to-style offerings in an intentionally wide variety of products and influences. NearVarna IPA is a hophead's delight, and Beehave is a refreshing blonde ale made with barley, hops, and local basswood honey. Shire Ale is fermented with Scottish Edinburgh yeast, and Bourbon Shire, the barrel-aged version of Shire Ale, develops a warming whisked finish while resting in barrels from the Buffalo Trace Distillery in Frankfort, Kentucky.

Craft brewers have, of course, been at the forefront of the locavore movement, and at Hopshire, Lacey makes that extra connection with hyperlocal ingredients. In addition to malted grain and hops, honey, ginger, maple syrup, and other ingredients are sourced from local farms and producers. He partners with Hollenbeck's Cider Mill in the Cortland County town of Virgil to produce a hard cider called Hoppenbeck with a dozen or so local apple varieties. A signature Shire cheese, adding Hopshire's Scottish Ale into the curd before pressing, is produced in collaboration with Lively Run Goat Dairy.

Lacey has set out to create a welcoming, comfortable gathering place, more than just a taproom. And over the brewery's first ten years, local folks have found many reasons to stop in here for a social lubricant, sometimes on music nights or trivia nights. Hopshire has become a cultural hub for the local Rotary, yoga classes, even the local book club, all of which makes the brewery a community cornerstone.

REVELRY YARDS
111 North Aurora Street
Ithaca, NY 14850
www.revelryyards.com

The only predictable thing about Ithaca's weather is its unpredictability. But when the weather here warms up, locals and tourists gather at the Yards, an urban beer garden that appears in the far side of a row of Aurora Street buildings. The brainchild of Kevin Sullivan and Matthew Cleveland of ITH Hospitality features a wood-fired oven and a mobile bar fabricated out of a shipping container. There are a dozen rotating beers on tap brewed on the second floor of the restaurant, the fermentation tanks visible through large windows above the Aurora Street storefront.

The menu is beer-centric—think pizza, wings, beer cheeseburgers, hefeweizen chicken sandwiches, and pretzel sticks.

Brewing on a ten-barrel system, Taylor Trenchard, formerly of the Cortland Beer Company (see page 199), produces a flagship called Layed Back, a West Coast–style IPA, and Betty White, a spicy hefeweizen. Other must-try styles here are Pothole, a lightly hopped American pilsner, and One Way Street, a hop-forward New England IPA, both names inspired by the wonders of downtown Ithaca.

LIQUID STATE BREWING COMPANY
620 West Green Street
Ithaca, NY 14850
www.liquidstatebeer.com

Adventurers and alchemists Ben Brotman and Jamey Tielens arrived in Ithaca from the Pacific Northwest hooked on craft beer. Both trained biologists, Brotman earned his brewing spurs at start-ups in Washington State, New Jersey, and Downstate New York before a stint at Ithaca Beer Co. (see page 174), and Tielens was a well-practiced home brewer, hop grower, and project manager at Cornell's Lab of Ornithology. In 2016, the two friends opened Liquid State Brewing Company, a convivial beer hall and seventeen-barrel brewhouse in Ithaca's West End, the same space where Cornell Laundry once washed the linens of local hotels and restaurants. Since then, it has become a beloved community watering hole, something you can feel when you walk through the doors. It's noisy and bustling, communal tables filled with locals and visitors who've worked up a thirst. They ogle huge fermentation tanks, visible behind a glass wall, where the prolific and versatile duo craft some of the region's best beers.

Liquid State does just about every style well, but a hazy New England IPA called Liquid Crush is the brewery's bread-and-butter beer, developed after boundless experimentation. Creativity goes into naming the beers. Just two examples: a fruited sour called Hula Hoops and Bubbles and a double IPA by the name of Supercritical Fluid. Brotman and Tielens usually dream up these names over breakfast at nearby State Diner.

From March through December, the resident Silo Food Truck serves beer-friendly buckets of fried chicken and sides.

Liquid State North Shore is a seasonal, off-site location in a sprawling complex among the wineries on Route 89 (see page 150).

PERSONAL BEST BREWING
321 West State Street
Ithaca, NY 14850
www.personalbestbrewing.com

Inside a renovated building that formerly held the City Health Club gym, Personal Best is the kind of place where you could easily lose a couple of hours. You can play shuffleboard; watch sporting events; listen to live music; and, oh, by the way, sip beers that are approachable and as diverse as the people who enjoy them. The concept of a community brewery on the city's West End is the invention of Anthony Cesari, sharing production of a ten-barrel brewhouse with Luke Thorley, whose experience includes prestigious stints at Good Nature Brewing in Hamilton, New York; Modern Times Beer in San Diego, California; and Big Mountain Brewing in Chamonix-Mont-Blanc, France.

Among the versatile styles designed to fill multiple niches, you'll find an Italian pilsner inspired by a Cesari family history. Rental Shoes is a nod to Anthony's great-grandfather who operated a bowling alley in Elmira during the 1950s. Imperial stouts and porters hang out in whiskey casks from Finger Lakes Distilling

Co. (see page 128), while saisons and braggots are resting in French oak barrels, having completed their mission at Usonia (see page 140), providing depths of aroma and flavor.

Ceiling fans whirl overhead, while craft-beer lovers fill the multicolored picnic benches inside. On good weather days, an overhead door opens to an outside beer garden, all the more reason to spend time here.

ITHACA BEER CO.
122 Ithaca Beer Drive
Ithaca, NY 14850
www.ithacabeer.com

Ithaca Beer Co. is to Ithaca what Sam Adams is to Boston and Boulder Brewing is to Boulder—the local craft-beer pioneer and regional institution. Founded by Dan Mitchell in 1998, beer production was initially outsourced; then as sales gradually increased, he was able to obtain the necessary resources to purchase his own brewing equipment.

This granddaddy of Finger Lakes craft breweries has built a loyal fan base that extends throughout the Finger Lakes and well beyond, cranking out provocative mainstays like Cascazilla Red India Pale Ale and distinctively crafted brews like Nut Brown Ale; Apricot Wheat; and, of course, iconic Flower Power.

Kick off your visit with a pint of Flower Power, and raise your glass to the beer that helped launch the Finger Lakes craft-beer revolution. While modern American IPAs evolved on the West Coast, in 2004, the brewery's first head brewer Jeff O'Neil introduced that style here with his formula for Flower Power. It was recognized as one of the first West Coast IPAs brewed in the Northeast, capturing the true power of the hop flower (the origin of the name) with its clover-honey hue, lush floral flavor, and robust fruity aroma from numerous hop additions in the kettle. Ithaca Beer's Flower Power was named one of the twenty-five most important American craft beers ever brewed by *Food & Wine* magazine, the only New York State beer to make the list. If you're looking for a truly enlightening beer, place it right at the top of your to-taste list when you visit the taproom.

The flagship location, an industrial-chic taproom, hums and at times roars with the sound of people having a good time. Featured beers are available in flights, so you can sample your way through the tap list. An open kitchen turns out wood-fired goodness, including creative pizzas.

A spinoff taproom is located at 409 College Avenue, just off the Cornell University campus.

OWASCO LAKE

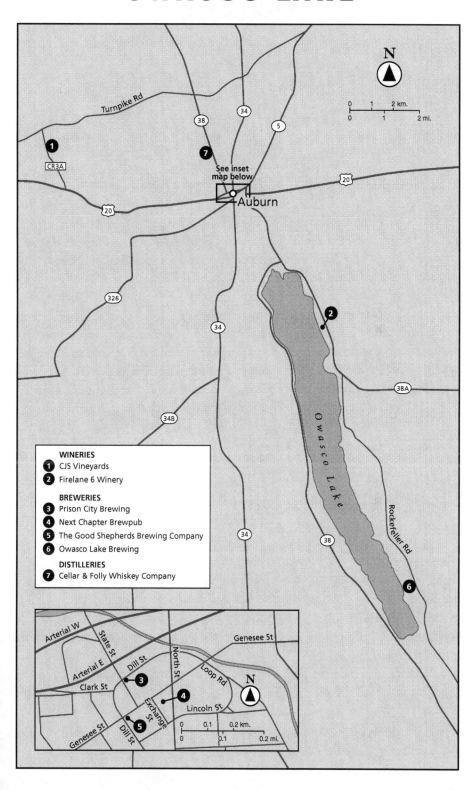

Turnpike Rd

CR3A

See inset map below

Auburn

Owasco Lake

Rockefeller Rd

WINERIES
1. CJS Vineyards
2. Firelane 6 Winery

BREWERIES
3. Prison City Brewing
4. Next Chapter Brewpub
5. The Good Shepherds Brewing Company
6. Owasco Lake Brewing

DISTILLERIES
7. Cellar & Folly Whiskey Company

Arterial W
State St
Arterial E
Dill St
North St
Loop Rd
Genesee St
Clark St
Exchange St
Lincoln St
Genesee St
Dill St

WINERIES

CJS VINEYARDS
6900 Fosterville Road
Auburn, NY 13022
www.cjsvineyards.com

The town that early settlers named after the Roman emperor Marcus Aurelius once included most of the northern half of present-day Cayuga County. The city of Auburn was established in 1805 from a portion of Aurelius. A short drive northwest of Auburn takes you to farm country, where in 1995 former steel-manufacturing engineer Chris Scholomiti began modest plantings of Riesling, Cayuga White, and Chambourcin grapevines on a property where nothing but brush had ever grown. He worked with Dave DeMarco at Seneca Shore Wine Cellars (see page 69) to see how another winemaker practiced his craft, before producing his own first vintage in 2001.

A range of CJS wines are handcrafted from the one-acre vineyard on Fosterville Road, with additional fruit sourced from family vineyards at Firelane 6 Winery (see below). Chris is a man committed to getting the most out of his estate's potential, and his greatest success has come with Chambourcin, a purple-skinned, French-American hybrid variety. Aged in Hungarian oak barrels for two years, his robust beauties deserve your full attention.

FIRELANE 6 WINERY
2960 Route 38
Moravia, NY 12118
www.firelane6winery.com

The art of making wine here is a truly personal pursuit. Corinne and Rick Ryan make their home on the two-and-a-half-acre vineyard; know each row intimately, vine by vine; understand the soils and high-risk microclimate; and hand-prune, hand-pick, then hand-sort the grapes, using surviving fruit to produce about one hundred or so cases of wine each year. This is the definition of a small-scale, mom-and-pop winery.

The couple began planting grapes in 2006 and during the first years sold harvested fruit to Rick's sister and brother-in-law Jan and Chris Scholomiti, owners of CJS Vineyards (see page 176) in Auburn. In 2020, with helpful guidance from Chris, they began handcrafting wines and officially opened Firelane 6 Winery, named for fire and rescue service access to their address.

Estate-grown Pinot Noir becomes a semidry rosé, and Rieslings are produced in two different styles. The sweet, foxy flavors of native Concord are tamed with black cherry and plum notes from French-American hybrid Chambourcin in a wine called Berry Blitz, the most popular among the winery's offerings.

Without a public tasting room, you'll need to search for Firelane 6 wines at wine shops or at one of their off-site tasting events around the region.

BREWERIES

PRISON CITY BREWING
28 State Street
Auburn, NY 13021
www.prisoncitybrewing.com

One of the oldest institutions in the city, Auburn Prison was constructed in 1816, the site of the first execution by electric chair in 1890. The prison put Auburn on the map, and in 2014, Prison City Brewing put Auburn on the craft-beer map. In a downtown building that once served as a Civil War–era armory, it was reconfigured by Marc and Dawn Shultz, and crowds are now knocking down pints.

At the helm of a five-barrel brewhouse during his first year, head brewer Ben Maeso developed a hazy, New England–style IPA named Mass Riot, flavored with Simcoe, Citra, and Mosaic hops, a beer that shook up the beverage world. In 2016, during a blind taste test of 247 IPAs, a panel of judges from *Paste* magazine selected Mass Riot as the best IPA in America. Mass Riot also captured a gold medal in the New England IPA category at the 2019 TAP New York Craft Beer and Food Festival. Before long, beer geeks got into the habit of getting in line for each batch of Mass Riot. Without the ability to keep up with demand, the brewery expanded its operations in 2020 to a nearby outpost (251 North Street) with a twenty-barrel brewhouse and a second taproom.

Brewing with a sense of adventure, Maeso creates a broad range of styles and inspirations. The success of Mass Riot has spawned a Riot series, each with a different mix of hops, including Quiet Riot, a low-ABV session beer, and Riot in Vermont, fermented with Vermont ale yeast.

The kitchen goes beyond the predictable bar-food options. Fried chicken comes with mashed potatoes and gravy; fish and chips, with French fries; and blackened tuna, with fingerlings, to name a few, but it's the beers that make Prison City one of the region's favorite places to quench a thirst.

NEXT CHAPTER BREWPUB

100 Genesee Street (at Exchange Street)
Auburn, NY 13021
www.nextchapterbrewpub.com

In 2018, Scott DeLap, an IT specialist for drinks giant Pernod Ricard, and Michelle Quinn DeLap, an interior designer, embarked on the next chapter in their professional lives, taking a leap from home brewing to commercial brewing. Inside a storefront across from the Auburn Public Theater, the couple has created a homey lounge area appointed with shelves of books and family photos, more like someone inviting you into their living room. Browse for something to read, sink into one of the well-placed comfy chesterfields near the fireplace, and settle in for one of Scott's craft brews.

Beer-wise, the emphasis is on sessionability—you know, sinking a few pints in one sitting. Don't leave without sampling Chapter Cosmic Too, a New England–style IPA crafted with regional barley, wheat, and oats. Juicy, fruit-forward beers include Watermelon Wheat, Blueberry Ale, and Blood Orange Blonde. Keep an eye out for Pumpkin Ale in the fall.

The pub menu includes wood-fired pizzas and plates of char-grilled chicken wings.

THE GOOD SHEPHERDS BREWING COMPANY

132 Genesee Street
Auburn, NY 13021
www.shepsbrewing.com

Garrett Shepherd honed his craft through the trials and tribulations of home brewing, apprenticed at CB Craft Brewers in Honeoye Falls, and built an arsenal of UK-inspired recipes for his fledgling, single-barrel nanobrewery in the old Nolan's Shoe Store. Good Shepherds was the first brewery in Auburn since Prohibition. The small scale affords Garrett an unusual degree of freedom to experiment with a range of personally crafted beers. His secret? He listens to Howard Stern when he brews, perhaps why he breaks some of the traditional rules. When he decided he needed a bigger space, Garrett purchased what locals call the "PB&J building," and the venture transitioned from nanobrewery to microbrewery.

Good Shepherds' lineup ranges from sessionable Hurricane Hailey Blonde Ale, perfect for sipping a few pints in one sitting, to Big Bang IPA, a beer that delivers the goods. But the beer that properly sums up the brewery is award-winning Shep's Flashpoint, a traditional wee-heavy Scotch ale, a malty and roasty classic and excellent winter sipper that'll warm your bones.

Sip five-ounce tastings, eight-ounce glasses, or sixteeen-ounce pints.

OWASCO LAKE BREWING
3241 Rockefeller Road
Moravia, NY 13118
www.owascolakebrewing.com

He was founder of the Standard Oil Company, a business magnate considered the wealthiest American of all time. John D. Rockefeller spent a share of his boyhood in a modest home just north of Moravia, and the road heading north along Owasco Lake bears his name. To some, the village of Moravia may seem like a long way to go for a beer. The good news is Owasco Lake Brewing has a style or flavor combination for just about everyone, and yes, it's well worth the drive.

The venture had its beginnings with the home-brew experiments of a local young man named Dillon Langtry. Inspired by WeldWorks Brewing in Greenly, Colorado, as well as homegrown successes, he worked his way up from intern to head brewer at Good Nature Brewing in Hamilton. In a refurbished 1800s-era barn on the Langtry family farm, just off Rockefeller Road, Dillon launched OLB in 2019. His two-barrel farmhouse enterprise captures a small-town America that we thought existed once upon a time, even though we were pretty sure it was long gone.

The look here is rustic, welcoming, and befitting Moravia's blue-collar history. One of the brews is called Work, something Dillon calls his "meat and potatoes" beer. With a positive reception from locals and a steady demand, the low-ABV, easy-sipping lager provides a working man's bridge from Budweisers to IPAs. And speaking of IPAs, Dillon's flagship is a dry-hopped New England–style double IPA called Lake Monster, its name inspired by the legendary serpentlike creature first spotted in Owasco Lake in 1889.

DISTILLERIES

CELLAR & FOLLY WHISKEY COMPANY
124 York Street
Auburn, NY 13021
www.cellarandfollywhiskey.com

In 1867, Auburn's favorite son, William H. Seward, US Secretary of State, negotiated the purchase of Alaska from Russia for $7 million. Despite the bargain price of roughly two cents an acre, the purchase was ridiculed in Congress and in the press as "Seward's Folly." That story and its local connection inspired the name of this 2022 start-up by drinking buddies Nick Streeter, Caleb Liber, and Colin Chilbert, who began experimenting with whiskeys in, you guessed it, Nick's cellar. The enterprise is a blendery rather than a true distillery, producing whiskeys by aging, flavoring, and proofing down corn distillate sourced from Black Button Distilling in Rochester.

The trio's signature spirit, Chai Fusion Corn Whiskey, is a bourbon-style whiskey gently flavored with cardamom, allspice, cinnamon, cloves, and ginger. Besides house-made whiskeys, the tasting room offers gins, vodkas, and other spirits from regional distilleries, served neat or in cocktails. Open weekends or by appointment.

SKANEATELES LAKE

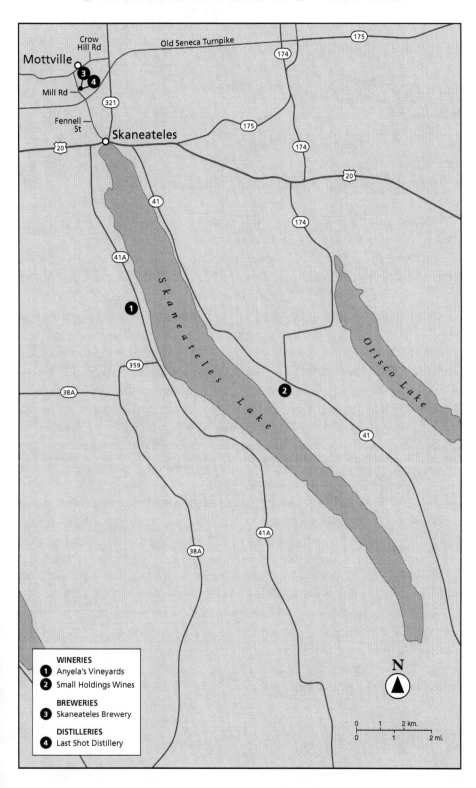

WINERIES
1 Anyela's Vineyards
2 Small Holdings Wines

BREWERIES
3 Skaneateles Brewery

DISTILLERIES
4 Last Shot Distillery

WINERIES

ANYELA'S VINEYARDS
2433 West Lake Road
Skaneateles, NY 13152
www.anyelasvineyards.com

William H. Seward, who served as Abraham Lincoln's secretary of state, once referred to Skaneateles Lake as the "most beautiful body of water in the world." A five-minute drive along the pristine lake's western shore leads to an impressive setting, one that reflects the moneyed reputation of Skaneateles and one that provides an opportunity to taste a creative range of wines.

The story of Anyela's began three generations ago in Eastern Europe and continues today on a hillside high above the lake. Owner/winemaker Jim Nocek, a nutritional physiology PhD by background, bought the land in 1996, planted his first vines on the one-hundred-acre plot in 2002, and named the venture in honor of his maternal grandmother who immigrated to the United States from Poland in 1918. The vineyard has an elevation of 1,100 feet and lacks the moderating effect that benefits vineyards along neighboring lakes, so after the winery's fall harvest, vines are removed from trellises and buried under mounds of soil to insulate the sensitive primary buds over the winter months.

The subtle art of building wines through blending calls on experience, memory, and the winemaker's taste buds. Jim enjoys the challenge that comes with seeking just the right composite of varieties and creating wines that reach the height of complexity and interest, much like an artist painting with many colors. The portfolio's strength is his proprietary blends, in which the winemaker adjusts proportions of contributing varietals to capture the true expression of each year's harvest. Best examples are Overlay, a Bordeaux-inspired blend of Cabernet Franc, Cabernet Sauvignon, Pinot Noir, and Shiraz, the winery's signature red blend, and Avail, an artful union of Riesling, Chardonnay, Cayuga White, and Pinot Gris. Deep-red, winter-hardy Noiret (pronounced *nwahr-AY*), made from productive hybrid grapes developed by the New York State Agricultural Experiment Station in 2006, is an excellent fit here, gracefully aged about one to two (and sometimes more) years to soften and fully develop flavor and character.

Once you're done swilling, drive back to the village and wander the village restaurants, shops, and art galleries.

ARTISANS AND CURATORS/SMALL HOLDINGS WINES

2508 Nunnery Road
Skaneateles, NY 13152
www.aplusc.com

Located on a bluff above Skaneateles Lake's eastern shore, Lot 10 Vineyard is one of the most northern and highest-elevation vineyards in all of the Finger Lakes. The parcel was originally the military tract awarded to Colonel Nicholas Fish for his service in America's Revolutionary War. This boutique enterprise is the brainchild of Christopher Bodell, a finance professional, and Alicia Tsai, founder of home fragrance brand Aerangis, with Lot 10 combining both homestead and boutique vineyard. In 2015, just more than seven acres of the eighteen-and-a-half-acre property were planted with Riesling, Pinot Noir, Cabernet Franc, and Grüner Veltliner on a site that has proved to benefit from ideal soil, slope, proximity to the lake, north-south row orientation, and latitude.

Part of the estate fruit is selected to produce limited quantities of wines under the Small Holdings label (a British term for a small farm that produces primarily for self-subsistence), with bottles offered for purchase online and at a few local shops and restaurants in and around Skaneateles. Remaining fruit is sold to other Finger Lakes wineries, earning coveted single-vineyard designation.

BREWERIES

SKANEATELES BREWERY
4022 Mill Road
Skaneateles, NY 13152
www.skanbrewery.com

In 2018, Christopher Fann arrived in this storybook village from an influential stint at Stable Craft Brewing in Waynesboro, Virginia, where he was named one of the best brewmasters in the state. Chris joined forces with consultant Mary Wiles, former brewer at Brooklyn Brewery, to launch Skaneateles Brewery in 2020.

There's an exceptionally good reason to make the trip a few miles outside the village proper. Housed in the same historic building as Last Shot Distillery (see page 187), you'll find a fine variety of beers produced in the seven-barrel brewhouse, with a dozen or more on tap for tastings. It's the perfect spot for an afternoon of sipping.

Chris has mastered beers with a settle-in-for-the-day, drinkable, and approachable style. Best examples are Lazy Day IPA and Skanny Dipper Blonde, both moderate-alcohol formulas, the kind of beers you can sip all day long. All his beers are crowd pleasers, but the flavored, barrel-aged stouts will make you swoon. Offered on a rotating basis, they're crafted with raspberries, chocolate, coffee, or whatever inspires the brewmaster.

DISTILLERIES

LAST SHOT DISTILLERY
4022 Mill Road
Skaneateles, NY 13152
www.lastshotdistillery.com

Skaneateles was home to several distilleries in the 1800s, most notably the one owned by Robert Earll, Jonas Earll, and Dorastus Kellogg near Skaneateles Creek. First producing spirits in 1840, the distillery was forced to close in 1864 under pressure from the local chapter of the Women's Christian Temperance Union. The shuttered building later housed a series of business ventures, including a grist mill and a paper mill. Then, in 2015, that very same building, shared with Skaneateles Brewery (see page 186), returned to its original purpose when Chris Uyehara and partner John Menapace opened the doors to the Last Shot Distillery.

After a thirty-seven-year career as a culinary professional, Chris brings the same work ethic and passion that fueled his fire in the kitchen to the chemistry of distilling spirits. He recognizes a parallel between his Japanese heritage and the distiller's craft. His father, also a chef, taught him that "quality is the first ingredient," and following the culture of his ancestors, he is an artisan always in pursuit of perfection.

As good as his gins, vodkas, and bourbons taste straight, they downright sing in cocktails. Visitors have the opportunity to sip an old-fashioned, gin and tonic, Moscow mule, or bloody Mary, with his spirits providing complexity and depth to these standards.

Japanese whiskey is influenced by the type of wood used to build the barrels in which it matures and by the quality and purity of the water used in distillation. It's with the Last Shot Japanese-style whiskey that Chris best expresses his craft. Distilled from malted corn; barley; red wheat; and triticale, a hybrid of wheat and rye, the Four Grain Whiskey is cut to proof with pure Skaneateles Lake water, then aged in charred, virgin American oak barrels. It was awarded first place in the *Master Distillers* TV series, while Chris was named master distiller.

BEST OF THE REST

WINERIES

CASA LARGA VINEYARDS AND WINERY
2287 Turk Hill Road
Fairport, NY 14450
www.casalarga.com

Andrew Colaruotolo grew up tending vineyards with his grandparents in Gaeta, Italy. After World War II, the seventeen-year-old immigrated to Rochester, New York, and started a home-building company. In 1974, he planted two acres of grapes on a hilltop between Canandaigua Lake and Lake Ontario, a site with moderate temperatures and a lengthened growing season, the beginning of a destination winery called Casa Larga. Now in the hands of Andrew's children, the estate includes forty-five acres of grapes, a wine shop, a tasting room, and banquet facilities, hosting tours and festivals.

Vibrant grapevines, arrayed in perfectly manicured rows beneath the tasting room campanile, regularly yield award-winning wines, including a blend of Cabernet Sauvignon, De Chaunac, and Cabernet Franc called Tramonto. The style, first created by the Colaruotolo patriarch in 1986, is a full-bodied, masculine wine with obvious Italian roots that represents the heritage of Casa Larga.

An ice wine produced from part of a dozen acres of Vidal grapes on the estate, Fiore Delle Stelle, is the jewel in the winery's crown. Dependably cold winters combined with the constant airflow from Lake Ontario means this wine can be made here nearly every year.

MURANDA WINE CELLARS
3075 Route 96
Waterloo, NY 13165
www.murandacheese.com

"We don't have the lakes," explains Tom Murray, "but we have the cows." Once the home of Schaffer Dairies, Tom and Nancy Murray purchased the 150-acre Waterloo dairy farm in 1991. The Murray family produces milk from a herd of ninety Holstein-Friesian cows, a breed whose high-fat, low-protein milk is well suited to Blane Murray, cheesemaker. The farm's mammoth hay barn, built in 1896, provides an atmospheric setting for tasting among seventeen varieties of cow's milk pasteurized cheeses, including flagship Red Buddy, a Swiss and cheddar blend, and Lady of the Lake, a gouda and parmesan cross.

To complement the offerings, the Murrays contract with Glenora Wine Cellars (see page 79) to produce Chardonnay, Niagara, dry Riesling, and Cabernet Franc wines under the Muranda Wine Cellars label. For beer drinkers, the brewery at Three Brothers Wineries & Estates (see page 99) crafts Moo-Randa, a lemonade Kölsch-style ale. Both wine and beer are available exclusively at the Muranda family farm.

HIGHLAND CELLARS
1556 Altay Road
Rock Stream, NY 14878
www.highlandcellarsflx.com

Born and raised in Seneca Lake wine country, Peter Oughterson earned a degree in agricultural engineering from Cornell University. After a stint at Hermann J. Wiemer Vineyard (see page 75) as vineyard manager and winemaker, in 2001 he set out on his own to establish Highland Cellars, its name suggested by Peter's Scottish ancestry.

Wines include dry Riesling, Cayuga White, and Syrah as varietals. Highland Glen is a Bordeaux-style blend of Syrah, Cabernet Sauvignon, and Merlot aged in French oak for two years before release. Rieslings, in a range of sweetness levels, are offered under the Finger Lakes Wine Company label.

Peter also provides a mobile service for fellow wineries in the region. Using equipment set up in the back of a tractor trailer, he bottles and labels wines and tops them off with corks or screw caps.

CHATEAU DUSSEAU WINERY & VINEYARD

5292 Erron Hill Road
Locke, NY 13092
www.chateaudusseau.com

Off the beaten path pretty much explains Chateau Dusseau. Drive a long and winding road all the way up Erron Hill, high above rural Cayuga County, and you'll find three acres of grapevines and the modest tasting room of a boutique-sized winery, cofounded by brothers Robert and Stephen Dusseau, local farmers and hobbyist winemakers.

That motorcycle parked outside belongs to Levi Dusseau of the second generation, who grew up surrounded by vines, tanks, and wine barrels. He is your gracious host for a tasting of limited-production, estate-grown Aurore and Frontenac, both cold-weather-hearty hybrids. These have proven to be the most productive of the grapes planted and have found a long-term home at Chateau Dusseau. Levi is a consummate storyteller, and he loves to talk about family history on the hill, an earlier enterprise as maple syrup makers. When he's not fiddling with bottles in the cellar or kicking up dust in the vineyard, he's on guitar with his band, Levi and the Wranglers.

The Dusseaus purchase Chancellor and Cabernet Franc grapes from nearby growers, supplementing Frontenac to produce Red Jack, a proprietary blend with all the dusty tannins of a rustic Italian table wine.

SONG HILL WINERY

521 County Road 9
Victor, NY 14564
www.songhillwinery.com

Song Hill Farm was formerly the home of Song Hill Thoroughbreds and the H. James Bond Racing Stable. In 2009, Conor Gallagher began converting pasture into vineyard and by 2013, as Song Hill Winery, brought in his first harvest. Gallagher received his certificate in winemaking from UC Davis. He first started working in the industry at Wild Blossom Meadery & Winery in Chicago. In 2011, he and his family moved to the Finger Lakes, where he worked as an assistant winemaker and vineyard assistant at Heart & Hands Wine Company (see page 164), before he and his wife established Song Hill Winery.

Estate wines are Diamond and Isabella for Petite Rouge. Gallagher sources Chardonnay grapes from Macri Vineyard on Canandaigua Lake for his French oak–fermented Chardonnay.

EMINENCE ROAD FARM WINERY
3734 Eminence Road
Long Eddy, NY 12760
www.eminenceroad.com

The winery began in 2008 as the passion project of a wine-loving couple. Housed in a converted cow barn in the Delaware County hamlet of Long Eddy, Andrew Scott and Jennifer Clark source sustainably grown fruit from Seneca and Keuka Lakes. Grapes are crushed by foot; fermented with native yeast; and bottled by hand, unfined and unfiltered, with the only addition being a minimal amount of sulfur for stability.

Varieties include Riesling, Chardonnay, Gewürztraminer, Pinot Noir, and Cabernet Franc. Production averages around one thousand cases a year.

ELEMENT WINERY
9790 Oak Hill Road
Arkport, NY 14807
www.elementwinery.com

In 2012, Christopher Bates was named best young sommelier in the world after winning best young sommelier in America in the same year. After passing his master sommelier exam a year later, he became only the 199th person in the world to do so and the first ever to achieve the accomplishment as an executive chef. Among his many irons in the fire, Element is Christopher's small-scale wine project, an opportunity to experiment with terroir effect, minimal intervention, and sustainable methods.

Varietals include Riesling and Chardonnay, but what's really interesting is Can't Stop/Won't Stop, a blend of Cabernet Sauvignon, Cabernet Franc, Merlot, Pinot Noir, and Syrah. A second label, Colloquial, represents estate wines from the Bates vineyard on the west side of Seneca Lake.

Off-site tasting rooms are located at F.L.X. Provisions on 16 Linden Street in Geneva and at 2-4 East Market Street in Corning.

CHATEAU RENAISSANCE WINE CELLARS

7494 Fish Hatchery Road
Bath, NY 14810
www.chateaurenaissancewinecellars.com

Patrice DeMay's roots run deep. He was raised in a family of winemakers in the Loire Valley region of France, and his passion for wine was stoked in his youth. The philosophy here is that wine is liquid art. His portfolio at Chateau Renaissance includes a handful of vinifera varietals, creative blends, and fruit wines, but visitors are drawn here to taste the sparkling wines.

When he's not crafting these small-batch, personal wines, Patrice can be found in a classroom at SUNY Corning, teaching viticulture to aspiring winemakers.

WILD BRUTE WINERY

8629 Oak Hill Road
Arkport, NY 14807
www.wildbrutewinery.com

After earning a degree in viticulture and enology at Cornell, Justin Recktenwald acquired hands-on experience at Dr. Konstantin Frank Winery (see page 32). Wild Brute, established in 2013, refers to Justin's wild-fermented wines using native yeasts found on the fruit and in the vineyard, and his wines are nurtured to the bottle, unfiltered and unfined. Justin and his wife, Kyleigh, opened the Brute Wine Bar at 99 Main Street in Hornell, pairing Wild Brute wines with locally grown, raised, and foraged foods.

20 DEEP WINERY

187 Mendon Ionia Road
Mendon, NY 14472
www.20deep.com

The roots of tenacious, old-growth grapevines can extend down into the earth to a depth of twenty feet. On a country road, just outside the town of Mendon, the most affluent suburb of Rochester, Michaela and David Gascon, along with Matt Cassavaugh, established 20 Deep Winery. From just more than five acres planted on their eighteen-acre property, Matt, former head winemaker at Casa Larga Vineyards (see page 189), crafts Chardonnay, Riesling, Gamay Noir, Pinot Noir, and Grüner Veltliner from estate-grown grapes.

The tasting room is at one with wine production, a space the owners describe as a "winery with brewery vibes."

WAGGONER LOCAL FARE

1034 Coddington Road
Ithaca, NY 14850
www.waggonerlocalfare.com

The Waggoner family has made the Finger Lakes region home ever since Englehardt Waggoner arrived from Germany in 1750. Several generations later, Alan Wagner arrived in Ithaca as a business student at Ithaca College. After a brief postgraduation stint in New Jersey, he and his wife moved back to Ithaca and raised a family, while Alan dabbled in multiple business ventures. In his most recent endeavor, Waggoner Local Fare, Alan has become a gentleman wine grower, tending fifty vines of Marquette grapes at his home property, sourcing other varieties from Randall-Standish Vineyards in Canandaigua, and producing small-batch wines.

VAGABOND WINE CELLARS

www.vagabondwinecellars.com

A harvest intern at Bloomer Creek Vineyard (see page 114) was Alexandra Bond's first rung on the winemaker ladder. She worked in both cellar and vineyard at Thirsty Owl Wine Company (see page 139), before dual assistant winemaking positions at Hector Wine Company (see page 111) and Forge Cellars (see page 115). She brought those earned skills to Damiani Wine Cellars (see page 118) in 2021, where she is currently assistant to head winemaker Katey Larwood.

As a side project in 2022, Alexandra purchased a small lot of Marechal Foch grapes and produced the first vintage of wines under her own start-up Vagabond label. In addition to varietal Foch, she used the leftover skins, fermenting what was left of the sugars, to make a piquette. (The centuries-old method is traditionally enjoyed by vineyard workers and family members.) The next year, she turned out beautiful examples of Riesling, Blaufränkisch, and a bit of Merlot, as she continues to develop her own brand.

Alexandra's wines are available for purchase online. Check the website.

MARK T. WILTBERGER CELLARS
www.marktwiltbergercellars.com

Simply said, Mark Wiltberger grew up at Keuka Spring Vineyards (see page 46), helping his family clear the land, planting the vines, and learning to make wines from his father. He went on to work at wineries in the Rheinhessen region of Germany, as well as New Zealand. In 2014, he returned to the Finger Lakes, purchased property near the former family estate on Keuka Lake, and began making his own wines.

Mark's small-batch beauties include two medium-dry Rieslings, Grüner Veltliner, and Chardonnay, available for purchase exclusively online.

ONYARE
www.onyarewine.com

In 2006, Minnesota native Katie Cook traveled to Quintessa Winery in Napa Valley to help with the harvest. She was accepted to the University of Burgundy the following June, and by 2009, she completed a master's-level program in enology. Thijs Verschuuren was born in the Netherlands, moved to France when he was six, and was raised in the Loire Valley. There, after working a harvest at Domaine Michel Bertin, he enrolled at Campus Briace, earning a "Brevet Technical Superieur" degree in viticulture and enology. He then worked at wineries in Loire Valley, Bordeaux, and Alsace. Katie and Thijs crossed paths in Alsace, and in 2014, they arrived together in the Finger Lakes to take jobs at Hermann J. Wiemer Vineyard (see page 75). Katie became assistant winemaker; Thijs, the vineyard manager.

In 2015, they produced two small batches of Riesling under their own Onyare label. The first released, Riesling Beautiful Little Fool (in *The Great Gatsby*, Daisy describes her hopes for her infant daughter: "I hope she'll be a fool—that's the best thing a girl can be in this world, a beautiful little fool."), is crafted in a full-bodied style. Riesling Nostalgie is an austere, Muscadet-style wine. The wines are available for purchase exclusively online.

BREWERIES

FALL STREET BREWING CO.
95-97 Fall Street
Seneca Falls, NY 13148
www.fallstreetbrewing.com

Just down the street from the *It's a Wonderful Life* Museum, Brad and Anna Luisi-Ellis have created a micro–beer brewery, small-batch kombucha brewery, and community gathering place. Yes, Seneca Falls was the inspiration for Bedford Falls in the film classic, and George Bailey would feel right at home in this small-town café that serves soups, salads, sandwiches, and wood-fired pizzas.

Operating a modest two-barrel system, Brad has perfected recipes for the dozen or so offerings on tap, most notably Declared Sentiments, a hop-forward New England–style IPA.

FLEUR DE LIS BREW WORKS
3630 Route 414
Seneca Falls, NY 13148
www.fleurdelisbrewworks.com

This venture combines the passion of two couples, Jon Paul and Craig Partee and their wives, Beth and Jennifer. On a patrician estate that has been in the Partee family for three generations, visitors now quench their thirst on an assortment of beer styles with a nod to their French ancestry. Head brewer Jon Paul employs a seven-barrel brewing system, on full display in the beer parlor, a handsome tasting room with copper bar, historic barn boards, and Edison light fixtures. He has access to fourteen varieties of hops grown on two acres of the estate.

The brewery's flagships include Irish Red Ale, brewed using kilned malts and roasted barley to give the beer its red color, and Milkshake IPAs made with lactose, a sugar derived from milk. Other eclectic offerings range from refreshing, low-alcohol, French-inspired farmhouse ales to strong and boozy stouts, including Lost Bikini, brewed with chocolate and tropical coconut.

The setting resembles an enchanted garden. Stroll the manicured grounds and sip a favorite brew by the water fountain. Fleur De Lis is a road-trip-worthy, must-visit destination for the beer tourist.

SUMMERHILL BREWING
14408 Route 90
Summer Hill, NY 13092
www.summerhillbrewing.com

A visit to this nanobrewery is a lesson in local history and culture. With a skilled background in environmental chemistry and stints at Corning and Cornell's Synchotron Project, Kurt McDonald serves as head brewer in this family enterprise, established in 2016. Working in a seven-barrel brewhouse, he crafts Millard's American Ale as homage to Millard Fillmore, the thirteenth president of the United States and a native of scenic Summer Hill.

The town is known for its nudist camp, so Kurt's German Altbier-style beer is named Naked Neighbor Amber, and hop-heavy Paper Money IPA was provided inspiration by Summerhill's own Elbridge Spaulding, who created our national paper currency. If you can't decide between a light and dark beer, Farmer's Tan combines half Millard's American Ale and half Iron Plow Porter. (Yes, a local fellow named Jethro Wood invented the iron plow.)

Megan McDonald rules the kitchen, baking beer-friendly pizzas, including the Hillbilly Philly Cheesesteak Pizza and, at Sunday brunch, a Bacon, Egg, and Cheese Breakfast Pizza. Drawing from culinary inspiration, Megan was instrumental in selecting the proper recipe of Anaheim, serrano, and jalapeño peppers for just the right heat in Arriba Chili Pepper Ale.

Sip beers in nine-, twelve-, or sixteen-ounce goblets, and take home your favorite in a growler.

HOMER HOPS BREWING
700 Route 90
Homer, NY 13077
www.homerhops.com

Their original plan included growing hops for regional breweries, but Jason Kristoff and Shawn Potts were too ambitious to stop there. In 2018, enlisting the help of family and friends, the two pals launched Homer Hops Brewing, a community-friendly gathering place just outside the village named for the ancient Greek poet.

Homer Hops is the kind of spot where you could easily lose a couple of hours. On good-weather days, you might decide to spend some of that time on the patio overlooking a couple of rows of hop trellises on the fifteen-acre property, feasting from one of the rotating food trucks and sipping tasting flights from the rotating beers on tap.

The brewery might still be relatively young, but the partners don't seem interested in playing it safe with beers. Crafted in the five-brewhouse, you'll have fifteen choices, from pale ales to cream ales, pilsners, fruited sours, robust porters, and bold IPAs, more categories than drinkers know what to do with. Exit 12 Pale Ale might be considered the flagship, but the crowd favorite is Mother's Day, a New England–style IPA, named for the partners' first homebrew.

A few local wines and a couple of hard ciders are available, a little something for those who don't drink beer.

LIQUID SHOES BREWING
26 East Market Street
Corning, NY 14830
www.liquidshoesbrewing.com

Brothers David and Eric Shoemaker fill the shoes behind this microbrewery on Market Street in the historic Gaffer District of Corning. The pair are focused on a half-dozen or so of mostly hop-forward beers, including Kung Fu Bicycle, a hazy IPA made with Australian Galaxy and New Zealand Rakau hops. Sky's Out, Thighs Out is an easy-drinking, visually appealing blonde ale with no dominating malt or hop characteristics.

HORSEHEADS BREWING
250 Old Ithaca Road
Horseheads, NY 14845
www.horseheadsbrewing.com

After marching 450 miles in a massive campaign to destroy villages of the native Iroquois tribes who had taken up arms against the American revolutionaries, forces of General John Sullivan were obliged to dispose of a large number of sick and disabled horses. The natives collected the skulls and arranged them along a trail that became known as the Valley of the Horses' Heads. Opened in 2007 by Ed and Brenda Samchisen just outside the village of Horseheads, the brewery was acquired by Brian and Kevin Lilly, who maintain original recipes for quenching local thirsts, including Chemung Canal Towpath Ale (a cream ale) and Horseheads Hefeweizen.

CORTLAND BEER COMPANY
16 Court Street
Cortland, NY 13045
www.cortlandbeer.com

Known as the Crown City because of its location on a plain formed by the convergence of seven valleys, Cortland is home to the downtown Cortland Beer Company, opened in 2010 by three partners, including Tom Scheffler, a Cornell Aggie, who managed the twenty-barrel brewhouse, supplied kegs to many of the local bars and restaurants, and showcased a wide variety of beers in its own storefront taproom. In 2019, the brewery was acquired by John Saraceno, who maintains the original flagship brews. Industrial IPA and Firehouse Pale Ale (its name inspired by the 1914 firehouse across the street from the brewery) follow the strong ale tradition, but the brewery's strength is most obvious in a rotating style of stouts, including Black Widow Stout and 7 Valley Stout.

IRON FLAMINGO BREWERY
196 Baker Street
Corning, NY 14830
www.ironflamingobrewery.com

Inspired by family beer-brewing tradition in Scranton, Pennsylvania, Mark and Nadia Mauer transformed the former Becraft Tire Company building into Corning's first brewery to bottle and distribute beer. Offerings here range from low-ABV Blonde Ale to boozy Hello Darkness, My Old Friend, an imperial stout. A satellite taproom called the Barrel House is located at 54 West Market Street in Corning's Gaffer District.

MARKET STREET BREWING CO. & RESTAURANT
63 West Market Street
Corning, NY 14830
www.936-beer.com

Settle in for dinner at Pelham and Theresa McClellan's beer-centered eatery, established in 1997. Located on Corning's quaint Market Street, the ambitious brewpub lures you in with an excellent core of five house-brewed beers, from the lighter Mad Bug Lager to the more robust English-style D'Artagnan Dark Ale, along with dishes like beer-braised bratwurst served with a side of honey-beer mustard. Weather permitting, alfresco sipping is available in the biergarten.

DUBLIN CORNERS FARM BREWERY

1906 Main Street (Route 36)
Linwood, NY 14486
www.dublincornersfarm.com

On a farmstead that's been in the family for more than a hundred years, Justin and Heather Grant launched Livingston County's first brewery in 2016, its name a nod to the early Irish immigrants who nicknamed the area Dublin Corners or Devil's Half Acre. And—no surprise—the brewery's IPA is called Devil's Half Acre. There's one exceptionally good reason to make the trip out to the farm. Better Red than Dead is an amber ale that ran away with a gold medal at the New York State Craft Brewers Association Beer Competition. The Grants operate a satellite taproom at 116 Main Street in Geneseo (see page 4).

UPSTATE BREWING COMPANY

3028 Lake Road
Elmira, NY 14903
www.upstatebrewing.com

Mark Neumann studied mechanical technology at SUNY Polytechnic Institute, worked on construction projects in Los Angeles, and in 2011 returned to the Southern Tier and opened Upstate Brewing. As for the beers, it seems as if a new one pops up every few days. Upstate is constantly experimenting and producing one-off brews and filling style gaps. Common Sense is top dog here, a dark cream style of beer once popular in and around Louisville, Kentucky, from the 1850s until Prohibition. A satellite taproom (see page 93) is located at 17 North Franklin Street in the village of Watkins Glen.

HOP NOTCH BREWING CO.

2471 Hayes Road
Montour Falls, NY 14685
www.hopnotchbrewingco.com

Jeff Klossner opened a microbrewery called Hop Notch in 2022, but you'll have to hunt for it—a few miles south of Watkins Glen and up the hill just outside the village of Montour Falls. Housed in a former dairy barn overlooking the village, brewer Taylor Trenchard is growing the fledgling venture from nanobrewery to microbrewery. Sip a fresh Irish-style red ale called Brewski's Red and walk upstairs to shoot a game of pool. Hop Notch is a relaxed, rustic meeting place for beer lovers.

RUNAWAY BLUE BREWING COMPANY
102 South Main Street
Newark, NY 14513
www.runawaybluebrewing.com

One of the first breweries in Wayne County and one of the smallest producers in the state, Runaway Blue was opened in 2022 by Newark native Brian Bremer, a former assistant brewer at Young Lion Brewing Company (see page 17), who operates a single-barrel system. Among the offerings, Brian's focus is on Bluest Sky IPA and Hi-Fi Double IPA. And if there is any doubt about Upstate football loyalties, his batch list includes the Process, a Buffalo Bills–themed light lager.

REINVENTION BREWING CO.
9 North Main Street
Manchester, NY 14504
www.reinventionbrewing.com

After a twenty-year career as a biomedical engineer and almost as many years making home brews, George Aldrich reinvented himself as a professional craft brewer with the opening of Reinvention Brewing Co. in 2017. Most notable is Aldrich's Misperception White Stout, conditioned atop cacao nibs and coffee roasted at CDGA Coffee Company in Canandaigua.

MORTALIS BREWING
5660 Tec Drive
Avon, NY 14414
www.mortalisbrewing.com

Brewing partners Paul Grenier and Dave Luckenbach are faithfully devoted to breaking from tradition in the pursuit of unexpected flavors. They have gained a cult following for "culinary beers," using food items in the brewing process—everything from red velvet cake to almond paste cookies. There's a Gummy Kids Sour, a Pineapple Coconut Lager, and an Apple Pie Fruit Beer. These are beers that drink like smoothies. Yes, there are more serious beers here, including Strange Philosophies (8 percent ABV) imperial IPA and Thesmophoros (10 percent ABV) imperial stout. Mortalis operates taprooms at 21 Richmond Street in Rochester and 1250 Niagara Street in Buffalo.

NOBLE SHEPHERD CRAFT BREWERY

7853 Route 20A
Bloomfield, NY 14469
www.nobleshepherdbrewery.com

On a drive through the village of Bloomfield, it's impossible to miss the distinctive geodesic dome structure with a giraffe popping through the roof (the sister dome of the Wizard of Clay pottery workshop). Since 2015, this has been the home of the Noble Shepherd Craft Brewery. Operating from a nanobrewhouse in the adjoining dome, former chef Tony Moringello employs a range of culinary ingredients to make his beers. Oatmeal Stout is conditioned on toasted coconut, Peach Tea Hefeweizen uses white peaches and Earl Grey tea, and Cucumber Riesling Saison is brewed with Riesling juice and fresh cucumbers. Each summer, a batch of Watermelon Wheat Ale is made with 160 pounds of fresh watermelon.

SILVER LAKE BREWING PROJECT

14 Borden Avenue
Perry, NY 14530
www.silverlakebrewingproject.com

While not technically one of the Finger Lakes, Silver Lake was also formed from retreating glaciers as they moved across the region several thousand years ago. Just off Main Street and alongside the Silver Lake Outlet, the brewery is housed in a building with many past lives: a movie house, a luncheonette, a horse stable, and a printing production house for the Perry Shopper. What's most interesting about Silver Lake Brewing Project, this community venture has thirty-seven shareholders and three managing partners, including head brewer Tony Jones, who cranks out a range of rustic farmhouse-style beers in a three-barrel brewhouse, including Bavarian-style Rye Ale and a textbook cream ale called the Standard.

TUB TOWN BREWING
26 West Steuben Street
Bath, NY 14810
www.tubtownbrewing.com

Charles Williamson, land agent for the Pulteney Land Syndicate, planned a settlement near Keuka Lake to be named in honor of Sir William Pulteney's daughter, the Countess of Bath, a city in Somerset, England. While the origin of the town's name has nothing to do with the bathtub, every year local folks in Bath celebrate by holding a bathtub race that winds through obstacles past an enthusiastic crowd on Liberty Street. And "getting wet" in town often includes a visit to Tub Town Brewing.

Established in 2020, the brewery's bread-and-butter beers are Blonde Bombshell, an approachable, easy-drinking ale, and Grape Sour, a fruited sour made with Concord grapes, both good choices for washing down a tavern pizza.

REBEL SAILOR BREWING COMPANY
1715 Route 21
Shortsville, NY 14548
www.rebelsailorbeer.com

The name was inspired by the seafaring Scandinavian raiders of Viking history, sometimes called "rebel sailors," and the interlocking horns, Norse drinking vessels, provide the brewery's logo and theme. Operating on a three-and-a-half-barrel system, Robert Payne's small batches include Kveik Red Ale, crafted with Norwegian yeast, which lends notes of citrus to his refreshing take on the traditional ale.

CRAFTY ALES & LAGERS
2 Exchange Street
Phelps, NY 14532
www.drinkcraftyales.com

The town of Phelps is known as the "Sauerkraut Capital of the World" because of its long history of cabbage growing and sauerkraut production. So it's not surprising that Mike Darling of Crafty Ales & Lagers once made a batch of Gose-style sour ale brewed with the brine of fermented cabbage. This nanobrewery, housed in the oldest building in Phelps, provides the community with a selection of small-batch, seasonal craft beers. Mike's original recipe is an oatmeal stout called Dark Star, and his Crafty Cream Ale, made with local honey and honey malt, floats like a butterfly but stings like a bee.

RISING STORM BREWING CO.
5750 South Lima Road
Avon, NY 14414
www.risingstormbrewing.com

In 2018, Bill Blake and Jeff Riedl, SUNY Geneseo grads, opened Rising Storm with a five-barrel brewhouse, producing New England–style IPAs, including Liquid Swords, the Monarch, Let Me Fly, and a double IPA called Hopp Deep. The bistro menu includes assorted beer nuts, chicken tenders, cheeseburgers, and pork belly sliders. Rising Storm's satellite taproom is housed in the Mill at 1880 Blossom Road in Rochester.

CIDERIES

GRISAMORE CIDER WORKS

4069 Goose Street
Locke, NY 13092
www.grisamorecidewrworks.com

In 1927, Maurice Grisamore quit his conductor's job with the New York Central Railroad, uprooted his family from Chicago, and settled on a newly purchased farm in this Cayuga County village. Over the years, picking strawberries, raspberries, blueberries, and sweet cherries at Grisamore Farms has become an annual summer tradition for many families in the region. In 1975, Paul and Christine Grisamore added apple trees to the farm, and in 2016, with fruit growing so firmly rooted in their heritage, grandsons Simon and Jesse Ingall had a plan to make hard ciders from the fruit on those trees. While waiting for commercial-license approvals, the brothers packed their bags and flew to the United Kingdom to apprentice at Cam Valley Orchards in Hertfordshire County, England, where the cider orchards produce more than half the cider consumed in the United Kingdom. They came home as cider makers.

The main floor of the Grisamore barn houses a farm store filled with farm-made and locally sourced products—fresh-picked fruit, apple doughnuts, jams, jellies, maple syrup, cheeses—you name it. But you're here for the ciders, so walk up the stairs to the tasting room. The flagship cider is called Alice, a blend of a half-dozen or more mostly bittersweet varieties. Named after their former pet cow, Alice was originally destined for the family's dinner table until the children started to play with her. The brothers couldn't resist putting her image on the Cider Works' labels. A cider called 24.4-Squared, the Alice cider blend, is aged on citra hops and named after the number of square miles in rural Locke. Fillmore, named after the thirteenth president of the United States, who grew up in a log cabin down the road in Moravia, is a semidry pear cider.

EVE'S CIDERY
308 Beckhorn Hollow Road
Van Etten, NY 14889
www.evescidery.com

Autumn Stoscheck has been called the "Robert Mondavi character in the Finger Lakes cider story." Among the forerunners of the American craft-cider revival, she is one of the movement's most influential players. While Mondavi put California wines on the map, Autumn's artisanal ciders have helped make the Finger Lakes the "Napa Valley of cider."

Each step in her journey encouraged the craft-cider prodigy and inspired what would become an influential enterprise. A summer job at Butterworks Dairy Farm in Westfield, Vermont, introduced her to Anne and Jack Lazor, pioneers in organic dairying. After a semester in the plant science classrooms at Cornell's Ag School, she decided to take a more direct route to her vocation, working at Littletree Orchards in Newfield during the day and waiting tables at a downtown Ithaca restaurant at night.

After reading his story, she drove to Poverty Lane Orchards in Lebanon, New Hampshire, to meet Steve Wood. He introduced her to one of the most diverse collections of apple trees in America and sent her home with grafting wood for propagating cider apples. He advised her to enroll in the small-scale cider-making program in Herefordshire County, England, where ciders have been part of the local culture since the Middle Ages.

In 2002, at the tender age of twenty-one, Autumn purchased equipment with her waitressing savings. And with quiet confidence and down-to-earth focus, she established Eve's Cidery, named for Pete Seeger's song "Letter to Eve," where she crafts naturally fermented ciders made from apples foraged in James Cummins's orchard. She sold her first bottles at the Ithaca Farmers Market and the Union Square Greenmarket in New York City.

Autumn grows fruit in Newfield on the Cummins farm and on the farm that once belonged to her grandmother. Production takes place in the property's converted 1950s-era dairy barn. Noteworthy is the single-orchard Albee Hill cider, a field blend that varies from year to year, an approach that provides a wonderful lens through which to display the best expression of the growing season.

DISTILLERIES

BARRINGTON DISTILLERS
5040 Bill Bailey Road
Dundee, NY 14837
Find on Facebook

During the years of Prohibition, there was a history of bootlegging in and around Keuka Lake. It's said that the lake's unusual shape made it easy for smugglers to avoid detection by law enforcement. Distilling is no stranger to the region. The Jayne family enterprise, established in 2016, is a hidden gem located in the middle of nowhere—so far out of the way, in fact, this place feels a little like a moonshiner's cabin.

Jesse Jayne oversees small-batch production of spirits in Barrington's two-hundred-gallon still for his signature Vampire Slayer, a mellow, unaged corn whiskey. It provides the base for a range of flavored products, including Apple Pie Moonshine, blended with apple cider from Wager's Cider Mill in Penn Yan. Among the cocktails offered at the tasting room is Bitten, a bloody Mary made with—what else—Vampire Slayer.

DRAGONFYRE DISTILLERY
1062 Leonard Road
Marathon, NY 13803
www.dragonfyredistillery.com

Nestled in the rolling hills of Cortland County just outside the village of Marathon, third-generation distiller Vince Pedini operates a twenty-five-gallon, home-built copper still to produce corn whiskey, straight bourbon, apple brandy, and backwoods-style moonshine. The fantasy-theme tasting room is decorated with suits of armor; pixies; fairies; and, of course, dragons.

FOUR FIGHTS DISTILLING
363 East Market Street Ext.
Corning, NY 14830
www.fourfightsdistilling.com

The antique and classic cars are gone from the old Stonebridge Motor garage, replaced by Corning's first legal distillery in more than one hundred years. Back in the days of moonshine and "stills in the hills," it was said that if you drank a pint of hooch, you were likely to get into a fight, and if it was really good, you might get into as many as four fights. In 2015, Matthew Bowers borrowed that old saw for the name of a craft distillery where he hand-makes small batches of spirits, including bourbon, vodka, gin, and a moonshine-style corn whiskey with corn locally sourced from nearby Smithome Farms in Big Flats.

The tasting room bar offers curated flights and cocktails, including the Corning mule, a local version of the Moscow mule made with Crystal City Vodka, Ithaca Ginger Beer, and lime juice.

SMOKIN' TAILS DISTILLERY
3 Church Street
Phelps, NY 14532
www.smokintails.com

The name pays homage to the moonshiners whose run from the cops would leave nothing but a "tail" of smoke. Peter Cheney, owner of the Cheney Funeral Home in Phelps, parlayed his award-winning appearance on the Discovery Channel TV show *Moonshiners: Master Distiller* into a distillery of his own. Opened in 2021, Smokin' Tails Distillery specializes in flavored moonshine-inspired spirits, including Coconut Moonshine and Dill Pickle Moonshine. The flagship whiskey, Sinister Cinnamon, is a corn-and-rye-based spirit aged in American oak, appropriately labeled as Undertaker.

BIRDSEYE HOLLOW FARM AND DISTILLERY

8398 County Road 96
Hammondsport, NY 14840
https://www.facebook.com/p/Birdseye-Hollow-Farm-and-Distillery
-100068832965793/

With our climate, soil, and forestry, New York is naturally perfect for maple-syrup production, and the state is home to the largest resource of tappable maple trees in the United States. Twelve hundred of those trees thrive on a seventy-five-acre working syrup farm that has grown into what Steve Ferris calls his "art project." After five years of sugaring, in early 2024 he began fermenting part of the maple-syrup production for artful Maple Rye, Maple Bourbon, and a rum-inspired craft spirit. The log cabin stillhouse and tasting room was built using the timber from the property, then using the scraps to fire the evaporator for boiling the sap. It's an atmospheric spot to sip spirits that capture the essence of the maple forest.

APPENDIX

Listings by Lake

CONESUS LAKE

WINERIES
Deer Run Winery

BREWERIES
Little Lake Brewing
No BS Brew Company
Dublin Corners Farm Brewery

CIDERIES
OSB (Original Stump Blower) Ciderworks

HEMLOCK LAKE

WINERIES
O-Neh-Da Vineyard/Eagle Crest Vineyards

HONEOYE LAKE

BREWERIES
Birdhouse Brewing Co.

CANANDAIGUA LAKE

WINERIES
Raymor Estate Cellars
Bristol Valley Vineyards
Arbor Hill Grapery & Winery
Hazlitt Red Cat Cellars
Inspire Moore Winery

BREWERIES
Peacemaker Brewing Company
Frequentem Brewing Company
Young Lion Brewing Company
Twisted Rail Brewing Company
Naked Dove Brewing Company
The Irish Mafia Brewing Company
Other Half FLX
Engine 14 Brewery
Naples Brewing Company

CIDERIES
Star Cider

DISTILLERIES
Hollerhorn Distilling

KEUKA LAKE (WEST)

WINERIES
Vineyard View Winery
Yates Cellars
Hunt Country Vineyards
Stever Hill Vineyards
Deep Root Vineyard
Point of the Bluff Vineyards
Azure Hill Winery

Dr. Konstantin Frank Winery
Divided Sky Vineyard
Heron Hill Winery
Keuka Lake Vineyards
Bully Hill Vineyards
Pleasant Valley Wine Company

BREWERIES
Abandon Brewing Co.
LyonSmith Brewing Company
Steuben Brewing Company
Keuka Brewing Co.
The Brewery of Broken Dreams

CIDERIES
Apple Barrel Orchards

DISTILLERIES
Antler Run Distilling
Krooked Tusker Distillery
Barrelhouse 6 Distillery

KEUKA LAKE (EAST)

WINERIES
Keuka Spring Vineyards
Rooster Hill Vineyards
Barrington Cellars/Buzzard Crest Vineyard
McGregor Vineyard
Ravines Wine Cellars
Weis Vineyards
Domaine LeSeurre Winery
Living Roots Wine & Co.

BREWERIES
Laurentide Beer Company
Finger Lakes Beer Company

CIDERIES
Sylvan Farm & Cidery

DISTILLERIES
Krookid Leyk Distilling

SENECA LAKE (WEST)

WINERIES
Trestle Thirty One
Ravines Wine Cellars
Belhurst Castle & Winery
White Springs Winery
Lacey Magruder Vineyard and Winery
Billsboro Winery
Scout Vineyards
Fox Run Vineyards
Red Tail Ridge Winery
New Vines Winery
Seneca Shore Wine Cellars
Kemmeter Wines
Anthony Road Wine Company
Prejean Winery
CK Cellars
Miles Wine Cellars
Shaw Vineyard
Hermann J. Wiemer Vineyard
Missick Cellars
Tabora Farm & Winery
Fruit Yard Winery
Hickory Hollow Wine Cellars
Glenora Wine Cellars
Fulkerson Winery & Farm
Rock Stream Vineyards
Apollo's Praise
Magnus Ridge Vineyard and Winery

Toast Winery
Barnstormer Winery
Lakewood Vineyards
Castel Grisch Winery

BREWERIES
Lake Drum Brewing
F.L.X. Culture House
Twisted Rail Brewing Company
WeBe Brewing Company
Brewery Ardennes
Big aLICe Brewing
Relative Risk Brewing Company
Seneca Stag Company at the Brew Barn
Climbing Bines Craft Ale Company
Tin Barn Brewing
Upstate Brewing Company FLX
Seneca Lodge Craft Brewing
Seneca Lake Brewing Company

CIDERIES
WortHog Cidery

DISTILLERIES
Spirits of Miles
O'Begley Distillery

SENECA LAKE (EAST)

WINERIES
Ventosa Vineyards
Three Brothers Wineries & Estates
Zugibe Vineyards
Boundary Breaks
Terra di Lavoro Vineyards & Winery
Idol Ridge Winery

Lamoreaux Landing Wine Cellars
Wagner Vineyards Estate Winery
Silver Thread Vineyard
Caywood Vineyards
Shalestone Vineyards
Bagley's Poplar Ridge Vineyards
Standing Stone Vineyards
Penguin Bay Winery
Flatt Rock Wine Cellars
Rasta Ranch Vineyards
Hazlitt 1852 Vineyards
Leidenfrost Vineyards
Hector Wine Company
Red Newt Cellars
Nine-Four Wines
Bloomer Creek Vineyard
Forge Cellars
Chateau LaFayette Reneau
Atwater Vineyards
J. R. Dill Winery
Damiani Wine Cellars
Silver Springs Winery
Catharine Valley Winery
Ryan William Vineyard
Hillick & Hobbs
Osmote

BREWERIES
Watershed Brewing Company
War Horse Brewing Company
Wagner Valley Brewing Co.
Lucky Hare Brewing Company
Scale House Brewery
Two Goats Brewing
Grist Iron Brewing Co.

CIDERIES
Bombshell Hard Cider

DISTILLERIES
Alder Creek Distillery
Finger Lakes Distilling Co.

CAYUGA LAKE (WEST)

WINERIES
Montezuma Winery
Swedish Hill Winery
Lakeshore Winery
Knapp Winery
Goose Watch Winery
Buttonwood Grove Winery
Six Eighty Cellars
Cayuga Ridge Estate Winery
Thirsty Owl Wine Company
Usonia
Hosmer Winery
Sheldrake Point Winery
Airy Acres Vineyard
Lucas Vineyards
Shepherdess Cellars
Americana Vineyards
Frontenac Point Vineyard & Estate Winery
Glenhaven Farm
Boland Thomas Vineyards
Bet the Farm Winery

BREWERIES
Lakehouse Brewery
Liquid State Brewing Company
Garrett's Brewing Company

CIDERIES
Blackduck Cidery
Finger Lakes Cider House

Bellwether Hard Cider & Wine
Black Diamond Farm and Cider
Idiot Brothers Hard Cider
Redbyrd Orchard Cidery
New York Cider Company
South Hill Cider

DISTILLERIES
Hidden Marsh Distillery
Mushroom Spirits Distillery
Myer Farm Distillers

CAYUGA LAKE (EAST)

WINERIES
Izzo's White Barn Winery
The Apple Station Winery
Quarry Ridge Winery
Heart & Hands Wine Company
Long Point Winery
Bright Leaf Vineyard
Treleaven Wines
Ports of New York
Six Mile Creek Vineyard

BREWERIES
Aurora Brewing Co.
Salt Point Brewing Co.
Hopshire Farm & Brewery
Revelry Yards
Liquid State Brewing Company
Personal Best Brewing
Ithaca Beer Co.

OWASCO LAKE

WINERIES
CJS Vineyards
Firelane 6 Winery

BREWERIES
Prison City Brewing
Next Chapter Brewpub
The Good Shepherds Brewing Company
Owasco Lake Brewing

DISTILLERIES
Cellar & Folly Whiskey Company

SKANEATELES LAKE

WINERIES
Anyela's Vineyards
Small Holdings Wines

BREWERIES
Skaneateles Brewery

DISTILLERIES
Last Shot Distillery

BEST OF THE REST

WINERIES
Casa Larga Vineyards and Winery
Muranda Wine Cellars
Highland Cellars

Chateau Dusseau Winery & Vineyard
Song Hill Winery
Eminence Road Farm Winery
Element Winery
Chateau Renaissance Wine Cellars
Wild Brute Winery
20 Deep Winery
Waggoner Local Fare
Vagabond Wine Cellars
Mark T. Wiltberger Cellars
Onyare

BREWERIES
Fall Street Brewing Co.
Fleur De Lis Brew Works
Summerhill Brewing
Homer Hops Brewing
Liquid Shoes Brewing
Horseheads Brewing
Cortland Beer Company
Iron Flamingo Brewery
Market Street Brewing Co. & Restaurant
Dublin Corners Farm Brewery
Upstate Brewing Company
Hop Notch Brewing Co.
Runaway Blue Brewing Company
Reinvention Brewing Co.
Mortalis Brewing
Noble Shepherd Craft Brewery
Silver Lake Brewing Project
Tub Town Brewing
Rebel Sailor Brewing Company
Crafty Ales & Lagers
Rising Storm Brewing Co.

CIDERIES

Grisamore Cider Works
Eve's Cidery

DISTILLERIES

Barrington Distillers
Dragonfyre Distillery
Four Fights Distilling
Smokin' Tails Distillery
Birdseye Hollow Farm and Distillery

ACKNOWLEDGMENTS

The group of artisans who interrupted their busy lives to help with this book are detailed throughout these pages, and I wish to acknowledge a deep debt of gratitude to each of them.

Without the help of Carol Doolittle, Laura D'Amico, and Joshua Heller of the New York State Liquor Authority, this project would never have gotten off the ground.

I owe special thanks to Dennis Hayes, who first saw the potential of this book and championed it, and to Jake Bonar of Globe Pequot for making it happen.

INDEX OF WINERIES, BREWERIES, CIDERIES, AND DISTILLERIES

INDEX OF WINERIES, BREWERIES, CIDERIES, AND DISTILLERIES BY LAKE

SENECA LAKE (EAST)

DISTILLERIES
Cellar & Folly Whiskey Company, 181

SKANEATELES LAKE

WINERIES
Anyela's Vineyards, 184
Small Holdings Wines, 185

BREWERIES
Skaneateles Brewery, 186

DISTILLERIES
Last Shot Distillery, 187

INDEX OF BEST
OF THE REST

ABOUT THE AUTHOR

Michael Turback, a true Finger Lakes zealot and locavore before the word existed, was among the first to embrace concepts of farm to table and vineyard to table at his restaurant, Turback's of Ithaca—an achievement recognized nationally. He not only created and nurtured one of the region's first destination restaurants, but he also built a reputation around his ability to stalk, procure, and support the best of local food and wine. The *Los Angeles Times* called Turback's the "first Finger Lakes restaurant to really devote itself to New York's culinary and enological bounty."

Turback was trained as a restaurateur at the Cornell University School of Hotel Administration. His restaurant's mission combined inventiveness, passionate cooking with local ingredients, and the novel concept of a wine list with exclusively New York State products. He pioneered concepts at Turback's that sparked trends seen throughout the restaurant industry today. His loyalty to small local farmers and use of seasonal local produce helped to popularize American regional dining. Wine-tasting events and wine dinners inspired interest in a new generation of regional wines. The Turback's staff even picked their own local grapes for the restaurant's house wine.

Turback originated the Great Nouveau Race, in which long-distance runners carried each new vintage's first-released bottles of local wines to market, upstaging the arrival of Beaujolais Nouveau from France and nearly creating an international incident!

Turback's was at the epicenter of the rebirth of wine culture in the region. Konstantin Frank, Guy DeVaux, Charles Fournier, John Williams, and Hermann Wiemer came to pour their wines. Walter Taylor would sit at the bar, sip wine, and sketch drawings for his Bully Hill labels. André Tchelistcheff visited from California to see what all the fuss was about.

The restaurant's library of early vintages documented the progress of the growing local industry, earning attention and commendation from *Wine Spectator*, *Bon Appétit*, *Gourmet* magazine, the *New York Times*, the *Boston Globe*, the

Washington Post, the *Philadelphia Inquirer, USA Today, Wall Street Journal, Fortune* magazine, the Food Channel, and NPR's *All Things Considered.*

The restaurant's success discredited the prevailing snub of New York State wines by the experts and critics. *Wine Enthusiast* magazine named Turback's "one of the wine-friendliest restaurants in America," and the restaurant's daring all-local lineup was awarded best American wine list by *Restaurant Business* magazine.